Women's Worlds
in Shakespeare's Plays

Women's Worlds
in Shakespeare's Plays

IRENE G. DASH

DELAWARE

Newark: University of Delaware Press
London: Associated University Presses

Associated University Presses
440 Forsgate Drive
Cranbury, NJ 08512

Associated University Presses
16 Barter Street
London WC1A 2AH, England

Associated University Presses
P.O. Box 338, Port Credit
Mississauga, Ontario
Canada L5G 4L8

The paper used in this publication meets the requirements of the American National Standard for Permanence of Paper for Printed Library Materials Z39.48-1984.

Library of Congress Cataloging-in-Publication Data

Dash, Irene G.
  Women's worlds in Shakespeare's plays / Irene G. Dash.
    p.   cm.
  Includes bibliographical references (p.   ) and index.
  ISBN 0-87413-599-0 (alk. paper)
    1. Shakespeare, William, 1564–1616—Characters—Women.   2. Women and literature—England—History—16th century.   3. Women and literature—England—History—17th century.   4. Domestic drama, English—History and criticism.   5. Women—England—Social conditions.   6. Sex role in literature.   I. Title.
  PR2991.D26   1997
  822.3'3—dc20
                                                              96-2686
                                                              CIP

PRINTED IN THE UNITED STATES OF AMERICA

For
Martin and
Deborah and Deena

Contents

This is Illyria, lady.
—*Twelfth Night*, I.ii.2

PART ONE
Personal World

How might one do, sir, to lose it to her own liking?
—I.i.150–51

PART TWO
Political World

And with the juice of this I'll streak her eyes,
And make her full of hateful fantasies.
—II.i.257–58

PART THREE
Familial World

"Where's your father?"
"At home, my lord."
—III.i.129–30

The Thane of Fife had a wife; where is she now?
—V.i.42–43

PART FOUR
Economic World

Illustrations

Acknowledgments

It is a pleasure to say thank you to those whose support helped me in bringing this book to completion: friends, colleagues, family, and institutions, as well as students whose questions often led me to clarify my ideas. Less easily identifiable are the incidental conversations, the books or articles read but not listed, and sometimes even the new ideas floating through discussions. All enriched my work. For the errors and weaknesses that may appear here, I, of course, take full responsibility.

My first debt is to those who read and critiqued the manuscript at different stages. My daughter Deborah has read and reread every chapter from the earliest proposal through the latest revisions. Supportive, yet critical when sections were unclear, she encouraged me to continue sharpening the text. A historian and a feminist, she brought these elements to her approach. My friend and colleague, Gerald M. Pinciss, has painstakingly read every chapter and provided insightful criticism. A Shakespearean, he challenged some of my assumptions, yet with the generosity of a teacher convinced me to develop them more precisely. Single chapters have improved through the close readings of Barbara Mowat and John Shawcross. At a later stage, David Bevington was kind enough to read and comment on the entire manuscript. I profited greatly from his criticism. Finally, I want to thank Jay Halio, editor of the University of Delaware Press, and Frances Teague, who read the work and focused my attention on overlooked nuances of text. I greatly appreciate their observations and suggestions.

Others who did not read the manuscript but nevertheless influenced its final form include Sighle Kennedy, with whom I debated late at night over the telephone subtleties of interpretation or expression; Virginia and Alden Vaughan, scholars whose friendship and encouragement I appreciate; Elizabeth Hageman, whose wit and energy spurred me on when we shared times together at the Folger Library; Bernice Kliman who continued to ask, "Is the book completed yet?" assuring me that it was a work worth finishing. Janice Lull's invitation to the University of Alaska marked a shift in my perspective and provided an overarching insight. Her col-

league's casual comment, "This is Illyria, lady," seemed to epito-
mize for me just what I was searching for. I realized the breadth
and unpredictability of the worlds women inhabit both in Shakespeare's plays and in the larger society outside the theatre. It was
a wonderful moment.

Overlapping communities of scholars have broadened my hori-
zons and enriched my experience. Through the initiative of the
late Bernard Beckerman and Gloria Beckerman the Shakespeare
Seminar at Columbia University became a reality. That forum permitted me to test ideas subsequently refined in the chapter on *A
Midsummer Night's Dream*. For this I am grateful. Joseph Price has
on many occasions extended warmth and advice; invitations to
his Folger seminar influenced my thinking. In varying ways, other
scholars—particularly Thomas Berger, Jackson Boswell, Weldon
Crowley, Phyllis Rackin, Margaret Ranald, Lois Schwoerer, and
Georgiana Zeigler—have been supportive. This has meant a great
deal to me.

Libraries are more than just books. I have been fortunate to have
had open to me the extraordinary resources of several libraries,
first among them the Folger Shakespeare Library—that amazing
source of Shakespeare promptbooks without which this book could
not have been written. At the Folger I first encountered promptbooks taking me into earlier theatrical worlds. In those books,
reflecting different people's interpretations of the text, I met ghosts
of other times: David Garrick, John Philip Kemble, Henry Irving,
as well as Ellen Terry, Ada Rehan, and even more recent ghosts,
Judith Anderson, John Gielgud, and Lillian Gish. But the Folger is
much more than a resource of materials, it is a resource of people.
I want to thank the Folger staff who not only answer my requests
when I am in attendance in Washington but who, even at long
distance, are unfailing in their help: Laetitia Yaendle, Jean Miller,
Betsy Walsh, Rosalind Larry, and Harold Batie, as well as David
Ressa, who keeps finding me space when I must see the material
in person. Werner Gundersheimer has invested the library with
his generous spirit and his respect for scholarship.

Closer to home, the Billy Rose Theatre Collection of the New
York Public Library has been a major resource. I want to thank
Dorothy Swerdlove who was so helpful when I started work there;
and more recently Robert Taylor, Kevin Winkler, and Christine
Karatnytsky. The Wertheim Study at the New York Public Library's
central research division provided a quiet haven where I could

work without interruption. I have also been privileged to use the Film Stills Archives of the Museum of Modern Art and the William Seymour Collection at the Princeton University Library. Sometimes easy proximity gives one a false sense of confidence that a resource will always be available. Presided over with generosity by Serge Moglidat during Joseph Papp's lifetime, the Public Theatre's archives proved just such an ephemeral resource, closing after his death. Other libraries much further away that were most hospitable to me and whose collections I explored for this book are: the Harvard Theatre Collection of the Houghton Library where Jeanne Newlin graciously introduced me to new material; the Lilly Library of Indiana University; the Library of Congress; the Library of the University of California, Los Angeles; the Huntington Library; and in England, the theatre library at the Victoria and Albert Museum; the Shakespeare Centre Library; the University of Bristol Library; and the Ellen Terry Collection at Smallhythe. I appreciate their generosity.

Several grants gave me the freedom to visit those libraries and to discover caches of relevant material. Foremost was the National Endowment for the Humanities whose generous one year's research grant allowed me the time and resources to begin this project. I am grateful for a Folger short-term fellowship which came when discouragement was high, permitting me to finish the chapter on *Macbeth*. A travel-to-libraries fellowship of the National Endowment for the Humanities later enabled me to continue my research and writing. Finally, I wish to express my appreciation to the University Seminars at Columbia University for assistance in the preparation of the manuscript for publication. Material drawn from this work was presented to the University Seminar on Shakespeare.

Sometimes we realize too late the thanks that were due earlier. To the late Bernie Kaplan whose sense of design so enhanced my first book and whose creativity may be glimpsed here as well, I belatedly acknowledge a debt. Bernie was a fine designer and an artist of great skill whose modesty often masked his talent and generosity.

At difficult moments, my family has urged me to continue this study. For this I am deeply grateful. Although at a distance, my daughter Deena, during long telephone calls and periodic visits, has convinced me of the work's value. My sons-in-law MacDonald and Sidney, in very different ways, have spoken of the need to take the time to write this book. My grandchildren—Mordecai,

Mikhael, Aaron, and Ze'eva—have had to deal with the idea of a grandma who wants to keep going without cease. And my mother, Bella Golden, from a very different perspective, wonders what drives me, forgetting the early and intensive theatre-going fostered by her and my father, Samuel Golden. Surely those experiences, too, contributed to this book.

Finally, I want to thank my husband, Martin, who has continued to make life a challenging adventure and who constantly illuminates the complexities of relationships between women and men.

Women's Worlds
in Shakespeare's Plays

Cabinet photo of Ellen Terry as Ophelia in the "nunnery scene." Her pearls and costume are closely imitated in the 1964 *Hamlet* production with Julie Harris, suggesting the persistence of traditions—even in costuming. Courtesy of the Folger Shakespeare Library.

CHAPTER ONE

Introduction

WORLDS WITHIN WORLDS

This is Illyria, lady.
—*Twelfth Night*, I.ii.2

Bright, confused, assertive, compliant, sometimes self-hating, often independent women characters move through Shakespeare's plays. When interacting with one another, they illustrate women bonding; women arguing; and, in disguise, women engaged in a wooing game with one another. More often, however, women in the plays interact with men, either accompanied by other women, or appearing alone as single, solitary figures in a man's world. Drawing on their inner resources, women must then confront the challenges of the male hegemony or pliantly give way to its power.

Through these multifaceted portraits, Shakespeare raises questions about women's lives. Although not a revolutionary, he recorded what he saw and heard with such extraordinary skill that his works, probing motivation for human action, continue to challenge interpretation. Audiences, readers, producers, and directors still argue about the plays' meanings, the artist's intention, and how best to project the texts on the stage. For, despite their apparently nonpolemical nature, Shakespeare's dramas address issues, even if obliquely, about the human struggle.[1] And this includes, of course, the struggles facing women as well as men.

Because women's worlds differ from those of men, however, their struggles also differ. As daughters, sisters, mothers, wives, lovers, and widows, women confront specific gendered pressures. They must make decisions about their physical selves—their bodies, their sexual choices; they must evaluate their political relationship to men where men control the major sources of power; and, most confusing for women, they must weigh the conflicting allegiances arising from their position.[2] Here questions multiply as women attempt to understand the relationship between the power of others over their lives and decisions about moral responsibility for action. If men control the power, are they therefore morally responsible for women's actions—questions asked in *Macbeth* and *Hamlet*—or does moral responsibility revert to the individual engaged in the action? Shakespeare dramatizes this dilemma for his women characters; sometimes it leads to their silence, sometimes to madness, but sometimes also to triumph as women achieve a sense of self.

In their complexity, such portraits tend to defy accepted stereotypes. Criticism as well as staging then seeks to reshape them. On the stage, lines are cut, scenes transposed, or, in some cases, chunks of text are added. The women characters are then reduced to simpler dimensions, conforming to preconceived notions about women's behavior. Promptbooks, records of actual performances, offer invaluable clues to these changes, illuminating how the women's roles have been skewed to make them culturally more acceptable.

All's Well That Ends Well, for example, the first play discussed in this book, raises the question of a woman's right to choose her husband—even against his will. In a world in which marriage was the only "vocation" for a woman, the drama asks why a woman may not pursue her vocation.[3] Moreover, with the play's unpopular notion of woman as wooer, we discover that Helena, a young woman of wit and intelligence, is often presented as cold, unimaginative, or humorless, her lines trimmed to fit such a portrait while the play's emphasis shifts to the comic scenes revolving around men and armies and games.[4] Supplementing the staging, criticism has faulted Helena's aggressiveness. Scholars find flaws in the play's structure, particularly reports of a young man's obliviousness to the identity of the woman he bedded (one is surprised by the vehemence of these protests), or, by referring to obscure Renaissance laws, argue in support of the actions of the cad, her husband.[5]

Other questions also arise. In *A Midsummer Night's Dream,* the impact of male political power on women is explored. Here, we witness, beneath the fluff of fairy magic and an enchanted wood, the "taming" of an outspoken female character—the fairy queen.

What remains when individuality and fire are stripped from such a character? Is compliance really attractive or desirable? The play challenges easy acceptance of such qualities. In addition, one discovers the effect of performance—the staged play—on reactions to the text. Here music, dancing, and concentration on the comic characters obliterate the harsher language of power.

Macbeth relies on yet other theatrical alternatives to interfere with questions about women raised by the text. Skewing occurs not only by diminishing the fiendishness of the witches—in the eighteenth and nineteenth centuries flocks of "dancing witches" inhabited the stage—but also by omitting major lines and scenes such as the murder of Lady Macduff and her children on the stage. Indeed, she has frequently been completely cut from acting versions. As a result, Lady Macbeth becomes the play's only unambiguous woman. As I point out in chapter 5, criticism labeling her a fiend, while it may reflect reactions to such a strong woman who supports, encourages, and even pressures her husband to move in the "way" that he "was going," also simplifies the text. Moreover, such criticism fails to take into account the contrast provided by the actual fiends—the three weird sisters—and of Lady Macduff, all of whom help delineate and refine the portrait of Lady Macbeth.

Criticism and staging interact synergistically as well as responding to contemporaneous cultural, political, and technological developments. It is well known that *Henry V* has been variously perceived as pro- or anti-war, depending on the climate of the times. Moreover, film has magnified the intensity of these variations. During World War II, for example, Laurence Olivier's production glorified the English victory at Agincourt, implying that contemporary Englishmen could once again defeat their enemy—this time the Germans—on the fields of France. Kenneth Branagh's 1989 production, on the other hand, exposed the dirt, fatigue, and uselessness of war.[6] Still other plays, such as *Othello* or *The Merchant of Venice*, have reflected shifting contemporary ideas about blacks or Jews in a particular cultural environment.

Attitudes towards women have a different kind of history—at once more constant as well as more varying. Thus we may read that a totally new production of a Shakespeare play occurred and then discover that although the scenery and costumes were new, the attitudes towards its women characters were old and familiar. The same lines had been excised, the same scenes transposed. Two factors explain this consistency: first, the perception of women in the larger culture; and second, the theatrical custom of transmitting promptbooks, their excisions intact, from one actor-manager or director to another. A Garrick prompt might be enlarged and slightly altered by Kemble. Or an Augustan Daly promptbook might include notes on the book's previous owner's recommended methods of production. Occasionally promptbooks contain references going back a whole century as occurs in a prompt of *Macbeth* with a Henry Irving bookplate that discusses David Garrick's interpretation. Appearing immediately before the second witch scene (I.iii), where Macbeth and Banquo first hear the predictions, the comment notes:

> Garrick threw an air of dejection over the character instead of the old daring and intrepidity. (Prompt *Mac* 48)

How long a tradition may persist! It is no surprise, therefore, that promptbooks even crossed the Atlantic, long before the days of airplanes.[7]

Another type of constancy also has persisted. In a society where men control the major sources of power, a bias against women and prescriptions for their proper behavior remain, although the excuse for a particular critical position may shift. Reactions to *Measure for Measure* illustrate this dualism. There a young woman, Isabella, a novitiate, about to take the vows of a nun, has been summoned to plead with the acting ruler for her brother's life. When, suddenly smitten with her, this ruler, Angelo, offers to commute the sentence if she will sleep with him, she refuses. Earlier critics questioned the sincerity of her religious commitment in this refusal—suggesting that a truly religious young woman would have sacrificed her virginity to save her brother's life. Later critics have condemned her for her overweening commitment to sexual abstinence. Ernest Schanzer, for example, quotes a characteristic 1933 comment by Lascelles Abercrombie:

> When we come to Shakespeare's use of the feeling against puritanism in *Measure for Measure,* we find that the antagonist who brings into odium the popular idea of puritanism in Angelo is actually puritanism itself—the splendid and terrible puritanism of Isabella. (Schanzer, 109)[8]

Schanzer himself protests that "Isabel is no hypocrite, nor is there anything ugly about her Puritanism" (110). Rather he sees it, in Abercrombie's phrase, as "splendid and terrible."

However, Schanzer believes that the dramatist is "manipulating our feelings towards Isabel by alternately engaging and alienating our affection for her" primarily by leading us to "question her decision to sacrifice her brother rather than her virginity" (110). Although admitting that "the majority of critics, especially R. W. Chambers, have, in fact, felt that Isabel could have acted in no other way than she did," Schanzer nevertheless speculates that the dramatist himself "preferred" the choice of Cassandra, the "Isabella" character in one of Shakespeare's sources (110).[9] Unlike Isabella, however, who triumphs at the play's close, Cassandra sacrifices her virginity to save her brother, and then, on hearing of his death, attempts suicide.[10] It takes a lot of rationalization to arrive at the conclusion that Shakespeare wrote one ending but really would have preferred its opposite. Nevertheless, such thinking characterizes responses to the play.

Finally, the more classic accusation against the "sexually harassed" woman appears in the following comments. "I think we are eventually meant to understand that she herself offers unconscious sexual provocation," writes Arthur Kirsch (96). Or, as expressed by Brian Gibbons in the 1991 New Cambridge edition of the play where the attacker and the victim are coupled together in a section entitled "word-play and self-betrayal," "Isabella is similarly prone to use, unconsciously, sexually suggestive language." The editor cites her lines "I would to heaven I had your potency, / And you were Isabel," then comments on "her choice of word":

> influenced by her contradictory feelings about her brother's potency ... but also perhaps registering the *subliminal awareness of Angelo's sudden sexual attraction to her, even perhaps of her to him.* (31–32, emphasis added)

Thus whether condemning her for lack of sincerity, for a "terrible puritanism," or for being sexually provocative, criticism agrees on one thing: the man's life is primary. The implications of rape or the threat of rape to a woman are irrelevant.

Unsurprisingly, this reaction to Isabella has contributed to the play's rocky stage history. The version that prevailed during the eighteenth century (Gildon's) substituted avarice for sexual promiscuity, the crime for which Claudio—Isabella's brother—was to lose his life.[11] No longer needed, therefore, were his lines explaining his relationship with Julietta:

> upon a true contract
> I got possession of Julietta's bed.
> You know the lady; she is fast my wife,
> Save that we do the denunciation lack
> Of outward order.
>
> (MM, I.ii.145–49)[12]

In Gildon's version, Claudio marries Julietta in secret so as not to endanger her rights to a dowry. Thus Gildon eliminates one challenge raised by the text and debated in twentieth-century criticism, the legality of Claudio's actions according to English Renaissance law.[13] More importantly, however, Gildon's Claudio never pressures his sister to accede to Angelo's demand as does Shakespeare's Claudio, who rationalizes:

> Sure it is no sin,
> Or of the deadly seven it is the least.
>
> (109–10)

Gone is the begging of the persistent brother:

> Sweet sister, let me live.
> What sin you do to save a brother's life,
> Nature dispenses with the deed so far,
> That it becomes a virtue.
>
> (132–35)

In the comparative portraits of the brothers, the issues raised in Shakespeare's play disappear. Gildon's Claudio places his sister in no such moral dilemma, insisting rather, "No,—my sister,—I have no thoughts of living on your ruin" (24). How much more difficult Shakespeare makes the choice, dramatizing not only the closeness between brother and sister as well as her knowledge of his weakness, but also the strain such a choice places on a young woman.

However, Isabella's rejection of Claudio's request here defies stereotypically expected responses. And staging, like criticism, has variously sought to bypass this characterization not only by rewriting the play, as occurred in the early centuries, but by concentrating on its comic characters, or translating that Puritan tint in criticism into acting and dress, presenting a cold, sexually frigid, unattractive young woman. In every case, her dilemma has been minimized. Moreover, by examining promptbooks, one becomes aware of the troublesome areas of text—those sections bothering producers, actor-managers, and directors. They disappear or are rewritten. Thus stage history can focus attention on lost or blunted textual cruxes in terms of women.

Revealing the dramatist's insight, for example, is the confrontational scene between Angelo and Isabella. It exemplifies what we now recognize as "sexual harassment." And like the blindness such confrontations have met in our own time, this exchange has received comparatively little critical attention although it underlines Isabella's reaction. Responding to Angelo's proposition, she exclaims in momentary triumph: "I will proclaim thee, Angelo. . . . I'll tell the world aloud / What man thou art" (II.iv.151–54). Sneeringly, he asserts:

> Who will believe thee, Isabel?
> My unsoil'd name, th' austereness of my life,
> My vouch against you, and my place i' th' state,
> Will so your accusation overweigh,
> That you shall stifle in your own report,
> And smell of calumny.
>
> (II.iv.154–59)

Confident, self-assured, and threatening, Angelo perfectly gauges societal response. But Shakespeare, taking a classic tale, transforms it by cloaking Isabella in the robes of the church. Thus he intensifies her dilemma as well as clarifying that of women facing the threat of rape by politically powerful men. As true today as it is in the play is Angelo's reaction to her exclamation.

Presenting Isabella as a devout novitiate in a strict religious order gives an added moral dimension for her conduct. A correlation exists for her between the invasion of her body, her personal self, and death. Despite modern ideas about sexuality, women, victims of rape, continue to find validity in such a correlation.[14] Susan Brownmiller links rape to power and to the relationship between a man and a woman, suggesting that it became "man's basic weapon of force against woman, the principal agent of his will and her fear" (14). Since Isabella's life is pledged to God, she weighs her religious beliefs against her brother's life.

Because of her religious commitment, the play also raises the more subtle question of the relative value of women's and men's lives. The dramatist asks not "what should a woman do" but "what would a woman do" if she valued her own life—at this moment a life belonging to the church—as strongly as a man does his? By adding this extra element—the religious—into the scale, the dramatist not only balances the woman's worth against the man's but illuminates the question of woman's self-sovereignty, her right to retain control over her body, and ultimately of her life. Despite its ending and some of the more pious phrases spoken by the Duke, the play not only challenges accepted notions about men and women but explores the meaning of self-sovereignty for women.

In fact, thematically, woman's self-sovereignty is at the core of this study. The quote from *Twelfth Night* at the head of this chapter (although it has a specificity in this play) characterizes the enigmatic answers women receive as they seek to understand themselves and the worlds in which they move. The line is actually spoken moments after Viola, a young woman recently shipwrecked, arrives on a strange shore. The captain who has rescued her identifies the place as "Illyria," a name drawn from antiquity with little relevance to the contemporary world. Answering her question, "What country, friends, is this?" (I.ii.1), he informs her of her whereabouts—"This is Illyria, lady"(2)—and introduces a concept that resonates throughout the play. For Viola is searching not only for the easy answer—the name of the particular place— but also for answers about her own identity. Believing she has lost her twin brother in that storm at sea, she wonders how she relates to the larger cosmic world and what her place is in this specific Illyrian world of men and women. Temporarily donning pants, 'til she has made her "own occasion mellow" to better know her own position, Viola, in her quest, characterizes other women in Shakespeare's plays. They too must learn who they are, often going through a process of relearning as they seek to establish their own identity—sexually, politically, socially, or economically.

As I have already said, Shakespeare was not a revolutionary with a polemical message but an artist looking at the multifaceted life around him and dramatizing some of its puzzles. Surely among them must have been the presence of a strong woman on the English throne despite the general position of women in society. Shakespeare was born and grew to maturity during her reign. In my earlier book I wrote that although we know little about women in the Renaissance, many of whom seemed to have been lost to history, one woman was not lost, even temporarily—Elizabeth I. When I wrote this, I theorized that she must have not only influenced the young Shakespeare growing up and later working in the theater, but also presented him with an obvious contradiction between what was said about women, and what he witnessed.

We also know, however, that despite Elizabeth's strength and talent as queen, she referred to herself as "Prince," combining in her person both male and female characteristics since she also considered her people "her children." Writing of her reign and her method of postponing marriage, one critic suggests that she was an "honorary male," and therefore effectively furthered patriarchal governance (Heisch, 45). However the writer then concedes that a male monarch would not have had to contend with the hostility of Parliament as did Elizabeth:

> It is absolutely evident that neither the challenge to Royal authority nor the intensity of that challenge could have occurred with other than a female monarch, for not only is it most unlikely that a king would have been opposed or compromised by his Privy Council, but it is also true that for a king marriage could not have been a problem, hence not an issue. (52–53)

Thus while Elizabeth, in many ways, may be perceived as an "honorary male," the fact that marriage and the necessity of providing an heir were, for so long, important issues during her reign, also suggests that she was still considered a woman, not only by her Privy Council but also by her people. As well as contending with a male parliament, she faced a church controlled by men, except as she headed that church. Moreover, we also know that by the time of her death the people were looking forward to the ascension to the throne of a male monarch surrounded by family. Surely a monolithic point of view on women could not have prevailed during the period. We now realize that it did not. Contradictions arose which a sensitive dramatist would have noticed and projected in his plays.[15]

Today we understand that Elizabeth was not a single phenomenon, except as she was queen, and that other educated, learned, aggressive, and thoughtful women lived then, too, providing a range of models from which the dramatist might have drawn his characters. In 1929 Virginia Woolf theorized in *A Room of One's Own* that such a range of women must also have existed even when the first Greek tragedies were written. Today, as we delve deeper into the works and lives of women in the Renaissance, particularly women writers, we are astonished by their range. Their works, both printed and in manuscript form, are being examined with new enthusiasm.[16] We are discovering that women walked and thought and loved and wrote and anguished during Shakespeare's time. In their own voices they told us what it felt like, adding to our knowledge of the period—and giving us a further insight into the power of patriarchy. Interestingly, they validate some of the questions Shakespeare raised about women's lives.

An excellent essay on Elizabeth Cary, for example, the author of the first extant original English tragedy by a woman, *The Tragedie of Mariam, the Faire Queene of Jewry* (1613), discusses the problem for a woman of maintaining "integrity of conscience." The author notes how Cary places her character in a dilemma similar to that encountered by Cary herself—of maintaining this integrity while also satisfying the requirements of being a proper wife to a husband who is a tyrant.[17] Cary's heroine retains this "integrity of conscience" by dying; Cary does not. Life is less simple; people do not give up their lives this easily.

Unlike Cary's heroine, but more like Cary herself, Shakespeare's women characters also face dilemmas that ultimately require "integrity of conscience" or, in the language of Simone de Beauvoir, the woman must decide who is "primary" and what being "other" means. In the tragedies, the dramatist reveals the pressures women face as they attempt to find their way, noting how difficult it is for them to perceive themselves as separate from their husbands. Both Gertrude and Lady Macbeth, although functioning in patriarchal societies, are lulled into believing themselves their husbands' partners: "Our sometime sister, now our queen, / Th' imperial jointress to this warlike state" (*Ham.* I.ii.8–9), announces Claudius of his marriage to Gertrude; "my dearest partner of greatness" (*Mac.* I.v.11), confides Macbeth to his wife in a letter. In a society that preached subservience and obedience, but also mutuality, such implied equality was seductively enticing for the wives.[18] Their husbands knew this, as did the audience. In both plays Shakespeare shows the folly of succumbing to this flattery. In both cases the implications of partnership occur during the wife's very first appearance: Gertrude accompanying Claudius; Lady Macbeth alone reading her husband's letter well after he has appeared on stage, betraying his own ambition.

For Gertrude and Ophelia in *Hamlet,* their Illyria is a world of bewildering and conflicting male voices. Over the din, each woman must seek to hear her own voice—strident or tentative; assertive or whispering; alluring or forthright. For Lady Macbeth and Lady

Macduff, the two mortal women of *Macbeth*, Illyria is the individual space each inhabits—as wife, mother, and householder. Here too the woman must listen for the sound of her own voice, her own conscience. Occasionally, the women characters achieve a measure of self-knowledge, as does Gertrude. At other times, the playwright dramatizes the pressures of the social system and the self-hatred or confusion that results for women, as they retreat into madness, the fate of both Ophelia and Lady Macbeth.

In the comedies, too, the dramatist raises issues about the meaning of women's lives. Here, however, he tends to follow formulaic patterns in the endings, where marriages usually take place. Sometimes the unexpectedness and inexplicability of those marriages, however, help to focus on some of the women's problems. As I have said, Shakespeare's plays are not polemical although they raise questions about the status of women. Raising questions does not necessarily mean providing answers. Rather, such a technique heightens audience awareness of unresolved issues. The endings of the comedies explored in this book illustrate some of the ambiguities that remain. As Ejner Jensen has pointed out, a comedy's meaning does not lie solely in its ending.[19] The whole play may raise the audience's awareness of a specific situation without the need for a sharp message spelled out in the ending. As I point out in chapter 2 on *All's Well That Ends Well,* Bertram's "if" at the play's close leaves many unanswered questions, while in chapter 3, on *A Midsummer Night's Dream,* the critical silence surrounding Titania's awakening again provokes questions.

Like the comedies discussed in the following chapters, *Measure for Measure* also seems to settle for acceptable closure and offers a highly problematic ending. Having watched his surrogate, Angelo, inflexibly rule by absolute standards but then become corrupt himself, the Duke, disguised as a friar, finally reveals himself. Resembling the deus ex machina in classical drama, he rights many of the wrongs in the world of the play. However, some problems remain—among them, Isabella's silence to his proposal of marriage.

The dramatist has "thrown a curve" to the director and emphasized the importance of the acted play. The ambiguous ending rests on actions without words—therefore on the director's interpretation—raising questions for readers that must be resolved on stage. Are we to accept the formulaic comedic ending and allow Isabella to marry the Duke, who, as a friar, had been her advisor throughout the comedy? Or, since he gave her the false news that her brother had died, are we to accept her silence as a signal of rejection? *Measure for Measure* ends without a verbal clue as to whether or not Isabella accepts the Duke's offer of marriage although patterns for comedy in the theater suggest that she does.[20]

The problematic outcome, however, does not necessarily imply that a confused Shakespeare could not resolve his ending, as some critics have suggested. Rather, the dramatist can through this device emphasize Isabella's powerlessness, showing her as a sexual-political victim. The deliberate lack of closure helps stress her plight. Anne Barton believes that the split between the realistic play and the fairy-tale ending indicates that Shakespeare was "seemingly disillusioned with that art of comedy which, in the past, had served him so well" (549); it is also possible that he used this split to highlight Isabella's dilemma and to show the need to confront this inequity for women.

For Isabella as for each of the women characters in the plays discussed in this book, "Illyria" represents a reappraisal of the world as well as a new understanding of herself. By the end of the play, her "Illyria" is neither the Vienna of the play's setting nor the simple life of a nun of the order of St. Clare, where we first meet her. Having chosen the cloistered life, she believes that she has set the parameters of her world and has control over her own sexuality. But she soon learns that political power interferes with that control. Like Viola on the shores of Illyria, Isabella, caught suddenly in a land she does not know, must make decisions, relying on her own moral standards; she must determine her own identity.

The five plays included in this book explore the meaning of self-sovereignty to the women characters. The study moves from the most intimate kind of self ownership—of one's body—through the various social and political situations in which women find themselves—finally to the potential for realizing this sovereignty through economic independence and freedom from male domination. Closing with *Twelfth Night*, the book analyzes two women who seem to have won this freedom, noting the various measures each takes to protect herself as she attempts to enter the masculine world. Unfortunately, stage excisions diminish the strong parallels between the young women. Nor are we sufficiently aware of the extensiveness of the unconventionality of both women—Viola and Olivia. As the dramatist plays with the questions of dress—male disguise or female conformity—he develops a woman character in wimple and skirts more threatening to accepted behavior than the woman in pants. Confirming this sentiment, stage productions help to weight the sentiment in favor of Viola, as I discuss in chapter 6. In contrast Olivia, who defies societal mores, meets censure for actively pursuing "a youth younger than herself." Even here, however, where two women characters have the potential for independence, free of male control, the dramatist shows the limits of that independence when the women fall in love. And stage productions highlight critical antagonism to the more outspoken of the two women.

As I emphasize throughout this book, promptbooks along with printed acting versions are invaluable keys to the texts. Marked-up copies of plays used for particular performances, they not only open doors to past productions but allow guidance for the future. Their pages of text alternate with interleaved pages. There the director, actor-manager, or prompter has scribbled notes, inserted un-Shakespearean lines, marked stage directions and character movement, or sketched in placement of properties—a throne, steps, masses of soldiers about to enter, or even a color note on the backdrop. A prompt may reveal Ophelia weeping in the nunnery scene, even while Hamlet spies Polonius peeping out from behind the arras, as occurs in an E. H. Sothern book. Or it may betray a scornful attitude towards women as does a Daly prompt of *A Midsummer Night's Dream* where, upon awakening, Titania exclaims, "Methought I was enamoured of an ass" and hears the reply, "There lies your love," from Oberon. How is he to speak this line? Compassionately? Unresponsively? Or, as he does in this prompt, "sneering[ly]" [*MND* 5, p. 61]?

While the bias of a particular director may surface in such a stage direction, a more universal bias becomes apparent in excisions that continue over a period of years, adopted by one actor-manager after another. Because Shakespeare's works are long, they are frequently cut. But when the same sections always disappear, one begins to wonder why. And when these excisions involve women characters, as is often the case, one tries to discover what sequential arrangement of lines or scenes might have been changed, what insights into a character lost. In *All's Well That Ends Well*, for example, banter about "virginity" between Helena, the major woman character, and Parolles, a braggart, is frequently excised. The residual effect is to alter responses to the play, as I discuss in chapter 2. One wonders why the dramatist included that particular exchange and what further evidence it provides to the interaction within the play. Therefore, although I have concentrated on the women characters in my search for the full text, the women have served primarily as templates for what happens to the entire play. The omitted material often keynotes the play's challenges to conventional ideas about women.

In addition, sexual politics enters productions through performance and interpretation of a specific role. Seeking to understand the character of Lady Macbeth more clearly prior to playing her on stage, for example, Ellen Terry in 1895 pleaded with William Winter, then an important American critic and a close friend, for assistance. Her letter reveals her own perceptions of the character she was to play but also her reactions as an actress projecting a role. Filled with underlinings, double underlinings, and squiggley lines to emphasize particular words or phrases, her letter provides insights for us into a performer's reaction to a role:

> Sweet Sir—Welcome to America!!—.... We arrived here [New York] from Boston last night and are "in for" 5 performances of Macbeth== It is not a pleasant prospect for me-For I rather anticipate folk will hate me in it= Everyone seems to think MrsMcB is a monstrosity-and I can only see that she's a woman—A mistaken woman-& weak-not a Dove- of course not-but first of all a wife= I don't think she's at all clever ("Lead Macbeth" indeed!-She's not even clever enough to sleep!)

Terry of course is referring to the sleepwalking scene where Lady Macbeth, "in a most fast sleep" (V.i.8) reveals her great "perturbation" by talking of all the murders she and Macbeth committed. After discussing the unintentional way that Lady Macbeth stumbles into murder, the actress then develops a series of farfetched comparisons to emphasize her belief that Lady Macbeth was not a fiend:

> try how hard I may I cannot perceive that Madame Sarah Bernhardt is a "thin woman" "an eal" that the sunshines upon us at midnight-, or that Lady Macbeth was a monstrous fiend who urged her little husband against his will to be naughty.

She then flatters Winter and appeals to his superiority: "for 2 years I've wanted you to tell me things about Lady M to help me with her." Continuing, she differentiates between Winter the critic and Winter the friend, "I don't mean in the Paper-but for myself." The

PART ONE

Personal World

The affection between Helena and the Countess of Rossillion is clearly visible in this photograph of Zoe Caldwell and Edith Evans in the 1959 Tyrone Guthrie production of *All's Well That Ends Well*. Angus McBean photograph, courtesy of the Harvard Theatre Collection, The Houghton Library.

CHAPTER TWO

When Women Choose

ALL'S WELL THAT ENDS WELL

How might one do, sir, to lose it to her own liking?
I.i.150–51

Although the phrase "catch 22" had not yet entered the language, Charlotte Perkins Gilman in 1898 described the concept with precision—as it applies to women's lives. She noted that even though the young girl "is carefully educated and trained to realize in all ways her sex-limitations and her sex-advantages" with the ultimate aim of marriage,

> she must not even look as if she wanted it. . . . What one would logically expect is a society full of desperate and eager husband-hunters, *regarded with popular approval.* Not at all! (emphasis added, 581–82)

And the irony is compounded, for our hypocritical society practices a "cruel and absurd injustice of blaming the girl for not getting what she is allowed no effort to obtain" (582). The writer thus describes the contradiction immediately facing young women, contrasting their support system with that of young men, who are encouraged to pursue their goals. Moreover, she distinguishes between the aims of boys and girls, again attributing the differences to societal training: "Where young boys plan for *what* they will achieve and attain, young girls plan for *whom* they will achieve and attain" (emphasis added, 582). Because of the "sexuo-economic relation" of our society, the girl's objective is immediately linked with another person, a husband.

Although written at the end of the nineteenth century and meant for her own time, Gilman's statement may also be applied to the lives of women in the Renaissance. Ruth Kelso, too, in her classic study of this subject defines wedlock as the only possible career: "Only one vocation, marriage, was proposed for the lady" (78). While not exploring Gilman's idea of "pursuit of vocation" and limiting her study to middle- and upper-class women, Kelso's words suggest that the goal of marriage well predates the nineteenth century and speaks to much earlier limitations on women's worlds.[1]

In *All's Well That Ends Well*, Shakespeare personalizes Kelso's notion of "vocation" and dramatizes Gilman's observation. Concentrating on the interaction of characters, the dramatist opens his play with a glimpse of Helena, a young woman at first dedicated to merely "thinking about" the man she adores. The play then shows her altering her ideas after she becomes involved in a discussion on "virginity" with a boastful friend of her hero's. In the two soliloquies that frame the dialogue, the dramatist unfolds her amazing transformation. In fact, Helena addresses the fundamental contradiction pointed out by Gilman: the illogical concept of pursuing one's vocation by not pursuing it. The soliloquies reveal the mental and emotional turmoil that lead Helena to rethink her attitude and actively pursue the young man of her choice. But Shakespeare does more than merely develop the portrait of a young woman of brains and drive, characteristics of Helena: he also turns to paradigms and reworks them. Deviating from his sources, he emphasizes this woman's strength, creativity, wit, and courage while, at the same time, he demonstrates her idol's weakness and dishonesty, creating a sharp dichotomy between them. Developing an unconventional heroine and making the object of her affection an antihero, the dramatist turns the action into an even more unconventional situation, which points up the truth of Gilman's thesis. Even as she protests that she would rather not upset the status quo, Helena, quite deliberately and dramatically, does so.

Like Gilman, Shakespeare also introduces economics into the relationship. A social schism exists between the two young people: Count Bertram is heir to Rossillion—an adored and handsome only son; Helena is the orphan of a physician and in the care of the Countess of Rossillion, Bertram's mother. Along with everyone around her, Helena too idolizes Bertram. When later the Countess asks, "Do you love my son?" (I.iii.186) Helena's answer, "Do not you love him, madam?" (187) reveals her evasiveness at this moment but also the logic of her choice of this young hero of Rossillion.

Indeed, he is the one, to use Charlotte Gilman's language, "for whom" Helena would "achieve and attain" and "through whom" she would reach the woman's ultimate goal of marriage.

Unfortunately, however, her success has caused many critics to find *All's Well That Ends Well* a problem. They fault Helena's determination or aggressiveness. Reflecting the relevance of Gilman's words, such critics still frown on young women pursuing the goal for which they have been highly "trained." As recently as 1980, Richard A. Levin writes of Helena's "guile" and "cunning":

> The romantically inclined reader will accept the image of patience that Helena projects. Another reader sees only an elaborate facade, concealing an aggressive and self-centered nature. Supporting the latter view, I will show that Helen's success depends on guile; later, I will discuss how her cunning affects the play's comic form. (131)

The intensity of this criticism indicates a hostility to the young woman that goes beyond the text. While this critic attributes to Helena an almost Iago-like nature, I hope to show how to view her sympathetically and understand what is driving the hostile criticism of her.

From the first scene, where she is introduced as a person of education and promise, to the closing scene, when she wins her husband for a second time, Helena has the endorsement, love, and sympathy of most of the characters in the play. The dramatist develops a complex portrait of a young woman orphaned and left to her own resources who comes to realize that she cannot merely pine away for a young man, but must act. Shakespeare gives her an unusual number of soliloquies for a woman, and through these she reveals this shift from passive to active. For example, in the first scene her closing soliloquy begins:

> Our remedies oft in ourselves do lie,
> Which we ascribe to heaven. The fated sky
> Gives us free scope, only doth backward pull
> Our slow designs when we ourselves are dull.
>
> (I.i.216–19)

This decision to take action marks a change from her first soliloquy, which sounds very much like the lament of an unrequited lover:

> My imagination
> Carries no favor in't but Bertram's.

> I am undone, there is no living, none,
> If Bertram be away.
>
> (82–85)

Speaking of him as her "bright particular star" (86), the man she
longs to "wed" (87), she enumerates his attractive physical features,
"arched brows, . . . hawking eye," and "curls" (94), concluding
with an almost overwrought "But now he's gone, and my idola-
trous fancy / Must sanctify his relics" (97–98). Here surely is an
exaggerated example of passivity. This concept of treasuring and
worshipping as "relics" the memories and the mementos surrounding her in his mother's home illustrates the stereotypical
portrait of the young woman who patiently waits. Thus Shakespeare establishes at the start the norm from which Helena will
deviate to grow into a self-sufficient person.

Between these two soliloquies occurs that unusual conversation
on virginity. Parolles, a braggart soldier and Bertram's closest companion and adviser, engages Helena in the dialogue. The topic is
central to the theme of the play but, like Helena's subsequent
aggressiveness, considered inappropriate for a woman to discuss,
even in jest, with a man. Acting as a catalyst, this conversation
appears to alter Helena's self-perception and leads her to take
action.

"Are you meditating on virginity?" (110), asks Parolles, bursting
in upon her and interrupting her melancholy mood. "Ay," she
answers honestly. Then, allowing him to distract her by ex-
pounding on the topic he had introduced, she poses her own question: "You have some stain of soldier in you; let me ask you a
question. Man is enemy to virginity; how may we barricado it
against him?" (111–13). Suddenly, a scene formerly marked by the
tearful parting of mother and son sparkles with humor. Parolles's
answer to Helena, "Keep him out" (114), leads to further verbal
parrying. "But he assails, and our virginity though valiant, in the
defense yet is weak. Unfold to us some warlike resistance" (115–17).
When the wordy Parolles concedes, "There is none. Man setting
down before you, will undermine you and blow you up" (118–19),
Helena refuses to accept such a direct answer. "Is there no military
policy how virgins might blow up men?" she queries (121–22). He
then offers a dissertation on virginity, on its ultimate uselessness,
noting that "Virginity, by being once lost, may be ten times found"
(130–31), and exclaims triumphantly, "'Tis too cold a companion;

away with't!" (132) Continuing this banter, Helena adamantly claims, "I will stand for't a little, though therefore I die a virgin" (133–34). Once again she prompts a long speech by Parolles, this one on the increase in population bred by loss of virginity.

Still "meditating," she then poses the crucial question, "How might one do, sir, to lose it to her own liking?" (150–51). But Parolles fails to give a clear answer. "Let me see. Marry, ill, to like him that ne'er it likes" (152–53), he asserts, seeming to reverse what she says. Speaking of "her own liking," Helena in this conversation has indicated a woman's determination to have a say in the final outcome. Parolles, however, counters with a generalization implying that men do not like women to remain virgins and would seduce them rather than give them the choice of partner. The ambiguity of his comment, however, allows for a range of interpretation. Whereas Helena's reference, "to lose *it* to her own liking," clearly refers to "virginity," Parolles's response could be understood as "Marry, ill, to like the man who doesn't like you." Samuel Johnson chose to understand the comment as a play upon the word "liking." He interpreted the line as: "She must do ill, for *virginity, to be so lost*, must like him that likes not *virginity*" (7:376–77). The wit combat extends for one hundred and seventy-four lines, terminating only when a page summons Parolles to join Bertram.

Despite the substantial length of the exchange, its exploration of a subject relevant to the play, and its insight into Helena's thinking, it has seldom reached the stage in full. In the Bell edition, which probably reflected what was acted at Drury Lane under David Garrick's management, everything after Helena's "ay" was excised.[2] Kemble adopted many of these changes although he often altered the text further in later editions. For example, although his 1793 and 1811 versions differ slightly, the conversation between Helena and Parolles appears in neither. Nor is it found in most of the basic acting texts of the nineteenth century since they derive from Kemble. Thus the Cumberland edition of 1828, the Lacy edition, and, late in the century, the French edition all excised this section of text. William Poel eliminated it at the century's close, and even in the twentieth century most of the lines frequently disappeared. It was cut from the Lillian Baylis production in 1922 and as late as 1953 from Michael Benthall's for the Old Vic. Price (24) notes that the Garrick and Kemble texts differ in their emphases, the one on farce the other on sentimentality. However, neither adaptor retained the verbal jousting of Shakespeare's text that contributes to the portrait of a vibrant Helena and illuminates an important theme in the play: the right of a woman to do her own choosing.

The fact that the characters speak of sexuality—illustrated by this outspoken conversation between Helena, a respectable young woman, and Parolles—partially explains the disappearance not only of these lines but of the play itself from the stage, as I detail below. As for the question of sex, even at mid twentieth century it was common for critics to have reservations about this topic in the context of the play. John F. Adams, in 1961, for example, observed that three interrelated ideas permeated *All's Well That Ends Well*. However, he found the major, or "ground," theme the subject of sex and procreation. "Essentially this ... problem is that of understanding sex within civilized institutions. Paradoxically, sex can be a significant sin or a significant virtue, circumstances determining which" (261). Deciding whether sex is a sin or virtue, however, may depend on the perceptions of the character speaking or the person being addressed. For Helena, the conversation on sex evidently affected her subsequent action. To adaptors, however, the thought of it as sinful influenced their treatment of the text. Writing of the Samuel Phelps production in 1852, Shirley Allen notes that it was an "almost unknown comedy" by then and that despite its extreme abbreviation, a reviewer called the plot "indelicate, even beyond the limits usually conceded to Elizabethan dramatists" (222). In 1920 Odell in his *Shakespeare from Betterton to Irving* seems no more enlightened in his comments:

> *All's Well that Ends Well* has ever been a problem on the stage; the story is revolting, the heroine incapable of awakening sympathy, and the comic scenes either disgustingly low (to use an Eighteenth-Century expression) or mere reminders of earlier (?) successes in the Falstaff plays. Who would cut must needs wield an heroic axe. (2:21)

The conversation on virginity would surely fall before such an ax, for Odell calls it "the filthy talk of Parolles to Helena in the first scene" finding its equal only in the lines of "the Clown to the Countess throughout" (2:21).

But that first scene reveals Shakespeare's artistry as he develops the portrait of Helena and raises questions explored throughout the play: to what extent may a woman determine her physical self-ownership, and can a woman choose her husband or must she be passive? Ancillary to these is another question: what hazards must she expect to confront? This scene, which offers a sharp contrast between Helena's two soliloquies, opens with the Countess of Rossillion bidding farewell to her son, Bertram. His father's death requires that the young man depart for Court to be the King's ward. Standing by silently, Helena is introduced to us primarily through the Countess, who identifies the young woman as a famous physician's daughter. "This young gentlewoman had a father. . . . Would for the King's sake he were living! I think it would be the death of the King's disease" (I.i.17–23), observes the older woman having heard of the inability of the king's physicians to cure the monarch. This challenge Helena will herself undertake later on. Here, however, she remains quiet as the Countess continues: "Her dispositions she inherits, which makes fair gifts fairer" (40–41). During that conversation Helena merely listens, almost like an object that is spoken of but has no voice. When, finally, she does break her silence, it is with a single line, an aside, addressed to no one in particular, but reflecting her own deep feelings at the moment "I do affect a sorrow indeed, but I have it too" (54). What is the audience to think hearing this line? Obviously, Helena's thoughts are not perceived by the others in the drama. Moreover, her statement sounds ambiguous, confusing, and provocative. As soon as the stage is cleared however, Shakespeare enlightens his audience by giving Helena that first soliloquy, establishing her character at the start. Visually and verbally, she embodies the shy conforming young woman, illustrating the training Gilman described centuries later.

Thus Parolles's entry and their subsequent conversation initiates a new mode of thinking for Helena—a new sense of self. It is generally accepted that the main plot of *All's Well That Ends Well* derives from Boccaccio's *Decameron*, Day III, and that Shakespeare added three major characters: the Countess, Parolles, and Lafew—adviser to the king—as well as several minor characters (Bullough, 2:375–81). There is less agreement, however, about the function of Parolles in the play. Because of his similarity to Falstaff in Shakespeare's *Henry IV* plays, the tendency has been to evaluate Parolles in terms of his influence on Bertram, noting the contrast between Hal's awareness of Falstaff's weaknesses and Bertram's blindness to Parolles's shortcomings. Writes Bullough, for example, "Parolles was invented to help us explain—and excuse somewhat—Bertram's offences, and to afford a baser parallel to those offences themselves" (2:387). Attaching great importance to the Parolles-Bertram relationship, W. W. Lawrence finds the "subplot . . . singularly independent of the main action" (33). G. K. Hunter in the Arden edition, disagreeing with Lawrence, emphasizes Bertram's role as central and considers both Parolles and Helena as subsidiary:

> . . . [T]he Bertram story would not mean the same without the Parolles story. There is continual parody of the one by the other. Parolles and Helena are arranged on either side of Bertram, *placed rather like the Good and Evil Angels in a Morality.* (xxxiii; emphasis added)

For this editor, Parolles and Helena illuminate Bertram's character.

On the other hand, although the plot links the two men, Parolles and Helena have the longest and most important roles in the comedy. In addition, he plays a major part in revealing her character.[3] His lines catalyze her into action. No other character so clearly serves this function. She herself hints at this before their lengthy dialogue in the first scene. Observing him approach, she forgives him his weaknesses in advance because of his friendship with Bertram:

> Who comes here?
> One that goes with him. I love him for his sake,
> And yet I know him a notorious liar,
> Think him a great way fool, soly a coward;
> Yet these fix'd evils sit so fit in him,
> That they take place when virtue's steely bones
> Looks bleak i' th' cold wind. Withal, full oft we see
> Cold wisdom waiting on superfluous folly.
>
> (I.i.98–105)

Having itemized his weaknesses, she then concedes the possibility of learning even from "superfluous folly." Although I believe that the rationalization was meant to apply to the companionship between the two men, by the end of the scene, Parolles's "superfluous folly" has influenced her thinking. Like Hal with Falstaff, she recognizes Parolles's weaknesses, and like Hal she listens to the advice, transforming it to her own uses and endowing it with new qualities.

Parolles in this first scene connects with the overall conflict of the play, the one voiced by Helena: "How might one do, sir, to lose it to her own liking?" Their conversation illuminates the different perceptions of virginity by men and women. A word often used in humorous conversation, it also defines the standards of a woman's life, as we see later in the play in the scene between Helena and the King. Moreover, virginity and its loss, with proof of progeny, are central to the work. And it is to Parolles, that character who is later unmasked as a coward, losing his position and prestige with Bertram, to whom Shakespeare assigns the task of opening a not quite conventionally acceptable subject to the audience: virginity and women's perception of it.

The construction of the first scene also illuminates not only Helena's forthrightness and quick wit but also Parolles's insight. In contrast with the Countess and others in the first half of the scene who had simply assumed, hearing Helena sigh, that she was thinking of her father, Parolles makes no such mistake. "Are you meditating on virginity?"—his opening line—meets an immediate "Ay." Had he been wrong, she might easily have said no. Although before his arrival she had confided to the audience her intention of humoring Parolles because he was dear to Bertram, no such deception was necessary. Her arguments on behalf of the virgin fail to mask that immediate "Ay." And though she listens to Parolles's long-winded discourse on the subject, she does follow up her own query of losing one's virginity to one's "own liking" with the lengthy, wistful reference to Bertram at court. "There shall your master have a thousand loves / . . . . with a world / Of pretty, fond, adoptious christendoms / That blinking Cupid gossips. Now shall he—" (166–75). Then almost catching herself, she continues, "I know not what he shall" (176). Stychomythia ensues, "The court's a learning place, and he is one—" (177). Her hesitation quickly prompts his "What one, i'faith?" "That I wish well. 'Tis pity—" "What's pity?" (178–80). Regaining self-control, she once more distances herself from that "bright particular star" at the center of her world and speaks in general terms to Parolles, wishing both men well.[4]

His parting words, "Get thee a good husband, and use him as he uses thee"(214–15), precede her closing soliloquy where she determines to act. She will pursue the objective for which, as Gilman observes, women have been trained. Helena jettisons the lovelorn self of the scene's opening and opts for extraordinary action. "The king's disease—my project may deceive me, / But my intents are fix'd, and will not leave me" (228–29). She has decided to use the knowledge of medicine bequeathed her by her father to cure the King. She will follow Bertram to the French court.

Such decisiveness wins neither societal approval nor that of the play's adaptors, actor-managers, or directors. The Bell text cut this soliloquy, as did Kemble's. There the earlier passive, worshipful speech on her "bright particular star" closed the scene, after the briefest of conversations. No quips on virginity survived. Transposition combined with excision remolded Helena into a passive, quiet, modest young woman. Modifications in the rest of the text reinforced this portrait. The stereotype prevailed over Shakespeare's characterization.

For audiences today, the Helena-Parolles conversation on virginity is hardly offensive, although some critics decry it. The exchange indicates Parolles's tendency to speak of a subject he thinks amusing yet appropriate to Helena, a young unmarried woman. And it might show his awareness of her interest in Bertram, an interest inimical to his own. Shakespeare's choice of Parolles for this early unmasking of Helena's feelings suggests a desire to pair these two characters who stand on the fringes of the society of the play and have the two longest roles—almost equal in length.[5] Their encounter also stresses Helena's lack of reserve (despite her early silence), her intellectual vigor, and her tendency to consider herself the equal of men—a point that will become for some her major problem throughout the drama.

Nor is Helena alone in this confident sense of self, expressed through an easy, unself-conscious exchange with a man on the subject of sex. Two scenes later, the Countess of Rossillion engages Lavatch, her servant-clown, in a similar conversation. Again the subject is virginity and again a woman crosses class lines, ignoring the demands of decorum to question a crude character who revels in his own down-to-earth observations. When she wonders at his rationale for marrying so late in life, he explains, "My poor body, madam, requires it. I am driven on by the flesh, and he must needs go that the devil drives" (I.iii.28–30). This leads to a debate on the relationship of marriage to evil, Lavatch freely admitting that "I hope to have friends for my wive's sake . . . for the knaves come to do that for me which I am a-weary of. He that ears my land spares my team, and gives me leave to inn the crop. If I be his cuckold, he's my drudge" (39–46)—an admission of fatigue, but also a brash statement on his willingness to be cuckolded. Again, perhaps, Shakespeare is turning tradition upside down—the tradition of male possessiveness of women. Occasionally the Countess interrupts Lavatch with a reprimand. However, such interruptions seem more like dramaturgic devices to terminate a monologue rather than real expressions of shock or anger. For Lavatch then continues his biting observations using a new approach, story, or song.

The conversation between Helena and Parolles presented two views on easy loss of virginity, suggesting a virile, youthful perception; the exchange between the Countess and Lavatch betrays the speakers' age—they are tired, wistful, philosophic. Both debates contrast men's and women's thoughts on sexuality and illustrate women's moral stance challenged by men's flippancy. The fact that both conversations occur early in the play suggests the dramatist's intention of showing the women's awareness of the male point of view when they later attempt to deal with Bertram, the beloved of the younger and the son of the older. But the conversations do more. They introduce us to two strong, attractive women who, unlike later audiences, appear unperturbed by men's rowdy humor.

In this scene as in the opening, past productions have excised, transposed, and inserted new material in an effort to alter the woman's portrait. Again, these changes date back to the earliest promptbooks—of 1773—and, with only some slight variations, continue through the nineteenth century and into the twentieth. For example, the Countess's lines with Lavatch are reduced to directives to call Helena while his talk of marriage, losing its cynicism, centers on a wish to have "issue a' my body" (25) and an admission, "I have been, madam, a wicked creature, as you and all flesh and blood are, and indeed I do marry that I may repent" (35–37). Indeed, by the twentieth century, Lavatch disappeared completely from Tyrone Guthrie's (1959) production, seriously affecting audience perception of the Countess. His absence helps diminish her portrait to that of a conventional, gentle, old woman, her vigor in Shakespeare's text fading into quiet conformity.

The general embarrassment and dissatisfaction with these conversations of the two women and the desire to mask the nonconformist aspect of their portraits have a long history. As early as 1773 the John Bell acting text, which purports to record the play "as performed at the Theatre Royal, Drury Lane," presented the following complaint:

From the appearance of several pieces Shakespeare wrote, we cannot but think he catched at some single idea, or character, without considering what other materials there might be to work upon. Hence we find him frequently capital in a few scenes, where he is very trifling in others; of this observation, we think *All's Well that Ends Well* is no slight instance; tho' a little attention might certainly have made even this slight plan much better; as it is, this play can never live on the stage, and hardly in the closet; yet we are of opinion, that by judicious alterations and additions, it might be made much more tolerable, both in public and private. (Prompt *AW* 3, Introduction)

In 1793 Kemble introduced "judicious alterations" into scene 3— the scene between the Countess and Lavatch—that glorified the mother who mourns her son's departure, injecting a note missing from Shakespeare's text.

The adaptation offers insight into the deeper understanding of women that emerges from the original. As occurs so often in Shakespeare's plays, adjacent scenes contrast with one another, sometimes to illuminate character, sometimes to establish the passage of time, and sometimes to heighten suspense. Shakespeare's scene 2, wafts us away from Rossillion for a brief sortie at the court of the sick King of France, showing his despair and the hopelessness of his illness.[6] Back at Rossillion in scene 3, we are conscious of a new time frame when we listen to the Countess first with Lavatch and then in a wonderful dialogue with Helena. The scene's first lines, "I will now hear. What say you of this gentlewoman?" (iii.1–2), reflect the Countess's concern for Helena. The lines also indicate the scene's artistic unity since the opening question will be answered at the close, when Helena, with the Countess's blessings, departs for the court of the King of France. Unified around the concept of women bonding together and supporting one another, the scene as constructed reveals little concern or weeping of a mother for a departed son.

Kemble, who moved scene 3 so that it immediately followed scene 1, lost the indeterminate time gap as well as the sharp contrast between the two older people—the King and the Countess. The actor-manager did, however, establish a pattern for later adaptors and created a more acceptably sad mother. Kemble changed the scene's opening lines, inserting a brief soliloquy before the query about Helena. Rather than referring to the future, it dwells on the past: "He's gone; and 't is weakness, to mourn over his departure," the Countess reflects (1793 ed., p. 3; 1811 ed., p. 8). The stereotypical mother, suffering silently and waiting patiently, replaces Shakespeare's activist older woman supportively encouraging the younger female. Ironically, Kemble borrowed the word *gone* from another context, the Countess's directive to Lavatch to "be gone, sir knave" (85), a command rather than a wistful recollection of her son.

Memories of her own youth and the sexual stirrings the Countess then felt—not thoughts about her son—characterize the soliloquy Shakespeare gives her. Considering Helena's plight, the older woman reminisces:

> If ever we are nature's, these are ours. This thorn
> Doth to our rose of youth rightly belong;
> Our blood to us, this to our blood is born.
>
> (129–31)

Meditating on virginity and sexuality, she reveals a warm, sympathetic, and basically optimistic perception of the heat and passion of youth. She has known it, and it has been good. Her lines contrast with the weariness of life and the jealousy of youth expressed by the King in the previous scene. He speaks of "haggish age" stealing on him (even giving it a feminine persona), then quotes his deceased friend's wish as reflecting the King's own desire:

> . . . "Let me not live," quoth he,
> "After my flame lacks oil, to be the snuff
> Of younger spirits, whose apprehensive senses
> All but new things disdain."
>
> (I.ii.58–61)

The fear of youth's disdain of age characterizes the sick King, contrasting his point of view with the Countess's healthy perception of herself and sexuality.

In comparing men's and women's lives, F. Scott Fitzgerald wrote of the sense of hopelessness, "the inevitable fatalism . . . the almost lust for death" that "creeps into all womanhood" as compared with the excitement that dominates men's lives (445). In this play Shakespeare reverses Fitzgerald's equation despite the adventures of Bertram at the front. In fact, the text here reveals the vibrancy of women's worlds as they differ from those of men. By transposing the sequence of scenes, however, Kemble diminished the contrast between the Countess's vitality and the King's languor and illness. Earlier, the Bell text blurred the distinctive differences between the two older people's ideas on sexuality by eliminating the Countess's lines on the warm blood of youth beginning, "If ever we are nature's, these are ours." Kemble reduced the Countess's lines of reflection to their simplest essentials—a brief reference to the resemblance between the two women followed by a description of the approaching younger one:

> E'en so it was with me, when I was young:
> Her eye is sick on't; I observe her now.[7]

The full speech emphasizes the naturalness of sexuality and the sense of human identification with nature. It has an outspoken joyousness. Interestingly, although the lines reappeared towards the end of the nineteenth century, they were again cut in 1935 by B. Iden Payne and in 1953 by Michael Benthall. Rather than representing the cultural responses of one period, the excisions seem instead to reflect patriarchal ideas about women that have persisted well into the twentieth century.

Shakespeare continues to offer conflicting perspectives on stereotypes about women in the second half of scene 3. There his dialectic method undercuts prevailing views that see women as competitive and lacking mutual support. Aware of Helena's plight, the Countess tries to show her concern for the young woman by proposing: "You know, Helen, / I am a *mother* to you." The simplicity of the language contrasts with Helena's formal "Mine honorable mistress." The dramatist then explores various interpretations of "mother":

> Nay, a *mother*,
> Why not a *mother*? When I said "a *mother*,"
> Methought you saw a serpent. What's in "*mother*"
> That you start at it? I say I am your *mother*,
> And put you in the catalogue of those
> That were enwombed mine.
>
> (I.iii.139–44, emphasis added)

Six uses of the word in seven lines heavily emphasize the concept. Although she is also teasing Helena here, the Countess is rejecting the belief in the superiority of natural to adoptive parents. Yet her son, in contrast, will later insist on verification of his role as natural parent as the price of becoming Helena's husband in more than name.

"You ne'er oppress'd me with a *mother's* groan, / Yet I express to you a *mother's* care" (147–48), the older woman reminds the

younger. Again the word *mother* surfaces. And again the stage
direction in the speech clearly delineates Helena's actions:

> God's mercy, maiden! does it curd thy blood
> To say I am thy *mother?*
>
> (149–50, emphasis added)

We, as audience, know the purpose of the Countess's insistence—
to elicit Helena's confession of love for Bertram, to offer sympathy,
and ultimately to help the young woman. Nevertheless, the rhetori-
cal pattern, the repetition of *mother*, has deeper resonances in this
play. For although the King has spoken to Bertram of his father,
we will discover that mothers, mother surrogates, mothering, and
the proof of motherhood take precedence over fatherhood. To the
Countess, motherhood means care, love, concern, and nurturing
without mandating pregnancy. Here the dramatist seems to question conventional patriarchal ideas about mothers or the strong
ties of blood that they must feel for their children. Rather, the
Countess's choral repetition of *mother* to Helena affirms close ties
with this "adoptive" child.

Excisions in this section abound in stage adaptations. These cuts
straddle the centuries. They reflect societal opposition to the ideas
expressed by the Countess rather than squeamishness regarding
language, an argument often used to explain textual excisions in
earlier periods. Neither eighteenth-century refinement nor
nineteenth-century bowdlerization account for them since they
persist into our age. For example, the 1773 text excises parts of the
Countess's soliloquy before Helena's entrance, but so does the 1953
text. Again, the lines "Adoption strives with nature, and choice
breeds / A native slip to us from foreign seeds" (145–46) disappear
from the 1888 as well as the 1953 versions. In contrast the following
passage has always survived intact:

> What, pale again?
> My fear has catch'd your fondness! Now I see
> The myst'ry of your loneliness, and find
> Your salt tears' head, now to all sense 'tis gross:
> You love my son.
>
> (169–73)

Unlike descriptions of motherhood and mothering, these lines contain all the push-button words associated with women and love:

pale, fear, fondness, mystery, loneliness, and salt tears. The excisions undercut Shakespeare's remarkable portrait of an outspoken, attractive upper-class woman, one who defied acceptable cliches.

Tyrone Guthrie, who had eliminated the Lavatch section in his 1959 production, retained this particular encounter between the two women in full. Perhaps the stress on intimacy between mother-surrogate and potential daughter-in-law had a contemporary relevance; or perhaps references to birth and pregnancy by two women alone on stage no longer shocked audiences. Undoubtedly the presence of two remarkable actresses, Zoe Caldwell as Helena and Edith Evans as the Countess, also influenced the director, who tempered the language elsewhere. According to stage directions, Helena kneels, the Countess lifts up the young woman's face, the Countess then holds Helena's hand and slowly turns her so that they are looking at one another. Warmth and trust exist between them (see illustration). Photographs suggest the scene's visual influence on the 1981 BBC TV production of *All's Well*. There the two women meet before a fireplace; the lights and shadows in the room and on their faces capture the fluctuations of mood as Helena moves from kneeling on the floor to rising with the older woman's blessings:

> Why, Helen, thou shalt have my leave and love,
> . . . .
>   and be sure of this,
> What I can help thee to, thou shalt not miss.
>
> (251–56)

Helena, the activist, will go to the French court. Convinced that she can cure the King, she wishes to gamble her life on her medicine, explaining, "I'd venture / The well-lost life of mine on his grace's cure" (247–48)—a gamble she will repeat with greater vehemence to the King himself when he challenges, "Upon thy certainty and confidence / What dar'st thou venter?" (II.i.169–70). Her final offer comes late in the conversation, only after she has failed to convince him of her skill. For the audience, that last proposal is linked to her earlier conversation with Parolles where she speaks with such directness about sex.

At first, despite Lafew's strong introduction of her as the daughter of her famous physician father, the King rejects Helena's proposal. He assures her that others, far more skilled than she, have finally admitted defeat. There is no cure for his illness. "We thank you, maiden, / But may not be so credulous of cure, / When our most learned doctors leave us" (II.i.114–16), he protests. As she presses on, he warns her of her naivete, "But what at full I know, thou know'st no part, / I knowing all my peril, thou no art" (132–33). It is only when she offers her life, and perhaps more persuasively, her reputation, that he listens. It is her willingness to have her name bandied about as a strumpet that finally convinces him. The obverse of Isabella's unwillingness to sacrifice her virginity for her brother's life (*Measure for Measure*), Helena's proposal rests on a similar awareness of the price expected of women—one linked with sexuality. Because her eventual goal is marriage to Bertram, Helena gambles that combination—her life and her reputation:

> Tax of impudence,
> A strumpet's boldness, a divulged shame,
> Traduc'd by odious ballads; my maiden's name
> Sear'd otherwise; ne worse of worst—extended
> With vildest torture, let my life be ended.
>
> (170–74)

The above passage is one of the play's cruxes, its punctuation challenging editors. However, the general references to being called a strumpet, celebrated as such in ballads, having her name disgraced, and finally meeting death through torture, seem clear, especially the direct connection between loss of virginity and loss of reputation. Helena knows that this is the sharpest criticism a young woman can face, coupling sexual disgrace with death. As a result of the extremity of her personal risk, the King agrees to try her cure.

And then, once again she deviates from the expected behavioral pattern for women: she asks for a reward. Rather than being satisfied with the King's thanks or her own sense of accomplishment at having cured a seemingly incurable man, she sets a specific price on her labor. Although her story parallels Shakespeare's source and is said to have prototypes in early folk tales (Lawrence, Ch. 2), her request for marriage to the man of her choosing is clearly unconventional. And yet, she asks for neither money nor wisdom nor any more esoteric reward, but rather for the prize which young women have been trained to seek: marriage. Helena's bargain with the King reflects her directness; she will chance her life:

> . . . not helping, death's my fee,
> But if I help, what do you promise me?
> *King.*   Make thy demand.
> *Helena.*   But will you make it even?
> *King.*   Ay, by my sceptre and my hopes of heaven.
>
> (189–92)

The challenge for Helena, however, goes beyond winning a husband; it lies in overcoming the shift in values when women succeed in a patriarchal society. Suddenly the rules of the game change. Helena cures the King and wins the hand of Bertram in marriage only to discover that the highly acclaimed achievement loses its luster when performed by a woman. Because such success so surprises men, as Margaret Fuller observes, the term *miracle* then replaces *success*:

> Wherever she has herself arisen in national or private history, and nobly shone forth in any form of excellence, men have received her, not only willingly, but with triumph. Their encomiums, indeed, are always, in some sense, mortifying; they show too much surprise. "Can this be you?" he cries to the transfigured Cinderella; "well, I should never have thought it, but I am very glad. We will tell every one that you have '*surpassed your sex*.'" (43)

The critical word in the above quote is *mortifying*. Fuller then goes on to explain it as revealing men's inability to comprehend women's success when competing in men's sphere. In Shakespeare's play, Parolles's lines reverberate with the same incomprehension as those of Fuller's typical man: "Mort du vinaigre! is not this Helen?" (II.iii.44), he exclaims in shock when he discovers that she is the person who has cured the King's illness and is dancing a coranto with him. If she has surprisingly "surpassed her sex," Helena's problem is that the reward she has asked for expresses the traditional expectations of her sex—a husband—but it casts her as the active pursuer rather than the passively wooed.

After Parolles's exclamation, the King wastes no time in honoring his pledge. He calls the young men of his court to him and directs:

> Fair maid, send forth thine eye. This youthful parcel
> Of noble bachelors stand at my bestowing,
> O'er whom both sovereign power and father's voice

I have to use. Thy frank election make;
Thou hast power to choose, and they none to forsake.

(II.iii.52–56)

Shakespeare uses a sensitively tuned artistic device—a series of young nobles whom Helena will query—to show that not merely Bertram, but societal attitudes, conspire against her. She moves from one young man to the next: "Sir, will you hear my suit?"(76) she asks. "And grant it" (77), he replies. The words seem to imply acceptance. Helena, however, moves on to the next potential suitor. Here her opening observation offers a clue to what she sees: "The honor, sir, that flames in your fair eyes, / Before I speak too threat'n-ingly replies"(80–81). Nevertheless, she asks and he accedes. Re-jecting him, she moves on. As David Haley observes, "The young lords' icy politeness masks a contempt of which Helena is quite sensible" (49). Although there has been some critical disagreement as to the young men's reactions to Helena, the dramatist provides a first-hand observer in the King's trusted adviser, Lafew. Because verbal meanings may be colored by tonal inflections and even contradicted by body language, his indignant comment should be recognized as summarizing those young bachelors' responses: "Do all they deny her? And they were sons of mine, I'd have them whipt, or I would send them to th' Turk to make eunuchs of"(86–88). On the page, the men's lines may not appear cold; Lafew's speech, acting as a stage direction, tells us just how they must be spoken on stage. A third and yet a fourth "noble bachelor" is approached and then rejected by Helena. We know, just as she does, that Ber-tram is the man, right from the start. Surely part of the reason for this movement from one young man to the next is the laughter it can provoke. Through the double vision possible in the theater, audiences may watch the contradictory impulses driving Helena and, at the same time, keep an eye on Bertram.

This important scene illuminating her character, however, fre-quently changes shape on stage. Records of the omission of the other young men date back to 1773. Once more, excisions reduce her role. The audience may no longer observe her dramatic flair as she moves from one young man to the next. Nor may they hear her keen evaluation of each prospect and her sense of humor. Even worse, the cuts deny audiences the opportunity to witness Helena's timidity as she shies away from naming Bertram at once, perhaps in the wild hope that he may find her attractive and step forward.

The scene, which emphasizes the fate of a woman who wins in a society where she is not even supposed to compete, becomes instead another example of Helena's unfeeling forwardness since she moves immediately to Bertram.

Shakespeare's insight into this catch-22 for women, personalized and made specific in Helena in this scene, echoes in our own time. In her article "Fail: Bright Women," Matina Horner documents the decision of intelligent college women to sacrifice intellectual excellence for sexual appeal to men (36–39). In fact, in Tyrone Guthrie's 1959 production, this dichotomy between brains and beauty is clearly established by the introduction of additional lines in a ball scene preceding the entrance of the cured King with Helena. The guests are speaking. One guest refers to the "Wise Woman" in the King's chamber; another to the "good old King"; still another gives the impression that the King himself will not appear that evening. Then one of the guests says, "quite a young girl, quite young. Your age or less"—obviously addressing a woman—who responds, "Would I had her skill." "Or she your beauty," is the quick reply. Giving the conversation a too-modern twist, the woman then chides, "Nay sir, none of that. My husband will be angry." Helena's triumphant waltz from one young man to the next hardly wins applause. She has not learned to fail. But productions in the eighteenth and nineteenth centuries refrained from showing the scene Shakespeare wrote. Instead they reduced it to a single, undeviating choice, emphasizing her single-minded devotion, without humor, to Bertram.

As written, Shakespeare's scene has a complexity that questions some accepted stereotypes. It confronts us with the weaknesses of our social system and the cost to women of a limited perception of sexuality, one stressing a dichotomy between intelligence and physical beauty. The play seems to accept the possibility that these two qualities along with assertiveness can belong to one woman character. Many adaptors, however, failed to link these characteristics in Helena. Guthrie's production characterizes one of the problems: the influence of contemporary culture on staging the play. Nineteen fifty-nine belonged to the post–World War II period, marked by women's return to the kitchen and child-raising; normalcy was defined as treasuring the home life.[8] Betty Friedan had not yet completed *The Feminine Mystique* although women were living it. As she says, she "wasn't even conscious of the woman problem"(1) until she started writing the book in 1957. To give some idea of just what the period was like, and how, therefore, it could have influenced this production, even though Guthrie was working in England at the time, I quote:

> By the end of the nineteen-fifties, ... the proportion of women attending college in comparison with men [dropped] from 47 per cent in 1920 to 35 per cent in 1958. A century earlier, women had fought for higher education; now girls went to college to get a husband. By the mid-fifties, 60 per cent dropped out of college to marry, or because they were afraid too much education would be a marriage bar. (12)

In such an environment, responses to Helena, but more important perhaps, projections of her in the theater were distorted.

By omitting the other young men, or by creating a portrait of the brainy if sexually unattractive woman, adaptors and directors failed to hear the text's complexity in Helena's selection speech. Perhaps they found her movement from one young man to another painful or unladylike. Nevertheless, this withholding of her choice of Bertram appears in the text. Although her lines to Bertram sound submissive, her final four words—addressed to the King— do not:

> I dare not say I take you, but I give
> Me and my service, ever whilst I live,
> Into your guiding power.—This is the man.
>
> (II.iii.102–4)

She has employed neither seduction nor tricks. In a society that rewards achievement, she has won honestly, gambling her life. But she has defied the conventions. Although innumerable examples exist in fiction probably known to Shakespeare's audience of the wise woman who, given a seemingly impossible task, achieves it, this drama also illuminates the immediate and specific obstacles a woman character, no matter how wise, must face.

When Helena says, "This is the man," Shakespeare creates an explosive situation to move his audience. Although Charlotte Perkins Gilman writes of "what one would logically expect" as a result of a girl's training, she also knows that such logic is irrelevant. At this point in the action, *All's Well That Ends Well* illustrates that absence of logic. Helena has followed logic in pursuing marriage to Bertram. He, however, scorns her; he would choose for himself and not be the one chosen. As we later discover, he insists on initiating the choice. Although his training, unlike a woman's, may not have focused on the "vocation" of marriage, the social structure endorses him. The play, however—because of its sympathy for Helena and its alteration of the character of Bertram from the prototype in the source—questions that position.

Shakespeare's play also reveals how a "logic" based on power governs patterns of courtship in a patriarchal society. Responses to Helena's being the wooer or pursuer depend in part on the staging and in part on evaluation of the validity of her action. George Bernard Shaw cheered her as the precursor of the modern woman, calling the play "an experiment repeated nearly three hundred years later in *A Doll's House*" (*Our Theatres* 1:27). Others have condemned her.[9] Writing of *Othello*, Helen Gardner noted that passions are still strong concerning the play's subjects—among them jealousy, fidelity, and chastity—and considers this one reason why a "conflict of views about the play and its hero" exists (5).[10] The same may be said about *All's Well That Ends Well*. A conflict of views exists about one of the primary subjects in this play: the right of a woman to pursue a man with the objective of marriage. Implicit here is the pejorative accusation of "aggressiveness" applied to women for characteristics praised in men as "strength" and "self-confidence" (Broverman 34:1–7). Despite her success in curing the King and her right to a reward, Helena herself feels the social pressure and retreats to the expected womanly role, "That you are well restor'd, my lord, I'm glad. Let the rest go," a line never excised (II.iii.147–48). But it is too late, the contest has become one between the honor of two men; the elder and more powerful, the King, triumphs.

Married to Bertram, Helena discovers the irony of that first debate with Parolles, so relevant to the play and so often omitted. Once again virginity is the topic. Paradoxically, the challenge she faces is not that of protecting herself from a man who would "blow her up" but of legitimating her marriage through pregnancy by her husband. Having returned to Rossillion at his request, she receives his letter: "When thou canst get the ring upon my finger, which never shall come off, and show me a child begotten of thy body that I am father to, then call me husband; but in such a 'then' I write a 'never.'" She recoils at its finality. "This is a dreadful sentence" (III.ii.58–61). Eighteenth- and nineteenth-century actor-managers also recoiled. They found his conditions tasteless and therefore reduced the letter to Bertram's first demand: the ring.

Like variations on a motif, the pattern of this scene recalls the play's opening at Rossillion. Again the Countess dominates the conversation. This time, however, her praise for Helena is linked with disapproval of Bertram. "I do wash his name out of my blood, / And thou art all my child" (67–68), she exclaims to the young bride, condemning Bertram's defiance of a good King and "misprising of a maid too virtuous / For the contempt of empire" (31–32). Reacting with scorn to the closing line of his letter, "Till I have no wife, I have nothing in France" (74–75), she labels him a "rude" (82) boy, exploding, "There's nothing here that is too good for him / But only she," (80–81). Meanwhile, the parallel to the earlier pattern continues as Helena listens in comparative silence. Again, she reveals herself only in soliloquy after the others have left the stage. This time, however, she speaks as a wife reacting to her husband's letter. Nor does her soliloquy capture the tone of passive adoration or exuberant confidence in the value of action heard at the beginning of the play. Despite reward, action had not brought the anticipated happy ending. The naive young woman who believed "Our remedies oft in ourselves do lie" has discovered that societal conventions subvert the self's achieving its goal. Feeling guilty at depriving Bertram of the right to come home and fearing that he may be killed in battle, Helena's adoration of him cannot be passive—as it was at the play's opening. More in despair than hope, she decides to leave Rossillion that night.

Shakespeare's modulations of the portrait of Helena continue, revealing his insight into women's lives as they seek to adjust and readjust to the restrictive rules of a patriarchal society. Disguised as a pilgrim, she arrives in Florence disconsolate and feeling defeated. Although critics have questioned her motives for going to Florence—some believing she is further plotting to "snare" Bertram—her reflections in soliloquy before leaving Rossillion, her subsequent letter informing the Countess of the decision to depart, and even Helena's later comments to the Florentine women all reflect her sense of defeat. At this moment in the play, she believes she has overstepped the boundaries of proper behavior and therefore deserves her fate.

Meeting three women who identify her at once as a pilgrim recently come from France, she accepts their invitation to join them in watching the parade of passing French troops. She listens to their talk of Bertram. "Here you shall see a countryman of yours / That has done worthy service" (III.v.47–48), says the eldest, the

Widow. When told that according to reports the King "married him / Against his liking "(53–54) and that Parolles speaks "but coarsely" of the wife, Helena agrees, "O, I believe with him" (56–57). Disagreeing with Helena, these women show more compassion for Bertram's wife than she does for herself. Observes the Widow's daughter, Diana:

> Alas, poor lady,
> 'Tis a hard bondage to become the wife
> Of a detesting lord.
> . . . .
> I would he lov'd his wife. If he were honester
> He were much goodlier.
> . . . .
> 'Tis pity he is not honest.
>
> (63–65, 79–80, 82)

She expresses her sympathy in three separate speeches, while Helena regains confidence after the Widow's comment, "This young maid might do her / A shrewd turn, if she pleas'd" (67–68). The disguised wife's quick response, "How do you mean?" (68), differs from her resigned acceptance of Parolles's unflattering comments earlier in the scene.

Providing comfort and support for her, these women also introduce still another perspective on virginity, one less concerned with "choosing to one's own liking" than with defense against the manipulative male. Before Helena's appearance, their conversation establishes the standards governing their actions. Diana's praise of "the French count" (Bertram) who had "done most honorable service" (III.v.3–4) is quickly interrupted by the warning, "The honor of a maid is her name, and no legacy is so rich as honesty" (12–13). The speaker, Mariana, then details men's methods of seduction:

> [T]heir promises, enticements, oaths, tokens, and all these engines of lust, are not the things they go under. Many a maid hath been seduc'd by them, and the misery is, example, that so terrible shows in the wrack of maidenhood, cannot for all that dissuade succession, but that they are lim'd with the twigs that threatens them. I hope I need not to advise you further, but I hope your own grace will keep you where you are, though there were no further danger known but the modesty which is so lost.
>
> (18–28)

All but the last sentence of this was excised from the 1773 Bell text and both Kemble adaptations. Benson, in 1888, printed the entire section in small type—indicating omission—and Bridges, in the 1922 production, deleted these lines. What remains is a brief "Beware of them [Parolles and Bertram] Diana" (18) followed by the response "You shall not need to fear me" (29). The specificity of the warning has been eliminated along with Mariana's hopelessness about women heeding her.

At the beginning of the play, Helena had asked in jest if there were a way to "barricado" oneself against the invading male; she had been assured there was none. Her conversation had concentrated on the physical aggression against a woman's virginity. Mariana includes the emotional and psychological, oaths and flattery, noting that women themselves cooperate in breaking down their own defences. Paradoxically, Shakespeare, here as elsewhere—in *Love's Labour's Lost* and *Romeo and Juliet*, for example—illustrates the ability of young women to perceive men's deception through oaths and flattery.[11]

Crossing social and intellectual lines, Helena gains a new sense of herself as a woman through this chance meeting with others who identify with "Bertram's wife." The Widow's comment about Diana leads the disguised pilgrim to further speculate, "May be the amorous count solicits her / In the unlawful purpose" (69–70). Her choice of words shows how carefully Shakespeare has developed the portrait of a woman who knows the man she has married. The texts "amorous," "solicits," and "unlawful" also seem to contradict one critic's theory that Bertram "must be educated to accept ... sexuality," or that his initial rejection of Helena included a "recoil from sexuality itself" (Parker, 100, 102).

Conferring with the Widow in her next scene, Helena asks for help in fulfilling the demands of the letter. She establishes her identity, then reveals, again, her knowledge of Bertram, a flawed man. Referring to the ring on his finger that she must acquire, she counsels:

> This ring he holds
> In most rich choice; yet in his idle fire,
> To buy his will, it would not seem too dear,
> Howe'er repented after.

(III.vii.25–28)

More than anyone else, she spells out his weaknesses. He is accustomed to getting what he wishes, then weighing the cost afterwards. According to her evaluation, her "bright particular star"—now her husband—is spoiled. In the first scene, she tolerated Parolles—"a notorious liar"—because of Bertram—"I love him for his sake." Here she offers more specifics. Although critics have tended to ask flippantly why someone as gifted and bright as Helena would want a cad like Bertram, the play emphasizes the irrelevance of that question. Rather, Shakespeare asks why a woman superior to a man in intelligence, ability, and moral strength may not choose to her own liking. He then explores the close relationship between power and sexuality. Helena has competed and won by society's rules. And yet she has not been able to claim her reward. Kate Millett writes: "Sexual dominion obtains . . . as perhaps the most pervasive ideology of our culture and provides its most fundamental concept of power" (25). Bertram's power supersedes the King's.

From the opening to the closing of this play, we hear the contrast between the way men and women "meditate" on virginity, noting its direct relationship to power. Helena opens with thoughts of Bertram. Parolles expounds on the philosophic reasons why women should hurry and lose their virginity. Helena decides actively to pursue Bertram at court. The Clown talks of his need for a woman and marriage; the Countess soliloquizes on falling in love, then shares her thoughts on childbearing with Helena. The King speaks of the girls of Italy, jestingly warning his young nobles against them. Helena at court chances being called a strumpet and disgraced as a whore if she fails in her cure. Meditating on virginity for her means winning Bertram. For Bertram, meditating on virginity means setting impossible standards for consummating a marriage. It also means deflowering Diana. For Diana, meditating on virginity means learning to distrust men's vows.

Diana's delightful scene with Bertram when she bargains for the ring and sets the time and place of the rendezvous illustrates her skepticism about the truth of men's vows:

> 'Tis not the many oaths that makes the truth,
> But the plain single vow that is vow'd true.
> . . . .
> If I should swear by Jove's great attributes

I lov'd you dearly, would you believe my oaths
When I did love you ill?

(IV.ii.21–27)

Reminiscent of Juliet's lines to Romeo, this speech gives insights into Diana's wit and sharpness. Often, however, merely a few lines remain, the scene's primary emphasis being on a comparison of his ring—"an honor 'longing to our house" (42)—and Diana's chastity—"the jewel of our house" (46). Gone too in many versions is most of her closing soliloquy, beginning "My mother told me just how he would woo, / As if she sate in's heart" (69–70) and ending, "Only in this disguise I think't no sin / To cozen him that would unjustly win" (75–76).

Since she and the Widow are important supports for Helena in the closing scenes, the audience needs to have some hint of their humanity and sense of values. Too often excisions blur the picture. Occasionally staging alters the intention of the text. Guthrie, for example, introduced a musical duet between Diana and Bertram at the scene's opening:

Bertram.	Pray thee take these flowers, maiden fair.
Diana.	Thank you sir for me they're blossoms rare.
Bertram.	Tho' they fade and wither yet stayeth green,
Both.	In my heart, forever my love unseen.

This was only part of the overall shift in characterization. According to Price, Guthrie also presented Diana as "a wartime factory tart who sits on the doorstep in nightgown and housecoat" and the Widow as an older version of her daughter (58). No longer is Diana a moral young woman supporting another woman's cause. She becomes, instead, someone involved in a trick because of possible reward, thus distorting the text.

The substitution of one woman for another in a man's bed has often troubled critics, who label it "the bed trick." Diana, after winning Bertram's ring, promises to meet him. Instead, her rendezvous becomes Helena's. Applying the test of realism to such substitution, some critics find the play deeply flawed. But realism does not affect the underlying truth expressed in the work. Nor is it relevant that Helena becomes pregnant after one encounter with a man—the complaint of one critic who called it "an extremely lucky hit" (Parker, 112). Shakespeare's portraits of women in *All's Well That Ends Well*, of their relationships with one another, of their

Transfixed by the passing troops, the women on the balcony momentarily leave their laundry while the Widow, on the street below, points out Bertram—in the 1959 *All's Well That Ends Well*. Angus McBean photograph, courtesy of the Harvard Theatre Collection, The Houghton Library.

perceptions of the male world, and of their sense of themselves have a validity that overshadows any realistic questions of plot—just as the presence of a ghost does not disqualify the insights in *Hamlet*. The women, particularly Helena and the Countess, are remarkable and complex. This comedy seems to ask, "What if men and women were equal?" It answers with a variation on Virginia Woolf's words, that "Anything may happen when womanhood has ceased to be a protected occupation" (41). Then women, like men, may choose to their own liking and make their own mistakes.

Moving into the Illyria of adulthood for women and chancing sexual disgrace, Helena discovers constantly new unanticipated obstacles even after achieving the "vocation" of marriage. While fulfilling the requirements of comedy, the play's ending, where she finally wins Bertram for a second time, seems hedged about with ambiguities. It includes his rejection of Diana, lying and accusing her of being a camp follower, and then, when confronted by Helena, who has fulfilled all the seemingly impossible tasks listed in his letter, he begins his speech with the word *If*. "If she, my liege, can make me know this clearly, [that she is pregnant by him] / I'll love her dearly, ever, ever dearly" (V.iii.315–16). While Bertram's concession in these closing moments may sound like a reprieve, his actions offer little support for an unconditional change of heart. As the King's final lines suggest, "All yet seems well, and if it end so meet, / The bitter past, more welcome is the sweet" (V.iii.333–34). This is hardly a strong affirmative statement. Shakespeare presents a portrait of a woman unloved by her husband. Audiences and readers recognize the irony of Helena's rejoicing in this momentary triumph since she surpasses Bertram in knowledge, skill, and virtue.

Helena's acceptance by Bertram, however, must be considered against the larger landscape of women's sexual options—no matter what their talents—when they come of age in a patriarchal society. Shakespeare's heroine has successfully challenged the pattern. Not only has she planned "for whom she will achieve and attain," but she illustrates the "eager husband hunter" regarded with approval in the world of the play. The problem for those in the world outside the play—audiences, adaptors, and critics—is that they still look with disapproval on such logical behavior.

PART TWO

Political World

A snake draped around her neck, and dressed in a coat of mail and a helmet, Verree Teasdale appears as the captured Amazon queen, Hippolyta, in this still for the 1934 Reinhardt film of *A Midsummer Night's Dream*. Courtesy of the Museum of Modern Art/Film Stills Archive.

CHAPTER THREE

Male Magic

A MIDSUMMER NIGHT'S DREAM

> And with the juice of this I'll streak her eyes,
> And make her full of hateful fantasies.
>
> II.i.257–58

Whether in the fantasy world of the forest or the equally fantastic world of Athens on a midsummer night, this play reveals how power, particularly political power, impinges on and shapes women's lives. Ranging from queens—Hippolyta, a character taken from mythology, and Titania, belonging to the fairy world—to youthful Athenian maidens in love, to a parodic heroine in an entertainment for the Duke's guests, these characters illustrate women's varied reactions to the imposition of power. One seems to adjust; one discovers new facts about herself; one serves as a lens for looking at the larger world; and one significantly reveals the tragic dimensions of the loss of power. Least mortal and yet seeming in her speeches and attitudes to mimic the mortal world, the fairy queen illustrates most clearly the loss of self— the abdication of autonomy—that may follow a woman's being victimized, even by fairy power.

In developing the early emotional relationship between her and Oberon, the fairy king, Shakespeare seems to have drawn on the world around him for models. Thus when Titania refuses to comply to Oberon's demands, he vows in pique and jealousy to "streak her eyes" with magic juice "and make her full of hateful fantasies" (II.i. 257–58). Moreover, moments before he carries out his threat, he becomes more explicit:

> Be it ounce, or cat, or bear,
> Pard, or boar with bristled hair,

In thy eye that shall appear
When thou wak'st, it is thy dear:
Wake when some vile thing is near.

(ii.30–34)

In fact, she does wake and call some "vile thing" her "dear." How then do we interpret this? Is it the act of magic that forces her to "fall in love" with an ass, or at least with a character who has been temporarily transformed into an ass? Or are we to accept much of the criticism that suggests her erotic desire for the ass reflects her true nature—the nature of woman? Does Titania at this moment "awaken from her dream," look at the monster, and desire him, as Jan Kott (228) suggests? Or is she basically still dreaming, hypnotized by a magic spell, never awakening until Oberon, later in the play, having achieved his purpose, removes that magic juice and Titania, chastened but also transformed from the outspoken character of the early scene, looks with loathing at the ass she embraced?

Although her disagreement with Oberon lies at the heart of the play, Titania does not enter until the beginning of the second act. Instead, Shakespeare first introduces other women more clearly caught in situations of political or social subordination than the fairy queen: specifically Hippolyta, the captive Amazonian queen; Hermia, the rebellious Athenian daughter; and Helena who, in her complete self-denigration, illustrates more indirectly the impact of patriarchal power on women. Interweaving a third plot strand culminating in the performance of "Pyramus and Thisbe," the comedy also provides a dual vision of women in patriarchy near the play's close. Parodying the tragic results of arbitrary parental power, this play-within-a-play in its metadramatic dimension offers insights into the mainly silent women, now married, in the audience.

Artistically, the dramatist weaves a complex multifaceted plot that exposes the political and domestic challenges confronting women while creating situations that throw us into the world of comedy. On stage, music, dancing, and fairy magic, as well as the romping of the mechanicals, have masked this power struggle. In criticism, the lure of the poetry, the concept of "topsy turvy," the illusion of dreams, and theories of mythology have often tended to blur any interest in the domination of women. Some critics have even proposed that the play was written specifically for a wedding although none has yet been found.

In fact, *A Midsummer Night's Dream* opens with anticipation of a wedding although it hardly reveals clearcut delight by both participants, Hippolyta and Theseus, the Duke of Athens, her captor but also her bridegroom:

> Now, fair Hippolyta, our nuptial hour
> Draws on apace. Four happy days bring in
> Another moon; but O, methinks, how slow
> This old moon wanes! She lingers my desires,
> Like to a step-dame, or a dowager,
> Long withering out a young man's revenue.
>
> (I.i.1–6)

His reference to "happy days" and the final fulfilling of his desire meets a noncommittal response from the bride. Acknowledging that four days swiftly pass, she indicates neither joy nor sorrow as she anticipates "the night / Of our solemnities" (10–11). Her ambiguous answer leads Theseus to search further. Still the host, if also the victor, he sends his master of the revels on an errand to:

> Stir up the Athenian youth to merriments,
> Awake the pert and nimble spirit of mirth.

He would have his bride be merry. Continuing, he relies on a strange metaphor to reinforce his invitation to joyous celebration:

> Turn melancholy forth to funerals:
> The pale companion is not for our pomp.
>
> (12–15)

Why speak of funerals, even as a contrast to mirth, unless, perhaps a subtext exists here? Although "pale companion" defines the personified "melancholy," contextually the words seem linked to Hippolyta, addressed in the very next word:

> Hippolyta, I woo'd thee with my sword,
> And won thy love doing thee injuries;
> But I will wed thee in another key.
>
> (16–18)

Is he apologizing for his earlier role? She fails to reply. His speeches suggest a shift in perception of woman from enemy to lover to wife, with the implication of woman's submission to man. As cour-

tesy books and religious tracts of the period indicate, that reference
to love and marriage, while including mutuality, also meant acknowledging man's superiority.[1]

This first scene, particularly the opening entrance and the ellip-
tical conversation between Theseus and his bride, have allowed
for a range of interpretations on stage because of Hippolyta's
silence. Directors and actor-managers have long manipulated both
the action and audience attitude toward a character or a situation
during such silences. Writing of this phenomenon recently, particularly as it affects productions, one critic observed:

> Hippolyta's silence is open not because Shakespeare lacked the skill
> to give her words but because he did not exercise that skill, did not
> employ the power of his "poet's pen" to give her silence precisely fixed
> meanings and effects. (McGuire, 17)

McGuire then cites examples from four productions since 1959.
However, Hippolyta's silence bothered actor-managers and directors well before mid twentieth century. Because her role is so brief
(she does not appear again until act 4) some, like David Garrick
in *The Fairies* (1755), have cut her lines although she is physically
present and combined Theseus's two speeches into a single long
address.[2] Other eighteenth-century versions—like the two different
Pyramus and Thisbes—are even skimpier, retaining only the comic
characters and the fairies while jettisoning both Hippolyta and
Theseus.[3] Earlier, during the Restoration, comic interludes, separated from the larger overall scheme, and abbreviated versions
held the stage, culminating in the opera *The Fairy Queen* (1692),
from which Hippolyta disappeared.[4]

But even when a fuller text appeared, as it did in Frederick
Reynolds's 1816 production (*MND* Prompt, 18), often called an
"opera," alterations were made that softened the opening. Some
occurred in the text itself, as, for example, when Reynolds not only
retained the conversation between the victor and his bride, but
elaborated on it. In this version, Theseus's fourth act directive to
a forester to provide "the music" of the "hounds," as entertainment
for Hippolyta (IV.i.110), is attached to that opening promise to
wed her in "another key" (I.i.18), an attempt to strengthen the
attractiveness of the bridegroom.[5]

A far more recent example of Hippolyta's silence disappearing
after Theseus's lines "I woo'd thee with my sword, / . . . But I will
wed thee in another key" occurs in the 1935 Max Reinhardt film

where he transposes the sequence of speeches. In the film, Theseus's lines precede, rather than follow, Hippolyta's single speech and therefore evoke her immediate and soothing comment "Four days will quickly steep themselves in night; / Four nights will quickly dream away the time" (7–8). Nor can Reinhardt's film be looked upon as a single aberration. Rather, the German director provides an important link between stage and screen, having produced the play eleven times (beginning in 1905) prior to making the film in 1934.

Free of the confining limits of the stage, he could, as film director, waft his viewers from one location to another, jumping from a distant scene to a close-up of a particular character. In a section of the film script later discarded, Reinhardt not only appears to have been testing the breadth of this comparatively new medium but also offers insights into the finished film. The script also reflects the director's penchant for interpretation. In quick succession, it carries us aboard Theseus's ship, drops us in the land of the Amazons, and involves us in the battle between Theseus and Hippolyta through visuals that act as prologue to the text. Broad shots of the sea and the distant castle of the Amazons are interwoven with close-ups of the two major figures. We read of Theseus standing on the prow of the ship, "a glamorous figure in shining armor, against the dark background of the sail" and of Hippolyta standing with a large wild dog at her side as she "sternly watch[es] the approaching ship" (*MND* Warners, 1934).[6] Stern Hippolyta is contrasted with glamourous Theseus. Finally, when he appears on land followed by his staff, she takes up armor and weapons and shoots at him. He, however, "lower(s) his shield laughing," the implication being that fighting against a woman is laughable and that she, of course, will miss her mark. Eventually, they end up in hand to hand battle, "shield against shield," his shield flat upon hers, pressing it backward. The sequence continues:

2. H[ippolyta].'s knee bending, interlocking with Theseus' leg
3. Th[eseus].'s shoulder pressing H[ippolyta].'s shoulder downward. . . .
5. H[ippolyta].'s head and shoulders going backward.
6. Th[eseus].'s arm across H[ippolyta].'s shoulder, knocks the helmet from her head. H[ippolyta].'s long hair falls about her shoulders.
7. H[ippolyta].'s head bends backward. Th[eseus].'s head comes into picture triumphantly.[7]

There we have the classic picture of the implied rape-seduction scene although as the opening of *A Midsummer Night's Dream* clearly indicates, Theseus waits to wed Hippolyta.[8] What remains of this sequence is a clue to a point of view and to the play's early moments.

In fact, as it was actually made, Reinhardt's film opens quite differently with a general celebratory air as crowds sing and cheer the returning victor, their Duke Theseus, with his captive queen who rides with him, her arm entwined by a snake, indicating her heathenish origins (see illustration). Later that snake will merely be a pattern on a "civilized" dress she wears. The strange look on her face during that opening entrance as well as her action in a subsequent scene probably owe their origins to this discarded "script." In the later scene, dressed like a lady, Hippolyta sits alone in a large open colosseumlike semicircular area surrounded by large columns (a Hollywood approximation of Athens) and looks wistfully across the water. Is she recollecting her former glory and envisioning again the burning towers she left behind? Moments later, Theseus enters and kisses her hand (see illustration). Her reaction seems to suggest that she feels a thrill at his kiss. The rape-seduction undercurrent first suggested by their hand-to-hand battle when her helmet fell off is sustained here.

In contrast, Liviu Ciulei's stage production, fifty years later, dramatically emphasized Hippolyta's role as a captive in that opening scene. Brought on stage where everyone is wearing white, Hippolyta enters in dark army garb. Moments later, screened from audience view by her captors, she is basically stripped, her clothes thrown into the fire—all except her boots, which she contines to wear—perhaps symbolically suggesting that some remnant of her former self remains—a remnant that allows her to express her hostility, by stamping her heels as an accompaniment to her sardonic laughter. Otherwise, she is redressed in a white gown. Someone holds a mirror to her. She turns away. When Theseus enters, there is laughter at his lines, as he says, "But I will wed thee in another key." She simply turns around, and sits, her physical stance exuding hostility.

Many versions simply eliminated this character, thus excising the frame and problems of interpretation, but also insights into how one queen eventually handles the humiliation of defeat. In her next appearance she has adopted an attitude of congeniality, quipping with Theseus about his knowledge of hounds. Moreover,

Civilized now, Hippolyta, with her blonde hair coiffed, smiles at Theseus, the snake design on her dress being the only remnant of her Amazonian past in this still for Reinhardt's 1934 film. Courtesy of the Museum of Modern Art/ Film Stills Archive.

in her final scene she takes on an even more complicated role as the only speaking woman in a world of men.

Out of the theater, the Hippolyta and Theseus relationship evoked still another reaction. Margaret Fuller, the midnineteenth-century American feminist essayist, in her outspoken work *Woman in the Nineteenth Century,* wrote: "Only a Theseus could conquer before he wed the Amazonian queen." Fuller compared Theseus to Hercules, who "wished rather to rest with Dejanira, and received the poisoned robe as a fit guerdon."⁹ Whether or not Fuller had the historical story in mind, or Shakespeare's play, she nevertheless does offer an alternative perspective on the play's first nineteen lines.

Hippolyta then fades into the background as another woman enters who must wrestle with her fate. Hermia is dragged in by her angry father, Egeus, who would have the laws of Athens enforced against her because she wishes to marry Lysander, the man of her choice, rather than Demetrius, her father's choice, although, as most critics agree, little difference exists between the suitors. As Muriel Bradbrook has observed, Shakespeare contributed to the development of comedy by breathing life into his characters through language. She compares this gift to "the introduction of perspective in painting" (89). Accepting her analysis, we realize that the similarity between the young men is intentional and meant to highlight Egeus's unreasonableness. "I am . . . as well deriv'd as he," protests Lysander, the suitor who is "belov'd of beauteous Hermia":

> As well possess'd; my love is more than his;
> My fortunes every way as fairly rank'd.

> (I.i.99–104)

But the father refuses to listen, insisting that he "may dispose of" his daughter as he wishes, "either to this gentleman [Demetrius] / Or to her death" (42–44). Nor does Theseus, who only moments earlier had pledged to wed Hippolyta "in another key" from that of conqueror, offer much hope to the young woman. Supporting her father, the ruler warns of the price of disobedience: "Either to die the death, or to abjure / For ever the society of men" (65–66).

Life in a nunnery, a retreat for Isabella in *Measure for Measure,* has little appeal for Hermia. It denies her normal sexuality. Moreover, she is a young woman in love. However, Theseus, the voice of political power, continues, unconcerned about her reactions.

Spelling out the meaning of the law, he details the young woman's choices:

> Therefore, fair Hermia, question your desires,
> Know of your youth, examine well your blood,
> Whether (if you yield not to your father's choice)
> You can endure the livery of a nun,
> For aye to be in shady cloister mew'd,
> To live a barren sister all your life,
> Chaunting faint hymns to the cold fruitless moon.
>
> (*MND*, I.i.67–73)

"Barren," "cold," and "fruitless" describe the sexual denial she must confront should she disobey her father. Theseus presents a frightening alternative for her. Taking the father from Roman comedy, Shakespeare creates a comic scene with undercurrents of possibly tragic dimension.

But sections of this speech as well as of Egeus's complaints against Lysander disappeared from the stage. Gone are such accusations against Lysander as "thou has given her rhymes, / And interchanged love tokens"; sung at her window "verses of feigning love"; seduced her "With bracelets of thy hair, rings, gauds, conceits"; and, finally, "Turned her obedience, which is due to me, / To stubborn harshness."[10] Only Egeus's demand for the privilege of the father remained—the right to "dispose of her" as he saw fit or to call for the death penalty. Although retaining this harsh sentence, those who excised lines had effectively diminished the speech's intensity through abbreviation.

Gone too from the stage are the closing lines of Theseus's admonition to Hermia defining the obligations of a daughter:

> To you your father should be as a god
> One that composed your beauties; yea, and one
> To whom you are but as a form in wax
> By him imprinted and within his power
> To leave the figure or disfigure it.
>
> (47–51)

The image here, specifically the threat to "disfigure," disturbed critics and editors as early as the eighteenth century. William Warburton, for example, sought to change the last line, finding Theseus's statement inappropriate for comedy. In contrast, Samuel

Johnson, always one to favor the text over any change of language, defended the word although still bothered by the meaning:

> I know not why so harsh a word should be admitted with so little need, a word that, spoken, could not be understood, and of which no example can be shown. The sense is plain, "you owe to your father a being which he may at pleasure continue or destroy." (Yale Johnson, VII, 136)

If that rather chilling ultimatum contributes to the portrait of a powerful ruler asserting the ideas of his society, stage productions, by omitting the last three and a half lines of Theseus's speech, frequently altered the image. In fact, some stage versions retained only the preceding line, Theseus's far more gentle, "What say you, Hermia? Be advis'd, fair maid" (46).[11] Because the interaction of characters helps define them, a weakened portrait of Hermia results from the combination of excisions in Theseus's and Egeus's speeches. Facing less opposition, she need be less defiant. Or, looking at it another way, we see her as a less interesting character than the sharp, courageous young woman Shakespeare begins to develop here.

Illustrating just how complex this text is and how it may be read and reread for the stage, some twentieth-century directors have translated the relationship between the two women at this moment on the stage as one of bonding: Hermia, who faces an anguished choice, and Hippolyta, who stands on the sidelines, listening. And here too promptbooks offer evidence. Beerbohm Tree's, for example, indicates the Amazonian queen's sympathy for the younger woman by directing: "Hip[polyta] leads Herm[ia] to seat" (*MND* 7, interleaf facing p. 4). In Liviu Ciulei's production, the bonding takes another form. Since Hippolyta's strong personality had been developed at the play's opening, here she sneeringly laughs at Theseus's ultimatum, a clear comment on his actions and on the irony of his earlier words to her, "But I will wed thee in another key" (I.i.18). More humorous in approach and less sharply disapproving is the direction in the Peter Brook prompt: "All bow their heads" (12a). Brook dramatizes the rift between Theseus and Hippolyta by having them exit to opposite sides of the stage, "pausing at doors to look at each other." These twentieth-century directors found their cues in the text and responded, not with excision but with a new awareness of the play's subtlety and of the possibilities that staging might permit.

If Hermia's tragic fate is briefly understood by Hippolyta, the play quickly moves back to the world of comedy as the two lovers left alone on stage not only bemoan their fate but also engage in a conversation in which neither is hearing what the other says. Comforting his love, Lysander cites historical parallels of similarly fated lovers; Hermia, not listening, overflows with anger and frustration:

> *Lys*   The course of true love never did run smooth;
>   But either it was different in blood—

He begins, but she interrupts:

> *Her*   O cross! Too high to be enthralled to low!

Alternating lines, they continue:

> *Lys*   Or else misgraffed in respect of years—
> *Her*   O spite! Too old to be engaged to young!
> *Lys*   Or else it stood upon the choice of friends—
> *Her*   O hell! To choose love by another's eyes!
>
> (I.i.134–40)

The stichomythic pattern of the duet captures the intensity of the lovers' feelings, but also the humor of their reactions as each finds solace from a different verbal outpouring.

Nevertheless, the exchange disappeared from acting texts for over a hundred years.[12] Although the excision at first seems inexplicable, George Bernard Shaw's comments on an Augustin Daly production offer a partial answer. Unaware of how much Daly's version owed to his predecessors, and indignant over his mauling of the text, Shaw attributes the excision to Daly's uncomfortableness with Hermia's "Oh hell," then notes the impact of the cuts. Humorously he writes:

> Mr. Daly, shocked, as an American and an Irishman, at a young lady using such an expression as "Oh hell!" cuts out the whole antiphony, and leaves Lysander to deliver a long lecture without interruption from the lady. (*Our Theatres*, I, 180–81)

This "long lecture without interruption" also further denies audiences the partial portrait, later to be developed, of Hermia. Unsurprisingly, the lines disappeared from the Garrick-Colman and

Reynolds operatic versions since these works concentrated on songs loosely connected with one another by speeches, rather than on short exchanges. But the absence of Hermia's frustrated expression from the later stage versions is surprising.[13]

Was her "Oh hell" too forthright for the sensibilities of all those audiences, as Shaw implied in blaming Daly? A glance at the *Variorum*, strong in nineteenth-century criticism, suggests other, literary reasons, as well. Coleridge, for example writes:

> There is no authority for any alteration,—but I never can help feeling how great an improvement it would be, if the two former of Hermia's exclamations were omitted—the third and only appropriate one would then become a beauty, and most natural. (Coleridge [101], quoted in the *Variorum*, 18)

Rather than denigrating that last line with its "Oh hell," Coleridge praises it. Obviously, Hermia's annoyed exclamations bothered him more than the simple comment on the unfairness of choosing love "by another's eyes." Less generously, Halliwell, another critic of the time, believed Lysander's speech "would be improved by the omission of all of Hermia's interpolations" (18). Moreover, to support his opinion, he cited the editions of Dodd and Planché which actually deleted Hermia's lines.[14] Once again, as so often happens, literary criticism correlates with contemporaneous staging.

Why did her short speeches offend so? Was Lysander's single uninterrupted speech more appropriate? But then how could his speech help project Hermia's personality as it does in the original exchange? Stylistically, those clipped single lines suggest the exasperation and intensity of the young woman we are to meet later on in the forest. Moreover, the patter, or duet, of these two lovers complements the long heavy speeches of Egeus and Theseus, taking us back into the comic, romantic world of the play.

As critics have often noted, conflict between father and daughter arises here as it does in so many other of Shakespeare's plays, and here too the strength of the daughter is created by showing her resistence to her father's pressure; her lines in this duet are important. Shaw's review of Daly's production suggests a further effect of the "alternating lines" spoken by the "two star-crossed lovers"; he believes the alternating pattern sets "the whole scene throbbing with their absorption in one another" (133). It also explodes with their differing responses to the same situation.

Although a strong, self-confident, if frustrated, young woman emerges through the language here, not all of her lines reinforce this portrait. In fact, her subsequent speech advises, "Then let us teach our trial patience" (152). Between her two speeches, she has listened to Lysander's litany of lovers who, throughout history, have faced problems. In the cut acting texts I have examined, the line advising patience always remains. What a different Hermia we experience. The language has been modulated, the humor of the exchange lost, and the outspoken young woman tempered.

Artistically, too, a change occurs. No verbal echoes will sound for the audience when, a few lines later, Hermia and her best friend, Helena, indulge in a similar pattern of alternating lines. Nor will the audience hear how their conversation mimics and yet differs from that of the lovers. The repetition of the pattern, comic in its shift of topic, also defines and contrasts the young women. Helena pines for Demetrius. Hermia would most willingly relinquish him. Unlike the earlier duet, this one concentrates on each young woman's attitude towards Demetrius. Rhyming couplets mark their exchange of confidences, and again acting texts excise:

> *Her.* I frown upon him; yet he loves me still.
> *Hel.* O that your frowns would teach my smiles such skill!
> *Her.* I give him curses; yet he gives me love.
> *Hel.* O that my prayers could such affection move!
> *Her.* The more I hate, the more he follows me.
> *Hel.* The more I love, the more he hateth me.
>
> (194–199)

Differing in their appeal to Demetrius, the women differ in their sense of self, Hermia confident with two adoring males, Helena disconsolate that the youth she loves has eyes only for her friend. Physically they differ too: Hermia being small and dark, at one point called "puppet" (III.ii.286), "dwarfish" (295), and an "Ethiop" (257); Helena being tall and lanky—"a painted maypole" (296). She is also probably fair.

Throughout this scene, Hermia exhibits a sardonic sense of humor, not only in her exclamations after her father leaves with Theseus, but even in her exchanges with her less confident friend. And once again, some texts delete Hermia's attempt to console her friend:

> Before the time I did Lysander see,
> Seem'd Athens as a Paradise to me;
> O then, what graces in my love do dwell,
> That he hath turn'd a heaven unto a hell!

(I.i.204–7)[15]

Although meant to emphasize the problems Hermia faces, the lines referring to "Lysander's graces" making Athens a hell also have a built-in irony. Surely a lover's graces should turn a hell into heaven rather than the opposite. Although differing from Theseus's comment to Hippolyta on altering their relationship from ex-combatants to lovers, Hermia's words here suggest a similarly thin and tenuous line between heaven and hell, springing from love.

Of the exchange, Samuel Johnson wrote:

> Perhaps every reader may not discover the propriety of these lines. Hermia is willing to comfort Helena, and to avoid all appearance of triumph over her. She therefore bids her not to consider the power of pleasing, as an advantage to be much envied or much desired, since Hermia, whom she considers as possessing it in the supreme degree, has found no other effect of it than the loss of happiness. (Johnson, *The Plays*, 1:98)

The comment also appears in a footnote in the Phelps promptbook (*MND* 13, 314). Since this was an 1805 printed text used for an 1861 production, it suggests that the lines were not only challenging in the eighteenth century but continued to be relevant in the nineteenth. When they disappear, as often occurs, they erase a problem for interpreters, but also an insight into Hermia's capacity for humor and sympathy.

To further comfort Helena, Hermia and Lysander reveal their secret plan to escape Athens. In soliloquy at the scene's close, Helena confesses her response. She will divulge the news of their flight to Demetrius, hoping to win his favor. Bemoaning her fate in rhymed couplets, she begins:

> How happy some o'er other some can be!
> Through Athens I am thought as fair as she,
> But what of that? Demetrius thinks not so;
> . . . .
> Love looks not with the eyes but with the mind;
> And therefore is wing'd Cupid painted blind.

(227–35)

But Helena does not think herself as fair as Hermia. Thus this reference to Cupid suggests a rather confused young woman. Continuing for twenty-six lines, the soliloquy ranges from analyses of love to a discussion of Hermia's strengths to a lament for the speaker's own plight:

> For ere Demetrius look'd on Hermia's eyne,
> He hail'd down oaths that he was only mine;
>
> (242–43)

She therefore resolves, "I will go tell him of fair Hermia's flight" (246), expecting a kind response. Here too excisions mar the portrait. Sometimes the lines are absent from printed acting versions; sometimes sections are crossed out or blocked for cutting.[16] As a result only the bare plot outline of this section remains, subtleties in characterization being lost.

Later, in the forest, the dramatist further develops the young women's personalities. There the popular Hermia, speaking with confidence, gently reprimands her lover, while the rejected Helena subjects herself to further humiliation, frustratingly following the man she loves. Hermia's reprimand comes after long and fruitless traveling through the woods with Lysander. Escaping Theseus's ultimatum, they seek refuge with the young man's aunt, beyond the range of Athens' law. Weary with wandering, Hermia would rest; Lysander then admits he has lost his way in the enchanted forest:

> We'll rest us, Hermia, if you think it good,
> And tarry for the comfort of the day.
>
> (II.ii.37–38)

Appreciating the idea, she then counters:

> Be't so, Lysander. Find you out a bed;
> For I upon this bank will rest my head.
>
> (39–40)

But he would have it otherwise. In fact, the lines indicate the action that has just occurred on stage as she chooses her sleeping site. A minidebate then ensues:

> *Lys.*   One turf shall serve as pillow for us both,
>   One heart, one bed, two bosoms, and one troth.

> *Her.* Nay, good Lysander; for my sake, my dear,
>   Lie further off yet; do not lie so near.
>
>   (41–44)

The adapters once again cut. Garrick's abbreviated musical version provides a record of the cuts in this speech, and, to some extent, sets the pattern for what subsequently occurred. The first eight lines of the exchange between the couple are retained (lines 35–42), followed by a duet (25). Then come lines not Shakespeare's, but believed to be composed by Garrick, which appear in a handwritten insert (*MND* 6).[17] In that version Hermia exhibits proper womanly fear:

> Now my Lysander, on that bank repose,
> That if perchance my woman's fears shou'd seek
> Protection in thy love and brav'ry,
> I may not call on love and thee in vain.
>
>   (*MND* 6, insert 21; Garrick, 25)

Lysander responds with the promise of protective care. The Garrick lines also appear in the Reynolds printed text (*MND* 8, 18). Later the pattern of excision continues although without the new, added material. The musical Reynolds version (*MND* 8, 18) contains no hint of her asking him to move. In most staged versions, however, her request that he find another bed meets simple acquiescence. Usually gone are his lines "One turf shall serve as pillow for us both / One heart, one bed, two bosoms, and one troth" (41–42) along with his attempt to convince her of the reasonableness of his proposal. Gone too is Hermia's perceptive "Lysander riddles very prettily. . . . / But, gentle friend, for love and courtesy, / Lie further off, in humane modesty" (53, 56–57).[18] Amusing, her response in Shakespeare's play highlights her realistic awareness of the physical attraction between lovers. Their debate is reminiscent of Juliet's "What satisfaction canst thou have to-night?" (*Romeo and Juliet*, II.ii.126) when Romeo protests, "O, wilt thou leave me so unsatisfied" (125). In both cases, the dramatist suggests that confidence in the loyalty of her lover does not blur each young woman's recognition of the reality of the sexual drive.

Unlike Hermia, her friend Helena nurtures no such fear. Groveling for some affection, she trails Demetrius. "I love thee not; therefore pursue me not" (188), he dictates. But Helena, like Emilia in

Othello so many plays later, has divulged the secret of Hermia and Lysander's flight in order to win a boon:

> I am your spaniel; and, Demetrius,
> The more you beat me, I will fawn on you.
> Use me but as your spaniel; spurn me, strike me,
> Neglect me, lose me; only give me leave,
> Unworthy as I am, to follow you.
>
> (II.i.203–7)

Nor do Demetrius's threats to her virginity (217–19) bother her. Rather they allow her to assert her confidence in his character. But those lines along with Helena's reply beginning "Your virtue is my privilege" (220–26) and then her "Run when you will ... " (230–34) disappear from the stage in many promptbooks.[19]

By cutting Helena's lines here and elsewhere, those versions tended to obscure the perceptiveness of Shakespeare's sketch of a young woman who is filled with self-doubt and self-hatred.[20] In fact, Shakespeare's insight here, although theatrically developed and placed in a comedic setting, has a contemporary counterpart in Kate Millett's more serious analysis of the lack of self-love that flourishes in women and minorities. She describes this as

> group self-hatred and self-rejection, a contempt both for herself and for her fellows—the result of that continual, however subtle, reiteration of her inferiority which she eventually accepts as a fact. (56)

Helena appears to have internalized this attitude. In an excellent essay on the play, David Marshall asks a relevant question concerning Helena. "Are we to be pleased by the success of Helena's subjection of herself?" (548), he wonders, challenging the idea that this is "one of Shakespeare's happiest comedies." [21] Actually, by the time we reach this section of the play we become aware of the various ways in which the women have been dominated by men— bridegroom, father, ruler, and rejecting suitor.

However, we have not yet met the strongest and seemingly freest woman character in *A Midsummer Night's Dream:* Titania, the fairy queen, who so delights us at her first entrance and later raises questions about women's roles. Is she the victim of male power, male irrationality, trickery, or jealousy? Is she merely a fairy? Or does she illuminate the feelings and attitudes of women reacting to dominating male behavior?

At its opening, act 2 stresses the conflict between her and Oberon, the fairy king. Quickly we learn the source of their dissension: control over an "Indian boy" at the time in her possession but desperately desired by Oberon. Representatives of king and queen, Puck and a fairy quickly sketch in the conflict, each hoping the other party will relinquish the field. "But room, fairy! here comes Oberon" (II.i.58), announces Puck. "And here my mistress. Would that he were gone!" (59) retorts the fairy. And then, king and queen enter. Do they make a grand entry from either side of the stage, magically from the air, with a train of followers, or simply alone?

The scene has allowed for a tremendous range of interpretations, some concentrating on the two principals, some surrounding them with troops of followers, many including the Indian Prince. Nonexistent in the play and seeming to symbolize Oberon's drive for dominance over Titania—or perhaps his jealousy of her—the prince materializes into an actual character. Not listed in the dramatis personae, he takes on a life of his own in nineteenth- and early twentieth-century productions, including the Reinhardt film. Although mystery surrounds him in the text—we don't know his age, his size, or his exact identity, except as he is described variously by Puck, Titania, and Oberon—he acquires theatrical substance on stage, frequently wearing a turban or carried in on a golden cushion.[22]

Suggesting the importance of this character to the relationship between the fairy king and queen are the stage directions written in pencil on the interleave to Kean's prompt:

> *Fairies enter dancing round Titania. 2 Bodies of Oberon's Train,—enter separately, . . . then 2 parties of Titania's—chorus first, who make an avenue of boughs, then a second troop of smaller fairies trip down through them,—on tiptoes—and run back thro avenue,—down L[eft] then round avenue and follow Titania with Indian Boy tripping down through avenue,—Oberon entering same time down slote, R[ight]* (MND 9, interleaf facing p. 21).

In another production, a dance of twelve fairies precedes Titania's entry "in a car drawn by swans" and accompanied by the Indian Prince. Paralleling their entry, Oberon descends to meet them (*MND* 20, verso of interleaf facing p. 12). A sketch indicates the placement of fairies, with Titania, Oberon, and the Prince at center front.

The presence of an actual prince also allows the director editorial commentary as he emphasizes the different functions of men and women, father and mother. Thus Titania is usually portrayed in a maternal relationship with that young child whereas Oberon is presented as giving the youth space and training for manhood. Consider, for example, the Reinhardt film where the young prince is practically smothered by attention from Titania's fairies and elves whereas later he is free to accompany Oberon. Even in criticism, this reference to the prince colors the perspective. C. L. Barber, for example, writing of Titania's later development, considers her giving up of the child as a maturing process. But one may question whether or not it is the child, as an actual person, or the symbolic importance of the debate between Titania and Oberon and its later outcome that is really at issue in the play especially since the prince's exclusion from the text helps stress the equality between king and queen.

Before turning to their actual verbal sparring, I want to cite other theatrical factors that further vitiated the strength of the debate, attracting eyes to the stage and ears to the music rather than attention to the words. I refer to the persistence of lavish musical accompaniments to productions. In fact, whether it was coincidence or not, the mid-nineteenth-century productions—beginning with that of Elizabeth Vestris and Charles Mathews in 1840, which included Mendelssohn's music—were highly successful and included more of the text than had previously appeared on stage. Discussing that production, one commentator suggested, "It would be an unpardonable mistake to any future performances . . . to omit . . . Mendelssohn's music" (*MND.* *NCP 18—, p. 6).[23] In Reinhardt's film, fairies, accompanied by the orchestral sounds of Mendelssohn's music, dance in on a cloud that spirals around a tree. Later productions, like that of the famous Old Vic Company in 1954 that featured Robert Helpmann and Moira Shearer, both professional dancers, as Oberon and Titania, also testify to the pervasiveness of a musical tradition and the emphasis on dance for the two principal fairies (see illustrations).

Finally, along with the music and the young prince, one stage property worked its magic on the audience: the mushroom from which Puck eventually emerged. The young Ellen Terry as Puck, for example, lay hidden in such a mushroom in Kean's production, springing into view as the mushroom rose. Following Kean's lead, Daly's Puck, hidden by a mushroom, was discovered when a fairy's wand brushed a plant (1888, *MND* 5, p. 32). Featuring complex machinery, Burton's production too had Puck spring from a mush-

Accompanied by a ballet company dancing to Mendelssohn's music, Moira Shearer plays Titania in the lavish 1954 production of *A Midsummer Night's Dream,* presented at the Metropolitan Opera House. Photo by Houston Rogers.

Wearing extravagant makeup, Robert Helpmann as Oberon angrily challenges Titania in the 1954 Old Vic Company production of *A Midsummer Night's Dream*. Photo by Houston Rogers.

room that rose from a trap then sank back down (*MND* 21, p. 15 and facing interleaf).[24] The rival Barry production featured a different, but equally enticing, entry for Puck:

> *A romantic Landscape, through which is seen a stream of water. (By moonlight.) A bush in the c[enter]. MUSIC—A troop of Fairies are discovered grouped. A Fairy touches the bush with her wand, it opens and Puck comes out; the bush disappears through the stage.*
>
> (*MND* 20, Act 2, p. 11)

Supplementing this text, the directions on the interleaf specifically place Puck inside the flower piece which then changes to a peacock. Accompanied by music, "the first fairy trips on from [the side entrance] . . . round the flower" waving the wand. "The flower opens and discovers Puck in a Peacock Car (with wand)." More music sounds as Puck descends from the car. Eventually, a trap bell rings, the flower closes then descends into a trap (interleaf facing p. 11).

I cite these extensive productions because they characterize what occurred on stage once the fuller text was presented. Whether this was because of the accompaniment of Mendelssohn's music or because the combination of the text with that music appealed so strongly to Victorians we do not know. Clearly, however, language and the verbal conflicts between men and women characters, whether fairy or not, were overshadowed by productions. Nor do the many references to a full text, as in the case of Phelps's production, which boasted of having omitted only three hundred lines, alter the general impression of the acted play. If these varied staged versions seemed to promise new perspectives, they failed to deliver; they still concentrated on the magic and wistfulness of the dream. Moreover, extant promptbooks testify to a disproportionate number of excisions of lines that blur Shakespeare's portrayal of the inequities that women faced whether in the real or unreal fairy world.

For it is in the unreal world of the fairies that the dramatist most clearly questions the patriarchal structure. Despite the extravagance of their entrances in different productions, Oberon's and Titania's opening lines sound more like those of humans than of fairies or otherworldly beings: "Ill met by moonlight, proud Titania" (60), asserts proud Oberon. We then encounter the queen of the fairies whom Shakespeare has endowed with dramatic and

evocative poetry. Unlike the other women thus far presented, Titania has a sure sense of self-worth and an independence of spirit.
Hippolyta was presented as defeated but enigmatic, Hermia as a
challenge to the rules of her society, and Helena as a self-doubting
person, questioning her own worth. But in Titania Shakespeare
offers a portrait of a queen, someone reliant on no one but herself
for her power. Her answer to Oberon in her opening lines rings
with contemporaneity:

> What, jealous Oberon? Fairies, skip hence—
> I have forsworn his bed and company.
>
> (61–62)

Why need a fairy assert she has "forsworn" another fairy's bed?
Since when do fairies discuss such mundane matters? Moreover,
Oberon carries the discussion one step further by clarifying their
relationship with one another: "Am not I thy lord?" (63) he asks.
"Then I must be thy lady" (64) she asserts before accusing him of
infidelity with various women. In his recent book *Road to Divorce:
England 1530–1987*, Lawrence Stone notes that until recently—but
particularly in the early period covered by this book—"all women
of childbearing age" were in a state of "constant anxiety about
their bodies. They worried about whether they were pregnant" (8)
and about such things as the possibility of dying in childbirth, of
coming to term, and of having a well child. Titania, being a fairy,
has no such worry although her conflict with Oberon has to do
with the child of a mortal who died in childbirth. "His mother
was a vot'ress of my order" (123), explains Titania. "For her sake
do I rear up the boy; / And for her sake I will not part with him"
(136–37). Moreover, in recent studies of women's writings of the
period, we become aware not only of women's quest for divorce
and of the problems they faced in confronting their husbands but
also of the real fears attending childbirth (Otten).

Titania's opening lines to Oberon may well have had specific
resonances for Shakespeare's audience. The phrase "separation
from bed and board" was applied at the time to a legitimate form
of divorce, whether "as 'de facto' grants of permission to remarry"
or merely following church ordinance that allowed a form of divorce but forbade remarriages (Stone, L., 304). Although Titania,
of course, had no particular plans to "remarry," her language mimics that of the time, with, however, a twist—an assertion of her
rights vis-à-vis an adulterous husband. Nor does Oberon's listing

of her less-than-faithful exploits affect her decision to foreswear his "bed and company." According to Stone, the pattern changed in the 1640s and 50s, which may explain an altered reaction to this section of text. He writes:

> The 1640s and 1650s were a period of disorganization and institutional chaos in the church. The ecclesiastical courts ceased to function in the early 1640s and in 1646 church control over marriage was abolished, authority being shifted in theory to secular authorities. But the bulk of the population seems either to have found ways to be married clandestinely by the old rituals of the Church of England, or were married by non-conformist clergy of their own religious persuasion, or reverted to marriages by verbal contract. As a result of this confusion, when the ecclesiastical courts were restored in 1660 they found themselves faced with an unprecedented torrent of petitions for separation which had been pent up for over a decade. (308)

Interestingly, what Shakespeare is doing here is using the vocabulary of divorce without presenting the actual situation. Moreover, unlike the usual separation between husband and wife of the time, this separation is instituted by the wife. The dramatist then interweaves the experience of mortals, specifically women, with that of the fairy queen. During the nineteenth century, the line referring to "bed and company" was often deleted. It disappeared from the Charles Kean printed text (*MND* 9) and was crossed through in the Beerbohm Tree prompt (*MND* 7). On the other hand, Garrick and Colman retained this line (*MND* 19) although slashing so much material on either side to make room for musical airs that the line's implications probably had little effect on the audience. In that text, the accusations by fairy king and queen refer merely to their specific favorites within the context of this play—Titania's preference for Theseus and Oberon's for the "bouncing Amazon" (70).

However, Titania's full speeches, although couched in "fairy terms," offer insights into the imperfect relationship between men and women. Describing the conflict between her and Oberon, she begins by mentioning jealousy:

> These are the forgeries of jealousy;
> And never, since the middle summer's spring,
> Met we on hill, in dale, forest, or mead,
> By paved fountain or by rushy brook
> Or in the beached margent of the sea,

To dance our ringlets to the whistling wind,
But with thy brawls thou hast disturb'd our sport.

(II.i.81–87)

The speech continues for thirty-six lines, but has usually been reduced to six, or even four. The remnant simply accuses Oberon of disturbing the gatherings of the fairies with his "brawls" whenever the two have met (87). As critics have frequently noted, the speech gives us a sense of Titania's breadth and sensitivity, connecting her with an Eden or a classical world of the gods, or even with nature deities of rustic sixteenth-century England. She refers to the effect of the dissension between her and Oberon on the elements, "The ox hath . . . stretched his yoke in vain, / The plowman lost his sweat . . . / The fold stands empty in the drowned field / And crows are fatted with the murrion flock" (93–97). Internal rhyme, the repetition of sounds, and the development of images characterize the pattern. Her concern for the maintenance of the rhythms in the animal world extends to the human world as well. She decries the effect of their arguments on the normal flow of the seasons and on human life.

The human mortals want their winter here;
No night is now with hymn or carol blest.
. . . . The spring, the summer
The childing autumn, angry winter, change
Their wonted liveries; and the mazed world
By their increase, now knows not which is which.

(101–14)

Images of nature's gifts and blights vie with one another, investing her speech with cosmic concerns beyond merely trading accusations with Oberon. When, later, she explains why she will not relinquish the child, she describes his mother, with whom she laughed and "gossip'd."[25] Titania's lines—"we have laugh'd to see the sails conceive / And grow big-bellied with the wanton wind" (128–29)—suggestively describe the pregnant woman herself. They too disappear, the verbal inferences coming too close to nature, pregnancy, and women's physical appearance.[26] Whittling down the lines narrows this portrait of Titania; she then more closely parallels Oberon who in this section has only brief comments.[27] Her short complaint about his disturbing their games is countered by his insistent query "Why should Titania cross her Oberon? /

I do but beg a little changeling boy, / To be my henchman" (119–21). Reinhardt's film cuts even further. None of Titania's lines remain except her response to Oberon's request for the changeling boy: "Set your heart at rest; / The fairy land buys not the child of me" (121–22). The scene's focus changes to the Indian boy.

Even when they retain practically all of the text, however, productions may alter the power of Titania's lines by stage directions, as did Peter Brook's in the wonderfully unisex-looking work. The performance had an exuberance and originality that captivated audiences. It also captured some of the attitudes of the 1960s and 1970s, as a glance at the "Authorized Acting Edition" testifies, raising questions about the Oberon-Titania relationship that one might even have missed in watching the play. Here, for example, is a detailed description of what went on during this scene of their first meeting which begins with Titania's crossing down stage center and kneeling (23a) before Oberon when she refers to their brawls. Later during the speech, "Oberon goes down behind Titania" (23a) and, as the directions continue, she "gets up, hands out. Oberon puts hands around her waist with wand" (24a). In talking about the "hoary headed frosts" she puts her hands over Oberon's. And at the lines "and the mazed world / By their increase now know not which is which" (24b) the stage direction reads, "Oberon's hands on Titania's breasts, with wand. Titania's arms out" (24a). As the scene continues, one sees more of physical sexual interaction between them until finally at her decision not to give him the boy, she pushes Oberon away. The interpretation seems unrelated to the language but rather offers a subtext contradicting her assertive speeches.

The comments accompanying the promptbook offer a partial explanation of this treatment of Titania. Brook had chosen to double the roles of Titania/Hippolyta and Oberon/Theseus. Alan Howard, who played Oberon/Theseus, discusses the point of view towards the relationship between his roles and the joint Titania/Hippolyta role:

> At the beginning of the play, Theseus/Oberon is worried about the moon being gone and that his desires are, in consequence, bottled up. And Hippolyta/Titania says: "Don't worry. Another moon will come in. Wait, and it will all be fine again." *Her kind of intensity is toward her knowledge of herself as a woman . . . in terms of whatever it is that women do that men don't.* Theseus/Oberon has somehow got to explain his case. (41, emphasis added)

Howard's comment indicates a perception of Titania as inexplicable "other" although her language clearly expresses her dismay at the destructiveness of their conflict. Oberon simply isn't listening. What is exciting about the play, however, is the way Shakespeare seems to be applying what he has been hearing, or observing, in the real world to this fantasy couple, embedding a contemporaneity within an otherworldly framework.[28]

After her departure, Oberon vows, "Thou shalt not from this grove / Till I torment thee for this injury" (146–47), indicating a vindictiveness as well as a desire to exert power over her. And here, perhaps because of the implication of equality suggested first by the conversation between the fairy and Puck and later by the confrontation between Oberon and Titania, we are unprepared for the trick he plays on her. Shakespeare's audience, however, may well have expected it, since Titania was behaving like the rebellious, dominant, independent wife who, according to Stone, might be breaking the code of the social group "concerning sexual or power relations within the family" (3). "Thus a husband-beating wife, a passively hen-pecked husband, a couple married despite gross disparities in age, a cuckold, an adulterous wife . . . were all liable to be treated to . . . humiliating demonstrations of public disapproval" (3). Titania suffers just such a "humiliating demonstration" later on when she falls in love with the first thing that she sees upon awakening, a mortal with an ass's head—the "translated" Bottom.

By endowing the situation with such human qualities and giving Titania wonderful lines, however, the dramatist may also be questioning the justice of Oberon's action especially where he seems to be motivated by revenge. When he directs Puck to fetch the magic herb called "love-in-idleness" (II.i.168), the fairy king explains:

> The juice of it on sleeping eyelids laid
> Will make or man or woman madly dote
> Upon the next live creature that it sees.

> (170–72)

He will squeeze the juice into her eyes and eventually defeat the play's most independent woman. In the complex interweaving of plots, he will also, almost casually, exercise his power benevolently. Although some critics have perceived Oberon as an even-handed ruler who insists on establishing a certain kind of obedience to his rule, his actions here seem arbitrary and tinged with jealousy.

When later on he acts more generously towards Helena, attempting to change her fate from that of cast-off woman to desired one, Oberon's actions seem to come almost as an afterthought to his more driven desire for revenge on Titania.

Having sent Puck on his way, Oberon, alone in the forest, sees Demetrius and Helena approaching. "I am invisible," he announces to his audience, as Hamlet's and Banquo's ghosts do not; rather on-stage characters provide the clues to the emptiness of the space even while the invisible character appears on stage. Alan Dessen discusses the implications of this "not seeing" or blindness of characters on stage as often metaphoric for the blindness or inability of the characters on stage to see and understand (130–55). Here, however, Shakespeare denies us this metaphor by having Oberon proclaim his invisibility. The dramatist, skilled in embedding stage directions in his text, chooses, instead, to characterize Oberon through this more direct statement, possibly with the aim of literalizing him, just as the mechanicals, later on, so carefully literalize their actions.

Observing Helena trailing Demetrius, the fairy king reacts with sympathy to her plight; he would have Demetrius sue for her love. The magic herb holds the key. What are we to make of Oberon's reaction here? If Titania is aggressive in rejecting him, Helena is aggressive in pursuing Demetrius. Ironically, Oberon, who would have the fairy queen exhibit the kind of self-abasement practiced by Helena, expresses great sympathy for the mortal woman and later sends Puck to find the Athenians while the fairy king himself will anoint Titania's eyes. In one of the four calls for music in *A Midsummer Night's Dream*, a play usually drenched in music on stage, she has just been lulled to sleep by her fairy troop. "Come, now a roundel and a fairy song. . . . sing me now asleep" (II.ii.1,7), Titania directs, becoming vulnerable to Oberon's scheme. Meanwhile, Puck, having sought Athenians in the forest and found only the sleeping Hermia and Lysander, squeezes the magic juice into the eyes of the wrong man.

Now Helena, the rejected Helena, is forced to face a new role— that of the chosen one, the pursued one, when Lysander, upon being awakened, expresses his undying love for her. This is difficult for a woman whose self-image has already been shaped. Speaking in soliloquy moments before his sudden and inexplicable pursuit, she weighs her virtues and strengths and finds them nonexistent.

She compares herself first with Hermia then indulges in close self-analysis:

> How came her eyes so bright? Not with salt tears;
> If so, my eyes are oft'ner wash'd than hers.
> No, no; I am as ugly as a bear;
> For beasts that meet me run away for fear.
> Therefore no marvel though Demetrius
> Do, as a monster, fly my presence thus.
>
> (92–97)

Helena doesn't like what she sees. Although the speech continues developing her profile, it too, like so many earlier speeches by the women, frequently loses its subtlety and color through excision.[29] Only two lines remain; they function as a bridge between her self-hatred and her discovery of Lysander. The full speech, however, explains her astonishment at his actions, and her inability to find any excuse for them. Lacking any sense of self-worth, she is bewildered. The play, however, provides a rationale. According to Lysander, one needs maturity to appreciate Helena's worth. "Reason" must be the guide:

> The will of man is by his reason sway'd;
> And reason says you are the worthier maid.
>
> (115–16)

He then expands on this, explaining, "Things growing are not ripe until their season, / So I, being young, till now ripe not to reason" (117–18). The scene also permits the dramatist to differentiate further between the two young women because even in these mere sketches, he assigns specific qualities to each. But once again major chunks of text are cut for the stage, eliminating all but the most obvious differences—the women's varying appeals to men.[30]

Illustrating the effectiveness of the magic juice, the brief scene between Helena and Lysander in its complete form anticipates the sharp reaction Titania will experience. Because so much criticism has interpreted the fairy queen's later actions when under the juice's spell as truly representative of her underlying feelings, one could test the validity of such a theory by applying it to Lysander, the first to be transformed. Does he really mean it when, responding to Helena's reminder of his love for Hermia, he refers to his former love scornfully as "the surfeit of the sweetest things" (137) and undesirable? Since he later returns to her, one must believe that this is merely his manner of coping, under the spell's influence.

Although some critics consider Oberon's potion a symbol of love, as it applies to Titania it appears to be more a symbol of power, or at least of revenge for her failure to release the child. In direct response to her unwillingness to acquiesce to his demand, Oberon induces the spell:

> The next thing then she waking looks upon
> (Be it on lion, bear, or wolf, or bull,
> On meddling monkey, or on busy ape),
> She shall pursue it with the soul of love.

(II.i.179–82)

No handsome youth or prince charming but rather a list of animals is intended as her fate. In fact some promptbooks—for the 1856 [*MND* 9] and Tree 1900 [*MND* 7] productions—excise these references to animals. In Garrick's production, she is never seen "enamor'd of an ass" (IV.i.77). Instead, the audience must rely on Puck's report:

> My mistress with a patched fool is in love.
> Near to her close and consecrated bower
> This clown with others had rehearsed a play
> Intended for great Theseus' nuptial day.
> When, starting from her bank of mossy down,
> Titania waked, and straightway loved the clown.

(III.i.2–7; Garrick in Pedicord, III:176)

References to the ass have disappeared; the substitute terms "patched fool" and "clown" soften Titania's fate.

Through the complex interweaving of plot strands in which fairies, tradesmen, and high-born characters from the world of Athens intermingle, Shakespeare can raise questions about women's roles. The dramatist draws on the third group, the mechanicals, for the "ass" who will humiliate, humble, and subdue the fairy queen. Entering the enchanted forest to rehearse their play, "Pyramus and Thisbe," these comic characters, hoping to perform before the Duke on his wedding day, inadvertently participate in Oberon's trickery. Reacting variously to the idea of performing—some with trepidation about learning the words, others protesting assignment of their roles—one in the group plunges into the adventure. He would play every role. Quickly we become acquainted with Nick Bottom, the weaver, who would shout like a bear and weep like a woman. He will, eventually, bray like an ass, a role not in their skit, but one he will take on in his unexpected adventure with the fairy queen.

Doomed to awaken "when some vile thing is near" whom she will take for her love, Titania hears the braying Bottom—anointed with an ass's head by Puck—and marvels at his musicality. She finds his music beautiful and his person appealing. But then she has been blinded by Oberon's magic spell. In the Ciulei production, she reacts to that juice by screaming as if hit by lightning. Few productions, however, dramatize the evil inherent in this type of magic. Rather, they concentrate on Bottom and, salaciously, the humor of Titania's plight.

More than anywhere else, it is in the effect of Oberon's trick on Titania, however, that one feels the tragedy for the women and the insights the dramatist gives us into the ways in which patriarchy manipulates women's options. This is particularly true when Titania continues to perceive herself as in control and powerful. During her first meeting with Bottom, the enchanted Titania praises his wisdom as well as beauty and musical skill, declaring that she loves him. When he wants only to leave the wood, she warns:

> Out of this wood do not desire to go;
> Thou shalt remain here, whether thou wilt or no.
> I am a spirit of no common rate;
> The summer still doth tend upon my state.
>
> (III.i.152–55)

The lines underscore the ironic contrast between her perception of herself and her actual situation. Like Lysander, she is trying to cope. Some versions eliminate her reference to power: "whether thou wilt or no." In many texts, her whole last speech, beginning "Come wait upon him; lead him to my bower," is excised. Thus audiences do not know that she entertains him in her bower, or that the moon, "when she weeps, weeps every little flower, / Lamenting some enforced chastity" (199–200). As a result, the full implication of Oberon's trick on Titania is lost to the audience.[31]

Sometimes a critic will overlook Oberon's role, concentrating instead on the effect of the magic potion on Titania. Jan Kott, for example, not only stresses the eroticism and harshness embedded in the text but also translates this eroticism in terms of the fairy queen. To him, her invitation to Bottom exemplifies woman's passion and hidden desire, rather than illustrating the male (Oberon's) exercise of power. Analyzing the staging of those scenes between Titania and Bottom, Kott also decries the tendency to play them for laughs rather than present them as black humor, an "English kind of humour, 'humeur noir', cruel and scatological, as it often is in Swift" (228). Most revealing, however, is Kott's final comment about the scene, as he describes Titania:

> The slender, tender and lyrical Titania longs for animal love. Puck and Oberon call the transformed Bottom a monster. The frail and sweet Titania drags the monster to bed, almost by force. (228)

This is the effect of the magic juice. Kott continues his male fantasy—the fantasy of women "never wanting to admit" to themselves that they really like being raped. In fact, Kott inverts this:

> This is the lover she wanted and dreamed off (sic); only she never wanted to admit it, even to herself. Sleep frees her from inhibitions. The monstrous ass is being raped by the poetic Titania, while she still keeps on chattering about flowers. . . . Of all the characters in the play Titania enters to the fullest extent the dark sphere of sex where there is no more beauty and ugliness; there is only infatuation and liberation. (228)

Obviously to Kott, beauty and ugliness vanish before infatuation and liberation.

Fuseli's eighteenth-century illustration captures much of the implied eroticism in this scene although it differs in point of view from Kott's (see illustration). In the painting, dominated by the two major characters, a large nude male figure, topped by a donkey head with large ears and sitting crossed legged with his arms clasping his knees, is being caressed by Titania, her nude breast amply visible beneath the outstretched arm around his head. Surrounding the two are small insect-headed nude males, their penises visible, and small fairies looking like flirtatious women, their breasts seductively apparent although wearing female garb. While Fuseli indicates the eroticism in the scene, bringing in the whole forest and suggesting, too, the male appetite, Kott concentrates only on Titania, perceiving her as a voracious female. Neither acknowledges the idea of her being tricked.

C. L. Barber provides a totally different perspective. To him, the

Surrounded by fairies and small insects, while the mischievous Puck looks on from behind the trees in the upper right-hand corner, the spellbound Titania embraces the ass-headed Bottom in Henry Fuseli's imaginative interpretation of this scene. Courtesy of the Folger Shakespeare Library.

Titania scenes with Bottom reveal a "growing up," as I mentioned earlier:

> It is when the flower magic leads Titania to find a new object that she gives up the child (who goes now from her bower to the man's world of Oberon). So here is another sort of change of heart that contributes to the expression of what is consummated in marriage, this one a part of the rhythm of adult life, as opposed to the change in the young lovers that goes with growing up. (FC 137)

Again the question arises of whether Titania experiences a "change of heart" or is victimized by Oberon and therefore no natural growth occurs, merely a change depriving her of her former sense of self.

Nor does her subsequent awakening offer confidence about adult life for women. Deluded, she courts the ass-headed Bottom, taking him to her bower. Meanwhile Oberon plans his next move:

> I'll to my queen and beg her Indian boy;
> And then I will her charmed eye release
> From monster's view, and all things shall be peace.
> (III.ii.375–77)

But shall they be at peace? Or worse, shall Titania's spirit have been broken? In _The Taming of the Shrew,_ Kate says, "My tongue will tell the anger of my heart / Or else my heart concealing it will break" (IV.iii.77–78). Shakespeare recognizes the effect on the human heart of bottling up resentment.[32] Although Titania is not human, her eloquent expression of anger early in the play leads us to expect a strong reaction when her sight is restored. But no such response occurs. Instead, she cares neither about the Indian boy, nor the trick that has been played on her, but only about the humiliation of having been in love with an ass. Are we to think of her as resembling the nonhuman witches in _Macbeth_ whose deeds do not upset them? Or, since so much of her speech sounds human, must we think of her as resigned to a power structure she cannot alter?

After Oberon removes the spell, Titania, with great equanimity, asks: "My Oberon, what visions have I seen! / Methought I was enamor'd of an ass" (IV.i.76–77). Nor does Oberon try to soften the answer. "There lies your love" (78), he asserts, pointing to the transformed Bottom. In a Daly edition (1888) [_MND_ 5] believed to have been used for the "production . . . tour of 1895–96," Oberon's "There lies your love" (77) is accompanied by the stage direction *"sneering" "Puck titters"* (61), reinforcing a sense of Oberon's power, his delight in having played this trick on her, but more importantly, of a director's point of view. Undoubtedly he reflected the attitudes of his time. Unfortunately, as we keep discovering, this delight in seeing a strong woman bested is not confined to a bygone age.

Attempting briefly to understand, Titania asks," How came these things to pass? / O, how mine eyes do loathe his visage now!"(78–79). But Oberon offers no direct answer. Instead, he orders Puck to "take off this head" [the ass's head] (80). Then, continuing to exert his power over Titania, the fairy king directs:

> Titania, music call, and strike more dead
> Than common sleep of all these five the sense.
>
> (81–82)

She complies: "Music, ho, music, such as charmeth sleep!" (86). Finally, as they fly off together, she once more returns to the subject of Bottom:

> Come, my lord, and in our flight,
> Tell me how it came this night
> That I sleeping here was found,
> With these mortals on the ground.
>
> (99–102)

But we never know if she receives an answer.

Although little has been written about Titania's character disintegration from a fiery, concerned fairy to a compliant partner, her change and lack of any clearly defined personality in the last scenes illustrate, on the one hand, the destructiveness of Oberon's action and, on the other, an inconsistency in characterization. Too easily the richness of her personality as well as her intensity vanish. Writing of the "linguistic and dramatic complexities and contradictions" in the play, Jay Halio observes that

> [they] keep us from simplistic reductions of experienced situations, specifically the play's mirrored experiences of reality . . . and force us out of . . . an artificial prison that R. P. Blackmur has . . . described as a tendency to set artistic unity as a chief criterion of excellence. (145)

Borrowing from Halio but concentrating on how language defines and sometimes creates ambiguities concerning characters, particularly the female characters, I find in Titania either an inconsistency or a tragic transformation. Since this is a comedy one must consider the former as more likely. Examining an early nineteenth-century musical version of the play that attempts to inject sentimental logic to the Oberon-Titania relationship, reconciling the behavior of Oberon through some staging and language, one realizes that Shakespeare probably intentionally allowed the ambiguity in characterization to stand. Reynolds's 1816 version provides an easy alternative. Oberon speaks:

> I'll to my Queen, and beg her Indian boy!
> Not, not so much from love of him, as her,
> I court this contest,—I'd put her to the trial—
> If she refuse, I know her love is on the wane;—
> But, if she yield! Ah! that she may! and still—
>
> (Prompt *MND* 18, 8 p. 40)

Music then is played. *"(Clouds descend and open.—A Fairy is discovered, who chaunts the following lines)"*

> *Fairy.*   Oberon!
> *Oberon.* Appear!
> *Fairy.*   Oberon! no more despair!
>   Titania wafts him to your care!
>   Borne by each propitious gale,
>   From India's shores her gallies sail.
>   Nor storms, nor quicksands can they meet,
>   For Zephyrs fan the Fairy fleet!
>   And silv'ry seas the treasure bear,—
>   The Boy!—The Indian Boy is near!
> *(Clouds begin to ascend again.)*
>
> (p. 40)[33]

This finale of act 2 in the Reynolds play confirms the portrait of an Oberon driven by love rather than jealousy and of a Titania who, on her own initiative, relinquishes the boy.[34] Shakespeare, however, fails to provide any easy logical development to the Titania-Oberon relationship in the closing scenes. In fact, the difference between this version and Shakespeare's play reminds one of the difference between Cibber's *Richard III* and Shakespeare's, between simple blacks and whites as compared with an extraordinary range of greys, between directness and ambiguity.

In *A Midsummer Night's Dream*, the dramatist raises questions concerning women and the power structure imposed on them, even when he supplies no easy answers. Having showed us Titania in her strength, he seems to turn to other concerns, returning her to her fairy role. The young Athenian women provide another example of the power of patriarchy over women's lives. Never confused in their affections for the two young men, Hermia and Helena gain insights into themselves and into the unpredictability of male behavior as a result of their experiences in the forest. Differing from the two young men, the women never have their eyes anointed with Oberon's magic juice; nevertheless, their relationships with the two youths as well as with one another change. Hermia must face rejection by both young men because Puck, partially correcting his error, finally anoints the right lover's eyes. Suddenly both Demetrius and Lysander are amorously pursuing Helena. Desired by both youths, she believes neither. Nor does her earlier passion for Demetrius convince her of his sincerity at this moment. She accuses them of mocking her. Disbelief, anger, and hurt mark her words: "Can you not hate me, as I know you do, / But you must join in souls to mock me too?" (III.ii.149–50).

Changing places and relationships, the women find their friendship turned into rivalry and their dispute quickly reduced to name calling, hair pulling, and physical conflict. Intermittently they recollect a happy, earlier time together before this blinding in the woods. Much cutting of lines, however, reduces this section to the outline of the contest between the men, diminishing any sharp character definition of the women. Large sections of Hermia's reprimand to Demetrius disappear. Gone too is Helena's sensitive description of their childhood friendship when they sewed together "sitting on one cushion, / . . . As if our hands, our sides, voices and minds / Had been incorporate. So we grew together, / Like to a double cherry, seeming parted" (205–9). Much later Shakespeare would develop this recollection of an early innocent friendship ruined by sexual jealousy, transmuting it into a description of the friendship between two men, Leontes and Polixenes in *The Winter's Tale*. Seldom heard on the stage, Helena's lines again individualize her, as she accuses her friend of conspiring with the men. Characteristically, Hermia counters with anger and frustration.

Because both suitors are fiercely pursuing Helena, Puck must lead them "Up and down, up and down," (396) to keep them apart, and because the role has its own magic, the scenes in the forest with the blinded lovers allow for farce, action, and humor. The two men pursue one another in the wood while Puck blankets it with fog and mimics each man's voice to mislead and confuse his opponent. Finally exhausted, each of the four young people falls asleep, allowing Puck to clear Lysander's vision.

The dramatist then switches focus from the youths to their elders. Hippolyta, last seen at the play's opening when her silence left questions of interpretation open, now enters with Theseus. Discord seems to have vanished. But here, unlike the Titania-Oberon exit when the fairy queen seemed so muted and transformed, the Amazon queen exhibits sparks of individuality as she jokingly debates the relative merits of Theseus's hounds. Stumbling on the sleeping young lovers, the older couple, upon awakening the youths, discovers two matched pairs. Oberon had never removed the magic juice from Demetrius's eyes; he will no longer pursue Hermia. Theseus's perspective alters. Rather than being the rigid, unbending Duke of Athens, he overrules Egeus's sentence on Hermia. Confused and uncertain, the couples leave the forest.

Bottom then awakens, the ass's head removed, and the spell lifted. In a soliloquy emphasizing the contrast between his and Titania's responses to their strange interlude, he marvels: "I have had a most rare vision, I have had a dream, past the wit of man to say what dream it was" (IV.i.204–6). His speech, as we know, parodies St. Paul's I Corinthians ii.9 ff. If Bottom's vision has been expanded, Titania's has been destroyed. Looking at him, she had reacted with revulsion. Thus, again, the victimization of a woman is implied.

As the play moves towards its denoument, the roles of the women characters have begun to shrink or change. Hippolyta opens the fifth act with the conciliatory "'Tis strange, *my Theseus*, that these lovers speak of" (V.i.1, emphasis added). Her term of address, like Titania's lines when she flies away with Oberon, reveals acceptance of her position although as the scene develops she is the one woman who constantly speaks out. Hermia and Helena, so vocal earlier, are strangely silent during the bridal entertainment hosted by Theseus. In contrast, the young bridegrooms, Lysander and Demetrius, along with Theseus speak a good deal, deriding the entertainment by Bottom and his friends. Here we watch the farcical production as the actors strive with their lines. The prologue begins the performance:

> If we offend, it is with our good will.
> That you should think, we come not to offend,
> But with good will.
>
> (V.i.108–10)

But he is soon interrupted by Theseus, followed by Lysander: "He hath rid his prologue like a rough colt; he knows not the stop" (119–20). Hippolyta too contributes: "Indeed he hath play'd on this prologue like a child on a recorder—a sound, but not in government" (122–24). Trying to outdo one another, the commentators keep interrupting the action as Pyramus exclaims against his fate:

> O grim-look'd night! O night with hue so black!
> O night, which ever art when day is not!
> O night, O night! alack, alack, alack
>
> (170–72)

As the play-within-a-play progresses and both Pyramus and Thisby commit suicide in a case of mistaken supposition, much like the deaths of Romeo and Juliet, the interruptions come more often and are more incisive. Whether it is Hippolyta protesting, "I am a-weary of this moon. Would he would change!" (251–52) of a character portraying moon, or Theseus's response, "It appears . . . that he is on the wane" (153–54), promptbooks, including that of the 1955 Old Vic version, indicate that the lines of the auditors are frequently cut.[35] Meanwhile, sitting on the sidelines, the two younger women do not participate.

Is it an accident that for so long, in the early years, it was *Pyramus and Thisbe* or other abbreviated versions that were produced?[36] Abstracted from its place in the context of *A Midsummer Night's Dream, Pyramus and Thisbe* was merely a farcical commentary on lovers who die for love, having been hindered by their parents from uniting. But as part of the larger whole, the play-within-a-play not only mocks the intensity of the Athenian lovers and the price of love, but also highlights, through this distancing lens of metadrama, the submissiveness (or at least silence) expected of women in marriage.

Perhaps aware of the implication of the young women's silence, Augustin Daly, having given the role of Helena to his favorite actress, Ada Rehan, reassigned many of the interrupting lines to the women. Altering the text and countering its implication of the silent women, Daly gave several of the lines of the commentators to Helena and Hermia, but primarily to Helena, creating in her an assertive personality. Specifically, the exchange on the moon is assigned to Helena and Hermia, as is another exchange between Hippolyta and Theseus. In fact, Daly's reassignment of lines spotlights the freedom of speech that Hippolyta, of all the women in the play, has gained. Did Shakespeare give her these lines because she was, even if won in battle, a former queen and Amazon? Or was the assignment based on her role as Theseus's wife? Hermia and Helena's last speeches occur in the fourth act when, delighted to have been united with the men of their choice, each marvels at the outcome, Helena still treasuring Demetrius, whom she has "found . . . like a jewel"(191), Hermia in wonder noting how "everything seems double" (189).

Of all the women characters, Titania has changed the most, accepting her role as Oberon's handmaid. Returning with the fairies, she sings and blesses the newly married couples' beds. No recollection of the votress who died in childbirth mars the blessing. Nor is the Indian boy ever mentioned again. As Stevie Davis observes:

> When Oberon reclaims his rule, and Theseus leads the characters into the reasserted status quo of the final Act, the issue of the changeling child is laid aside, the mother forgotten, as the play closes around the artisans' comedy it contains. But a reader may not forget nor really forgive the misappropriation of the boy-child by the law of the fathers, nor is the haunting music of Titania's elegy contradicted by a preferable ethic or emotion. (127–28)

Shakespeare's portraits of women here raise questions about the validity of the political and social structures that limit women's actions. At other times the dramatist challenges accepted notions by creating women characters, such as those in *All's Well That Ends Well*, who are more capable, clever, and intelligent than their male counterparts. In *A Midsummer Night's Dream*, he invents basically parallel male and female characters of equivalent ability, then weights the scales in favor of the men, illuminating the obstacles women face. Having presented the issues lightly, he then moves on to conventional theatrical treatment in the ending.

Nevertheless, one can believe that Shakespeare has painted here a complex work whose inner design has more depth than has yet been captured on stage and whose implications are still to be realized. Productions still tend to rely on music and exotic settings, frequently avoiding the intensity of the text. As John Simon wrote of a production in 1988 at the Public Theatre in New York, decrying its lack of lyricism, "What has been added is a lot of samba, bossanova, and Brazilian ambiance that often clashes with what is spoken." In that late twentieth-century production by A. J. Antoon, an important contemporary director, the text still seems to have been secondary to music and setting.

Perhaps an argument for the play's still untapped potential lies in the example of the recent revival of *Carousel* of which one critic wrote: "*Carousel* will be 50 next year, but as of this morning it is the freshest, most innovative musical on Broadway" (Richards). Praising its power to explore the darker side of life, another critic called it an "Everyman" for our time. Whatever *A Midsummer Night's Dream* might have been planned for in its own time—whether a wedding, a simple entertainment, a vibrant piece of stagecraft to amuse even those who were being examined—in its language, in its questioning of societal values, and in its brief portraits of several women suffering at the whim of a power structure they did not devise, the play holds the potential for being an "Everywoman" for our time, briefly exploring the "darker side of life." On the other hand, it remains for a work like *Hamlet* to focus more closely on that darkness—on the confusions that face women as well as men in their search for a clearer path in a patriarchal world.

PART THREE

Familial World

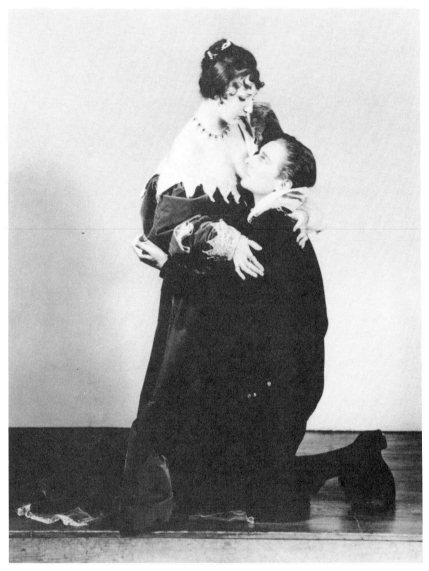

Freudian interpretation is apparent in this photograph of Judith Anderson as Gertrude and John Gielgud as Hamlet from the 1936 production directed by Guthrie McClintic. Courtesy of the Billy Rose Theatre Collection, New York Public Library.

CHAPTER FOUR
Conflicting Loyalties

HAMLET

"Where's your father?"
"At home, my lord."

III.i.129–30

In *Hamlet*, Shakespeare reveals the emotional pain and confusion that result when women, lacking a clear sense of self, rely instead on their various roles for identity. Mother, widow, and wife, but also queen, Gertrude must choose between conflicting loyalties to husband and son, the ghost of her first husband hovering in the background. Daughter, sister, beloved, and then rejected woman, Ophelia faces a more searing moral choice—between obedience to father and honesty to loved one. The multiplicity of roles and obligations women have to undertake may lead to confused values, total subordination, compliance, and even to madness, and death.

The dramatist exposes the problems facing women in a patriarchal society where men not only control the political and social avenues of power but also demand women's love, affection, and nurturance. These restrictions interfere with a woman's ability to see the world around her clearly and evaluate her own options. When Ophelia must answer Hamlet's query "Where's your father?" she faces just such conflicting demands. On the brink of maturity when the play opens, she begins with a positive, if fragile, sense of personal identity, which disintegrates when she must substitute the value systems of others for her own. Caught in the clashes between the men who govern her life—brother, father, and beloved—she goes mad. Gertrude too faces challenges peculiar to women. As a wife she is supposed to defer to her husband; but as a queen she also has certain powers. Nevertheless, at the play's opening she adopts the more dependent role, believing she can juggle her several functions. Only as the tragedy progresses does she discover the impossibility of that assumption and move toward a clearer definition of who she is.

Like Hamlet, the drama's protagonist, the women too struggle toward self-understanding: Ophelia stumbling, Gertrude growing. Unlike Hamlet, however, the women's struggles are interwoven with their socially assigned roles and with their attempts, whether consciously or not, to extricate self from role. In these characters, hedged about by a patriarchal society, Shakespeare shows not only that women's lives are hinged to those of the men but also that ultimately such a dependency hampers individual growth.

Warning against just such a submersion of the self, Margaret Fuller in the nineteenth century wrote that women must commune with themselves and know themselves:

> I wish Woman to live, first for God's sake. Then she will not make an imperfect man her god, and thus sink to idolatry.... [M]en do not look at both sides, and women must leave off asking them and being influenced by them, but retire within themselves, and explore the ground-work of life till they find their peculiar secret. (176, 121)

She then recommends: "Let her put from her the press of other minds, and meditate in virgin loneliness" (121). Neither Gertrude nor Ophelia ever retires within herself although Ophelia, through madness, escapes from "the press of other minds" and the Queen, at Hamlet's insistence, looks into her own soul.

Introduced in I.ii as "our sometime sister, now our queen, / Th' imperial jointress to this warlike state" (8–9), she enters with Claudius, in apparent control of her various roles. Although these lines suggest her position as co-ruler, the King's subsequent statement belies such equality, emphasizing instead his dominance in their relationship. When he speaks of having "taken" her "to wife," she does not protest—nor would one expect her to at this state function. The lines, however, tell us something about Claudius:

> *Have we,* as 'twere, with a defeated joy,
> With an auspicious and a dropping eye,
> With mirth in funeral, and with dirge in marriage,
> In equal scale weighing delight and dole,
> *Taken to wife.*
>
> (10, 14, emphasis added)

The audacious coupling of opposites—"mirth in funeral" and "dirge in marriage"—suggests his defiance of the ordinary rules of mourning. Attracted to Gertrude and planning to assure his solid position as King of Denmark, he marries her at once.[1] Only later do we discover how aware she was of the impropriety of their hasty marriage. Husband and wife appear as one, and the verbal sophistication apparent here offers a valuable example of Claudius's manipulation of language. But because of the speech's paradoxical wording, it seldom reaches the stage intact. Usually excised are all the words between "Have we" and "taken to wife" (11–13), a practice seen in the earliest record—the seventeenth-century Smock-Alley Promptbook—and still followed in the twentieth.[2] On the stage, only the simple statement remains. Of course the complexity of the speech may have contributed to its multiple excisions, and the fact that it suggests joint rule may have been incidental. Nevertheless, those first excisions deny the audience an early glimpse of the relationship between husband and wife.

Although the texture of this speech primarily affects our impression of Claudius, when coupled with the next major excision of his lines, the omissions skew the stage portrait of Gertrude. Following her husband's request that Hamlet remain at Elsinore, the Queen pleads:

> Let not thy mother lose her prayers, Hamlet,
> I pray thee stay with us, go not to Wittenberg.
>
> (118–19)

Her two-line speech follows an extraordinarily lengthy one by Claudius. Standing alone, her brief, simple statement should move Hamlet as well as the audience. It is the voice of the supplicant. In theatrical context, her words sound genuine. The mother would have her son near her. But Gertrude's speech, within the framework of the text, merely repeats in another key her husband's wish:

> For your intent
> In going back to school in Wittenberg,
> It is most retrograde to our desire
>
> (112–14)

Her "prayers," emphasizing free choice, replace Claudius's "retrograde" and "your intent"—words that stress the conflict of wills between the men. Coming near the close of a speech reprimanding

Hamlet for his overlong and too intense period of mourning, Claudius's reference to Wittenberg sounds threatening. Accusing the young man of "unmanly grief" (94), "a mind impatient"(96), "an understanding simple and unschooled"(97), and "a fault against the dead"(102), the speech through its piling up of phrases develops a sharp portrait of Claudius as an aggressive, insensitive, manipulative monarch. Although it opens by commending Hamlet for properly mourning his father, by the time Claudius has moved eight lines into his polemic, he is saying:

> ... 'tis unmanly grief,
> It shows a will most incorrect to heaven,
> A heart unfortified, or mind impatient,
> An understanding simple and unschool'd:
> For what we know must be, and is as common
> As any the most vulgar thing to sense,
> Why should we in our peevish opposition
> Take it to heart?
>
> (94–101)

Here he has twisted that first bit of praise into sharp criticism. More than that, he is accusing Hamlet of simply being perverse. Considering what we later discover about Claudius, we can regard the next line as showing his ease with his own villainy: "Fie, 'tis a fault to heaven" (101). And then we hear Claudius's rhetoric:

> A fault against the dead, a fault to nature,
> To reason most absurd, whose common theme
> Is death of fathers, and who still hath cried,
> From the first corse till he that died to-day,
> "This must be so."
>
> (102–6)

How skillfully he projects self-righteousness. But once again excision interferes. The above lines, from 94 to 106, usually disappear from the stage.[3] We fail to hear the strong antagonism between stepfather and stepson or to witness Gertrude striving, this early in the play, to mediate. Nor do we hear the linguistic skill that in some ways resembles Hamlet's and which may have contributed to Claudius's successful wooing of the widow queen.

Throughout, selectivity in excisions also marks this long speech. Following the dissertation on "a fault," appear three lines usually retained. Unlike the material excised, they are simple requests:

> We pray you throw to earth
> This unprevailing woe, and think of us
> As of a father, for let the world take note
> You are the most immediate to our throne.
>
> (106–9)

It is almost as if Claudius had shaped this part of the speech for Gertrude rather than Hamlet. Moreover, when only this section, along with the single line—"Our chiefest courtier, cousin, and our son" (117)—remains, Gertrude's lines function, as I have already indicated, primarily as a mother's request. In contrast, the full text presents a queen already challenged by competing forces. It also illuminates the appeal, beyond the physical, of this new husband. He has a gift with words even if, occasionally, he is carried away by his own verbosity. Gertrude's speech, therefore, functions as a wife's reinforcement and skillful reshaping of her husband's orders.

This rich stage portrait is reduced by the textual deletions. Only a passively loving wife and mother emerges. She conforms to stereotypical notions of women—specifically, that they are defined by their roles rather than as individuals with individual differences and individual value systems. (Of course other excisions also occur—such as the discussion later on of the deaths of Rosencrantz and Guildenstern where Hamlet admits his role in substituting one death warrant for another. However, because of my interest in the women characters, I have stressed cuts in language relevant to them throughout the chapter.) Often lost are the text's hints of Gertrude's struggle to reconcile conflicting loyalties. Stage versions retain the major outlines of the portrait of the supportive wife, but lose the incisive character definitions that are heard only briefly at the beginning of the play in her reprimand:

> Good Hamlet, cast thy nighted color off,
> .   .   .   .
> Thou know'st 'tis common, all that lives must die,
> Passing through nature to eternity.
>
> (68–73)

followed by their exchange:

> *Ham.* Ay, madam, it is common.
> *Queen.*   If it be,
>   Why seems it so particular with thee?
>
> (74–75)

Although she has posed the question, her husband follows it up, debating her son, while Gertrude waits on the sidelines for a resolution. Only much later does a fuller picture of her emerge.

Until that time, the audience must grasp at hints and innuendos. The Ghost's lines to Hamlet offer strong, if inconclusive, evidence of guilt. Although primarily attacking "that incestuous, that adulterate beast" (I.v.42), Claudius, who won to his lust that "most seeming virtuous queen" (46), the words, nevertheless, taint Gertrude. And what of the subsequent reference to "the royal bed of Denmark" as "A couch of luxury and damned incest" (82–83)? The ambiguities in the report and the implication of Gertrude's involvement with Claudius before her husband's death taunt Hamlet. But the audience must be more judicious. Does Claudius's earlier reference to Gertrude as "imperial jointress" suggest complicity? Or does the hostility of Claudius's other lines, including his long tirade to Hamlet while she hardly speaks, argue for her innocence?

When she next appears, in II.ii, audiences watch her actions and listen intently to her words. If she is coruler, is she also coconspirator? Exuding confidence and power, she welcomes "Guildenstern and gentle Rosencrantz" (II.ii.34) with lines paralleling and gently correcting Claudius's "Rosencrantz and gentle Guildenstern" (33). When, after expressing concern for her son, she then promises the two men, "Your visitation shall receive such thanks / As fits a king's remembrance" (25–26), she sounds guilty. The vagueness of her words arouses skepticism. Is this just a generous promise, or is a bribe implied? Nor does her sharp reprimand to Polonius— "More matter, with less art" (II.ii.95)—interrupting his long discourse on madness, allay suspicions.

However, the scene also offers contradictions. The unbroken unity of purpose of husband and wife shows cracks. They momentarily disagree. When told that Polonius has discovered the source of Hamlet's melancholy—rejection by Ophelia—Gertrude disagrees: "I doubt it is no other but the main, / His father's death and our o'erhasty marriage" (II.ii.56–57). Spoken confidently, her lines illuminate that earlier excision in Claudius's speech explaining the reason for their marriage. His queen had had reservations. But audiences never heard his words and those who read them seldom considered their possible later implications.

Henry Irving, whose acting versions of 1874 and 1878 cut some 1,200 lines, selectively excised in this scene (Hughes, 30). Following traditional patterns, he deleted all references to Voltemand and Cornelius, keeping them out of the scene; but he also deviated from tradition by excising the Queen's protest here—lines retained, for example, in the Smock Alley and other acting texts. Gone too are many of Polonius's lines. What remains primarily serves the plot as it revolves around Hamlet—the report of his strange behavior at Ophelia's closet, and the certainty that love is the cause of the Prince's melancholy. The full focus is on the Prince, diminishing other characters. As Alan Hughes in his study of Irving's Shakespeare productions writes:

> Inevitably his own part was overemphasized by omissions, simplifications and the sheer focusing power of his genius, but the production was probably not as oversimplified as most we see today. (29)

The comment is relevant to many *Hamlet* productions. It explains how women's portraits may also suffer when the text is abbreviated.

Excised by Irving, Gertrude's few lines disputing Polonius's theory and admitting a lack of decorum in her hasty marriage would certainly remind audiences at the play of Hamlet's first soliloquy and his later exchange with Horatio:

> *Hor.* My lord, I came to see your father's funeral.
> *Ham.* I prithee do not mock me, fellow studient,
>   I think it was to see my mother's wedding.
> *Hor.* Indeed, my lord, it followed hard upon.
> *Ham.* Thrift, thrift, Horatio, the funeral bak'd meats
>   Did coldly furnish forth the marriage tables.
>   (I.ii.176–81)

Echoing this conversation, the Queen's lines offer the first hint of her unconscious agreement with her son. She, too, had been aware of the impropriety of the action, but the King's gift in language had convinced her. In this momentary disagreement with Claudius, Gertrude shows a character at war with herself. Although her protest quickly slides into oblivion, it presages the future. Here, she delightedly accepts Polonius's prediction after he reads aloud Hamlet's love letters to Ophelia. "Do you think 'tis this?" Claudius asks. "It may be, very like" (II.ii.151–52), Gertrude quickly concedes.

In their next scene together, the emerging conflict of personalities or at least of points of view again appears—and again she subsides into compliance. Once more Rosencrantz and Guildenstern appear before the monarchs. This time, however, King and Queen no longer speak as one voice. Claudius sharply asks:

> An' can you by no drift of conference
> Get from him why he puts on this confusion,
> Grating so harshly all his days of quiet
> With turbulent and dangerous lunacy?
>
> (III.i.1–4)

Taking their cues from "Grating," "harshly," and "dangerous lunacy," the young courtiers speak of Hamlet's "crafty madness" (8), and would, perhaps, continue. But Gertrude interrupts, altering the direction of the questioning. She asks for a simple judgmental evaluation:

> Did he receive you well?
>
> (10)

Again responding to the tone, Rosencrantz assures her, "Most like a gentleman" (11) while his partner plays to the King, "But with much forcing of his disposition" (12). Gertrude then jogs the conversation one step further from turbulence and madness: "Did you assay him / To any pastime?" (14–15) Good friends should entertain and divert. She has placed the burden on the two courtiers. Reference to the players brings the interview to a close, and the King dismisses the two men. If Gertrude has broken the pattern of questioning at the beginning of this scene, Claudius quickly establishes his dominance when, moments later, he dismisses her too. "Sweet Gertrude, leave us two" (28), he begins, before explaining the plot. Ophelia will be the "springe" to catch Hamlet while monarch and adviser listen, "unseen," for signs of love.

Unhesitatingly Gertrude acquiesces in the directive. Responding to each point of his statement in sequence, she begins, "I shall obey you" (36), then addresses Ophelia:

> And for your part, Ophelia, I do wish
> That your good beauties be the happy cause
> Of Hamlet's wildness. So shall I hope your virtues
> Will bring him to his wonted way again,
> To both your honors.
>
> (37–41)

Despite a gap of nine lines between Claudius's command and her response, Gertrude manages to answer his speech in the order of its recital, acting her role of wife and Queen, then combining her varied other roles—mother, potential mother-in-law, and woman surveying another woman's youth. To Ophelia, the obedient daughter waiting on one side, Gertrude expresses her hopes for her son. Stereotypical behavior prevails—obedience to husband, praise of Ophelia's "good beauties," belief that a young man can be cured by "the love of a good woman," and even the hint of passion in the young people's love for one another.

Ophelia's simple answer, "Madam, I wish it may" (41), indicates an equally accepting attitude toward the men's plan. Neither woman considers its morality, honesty, or wisdom. Most important, neither questions the directives given her. Before the scene is over, that happy reliance on men's judgment—their "better wisdom"—is shown to be an ordinary weakness of these women. More particularly, the scene reveals the flaws in the patriarchal system where women's compliance to the directives of men overlooks the humanity of the women themselves. Their value systems are supposed to be non-existent, or, if existent, easily jettisoned in order to obey the rules of a male society. As the scene mounts to its dramatic close, we watch Ophelia caught in the net of the system as she struggles to answer Hamlet's question, "Where's your father?" finally lying, "At home, my lord" (III.i.129–30). The clash between the self and the outside forces ultimately destroys her. "O what a noble mind is here o'erthrown!"(150), its "noble and most sovereign reason / Like sweet bells jangled out of time and harsh"(157–58), she mourns at the scene's close little realizing hers will soon be the "mind . . . o'erthrown." Neither woman will appear again in such seeming equanimity as she does at the beginning of this scene. The next scene, at the play, will reveal a Hamlet coarse and insulting to Ophelia and sardonic to his mother as he seeks to identify her with the Player Queen.

Not until the closet scene do audiences finally begin to understand and empathize with Gertrude. "[A]lmost as bad, good mother, / As kill a king, and marry with his brother" (III.iv.28–29), Hamlet accuses. "As kill a king!" (30). Her line expresses her astonishment. Audiences have already heard Claudius's prayers, his admission that he still possesses "My crown, mine own ambition, and my queen" (III.iii.55) for which he murdered his brother. Gertrude's amazed reaction to Hamlet's accusation as well as Claudius's reference to the Queen, implying that she was not aware of his act of murder, finally indicates that she was not a coconspirator—a fact left in doubt in the early scenes of the play. But her dependence on the King for identity remains.

As the closet scene unfolds, she slowly begins to realize the necessity for separating herself and her identity from that of Claudius. Opening with the stichomythic gambit between mother and son—"Hamlet, thou hast thy father much offended" / "Mother, you have my father much offended" (III.iv.9–10)—the scene expands with Hamlet's lengthy speeches of accusation following his murder of Polonius. Before that, however, Gertrude relies heavily on her role as monarch, showing anger as well as fear: "I'll set those to you that can speak" (17), she threatens. When Hamlet responds with an order, his lines imply physical force:

> Come, come, and sit you down, you shall not boudge;
> You go not till I set you up a glass
> Where you may see the inmost part of you.
>
> (18–20)

She fearfully calls for help. The accidental death of Polonius leaves her alone in the room with her son. Realizing the enormity and frenzy of his actions, she may also begin to wonder about the truth of his accusations.

The hostility and acrimony threading through Hamlet's lines might be expected to alienate audiences and build sympathy for the Queen. Surely they offer a new picture of her as she counters her son's words. His language is raw; his accusations are intense: "Sense sure you have, / Else could you not have motion, but sure that sense / Is apoplex'd" (71–73), he charges, then speaks of madness, of "rebellious hell," that "mutine[s] in a matron's bones," and describes the heat of sexual passion, using parallels from the animal world. His overemotional reaction to the idea that his mother has remarried—that women her age can feel the stirrings of sexuality—might win audiences to her. But, dating from 1767, the last seventeen lines of this long speech have seldom reached the stage.[4] Although some of these lines were omitted from the Folio, there is no consistency between the excisions and either the first or second Quarto text. Rather, the excisions seem to be based on the intensity of the language. Gone are the lines:

> What devil was't
> That thus hath cozen'd you at hoodman-blind?
> Eyes without feeling, feeling without sight,
> Ears without hands or eyes, smelling sans all,
> Or but a sickly part of one true sense
> Could not so mope.
>
> (III.iv.76–81)

This enumeration of the senses and of their absence of feeling in a speech accusing Gertrude of overemotional sexual responsiveness has its own intensity that suggests Hamlet's lack of control. Most acting texts retain only the single line, "O shame, where is thy blush?" (81) but excise all that follows, including the young Prince's:

> Proclaim no shame
> When the compulsive ardure gives the charge,
> Since frost itself as actively doth burn,
> And reason panders will.
>
> (85–88)

Although in the eighteenth century, respect for audience sensibilities was often an excuse for excision, even in modern times, when sexual honesty is exploding in drama, this section often remains closeted in the text. Rather than audience sensibilities, those of actor-managers and stars govern the decision. The language of the text at this point presents a frighteningly high-strung, emotional, sexually preoccupied son intensively pressuring his mother. Finally the audience may tend to empathize with Gertrude, seeing the pain in a woman's split worlds.

Since the interaction of characters on the stage determines responses in the theater, the elimination of many of Hamlet's most corrosive lines to Gertrude affects both one's feelings for him and for her. When he spews out the language of steamy beds and sties—the language of the text—Gertrude wins compassion for her plight as a mother and her confusion as a woman. Hamlet's extraordinary passion seems touched by madness.

What does a mother do when a son sneeringly says:

> Not this, by no means, that I bid you do:
> Let the bloat king tempt you again to bed,
> Pinch wanton on your cheek, call you his mouse,
> And let him, for a pair of reechy kisses,

> Or paddling in your neck with his damn'd fingers,
> Make you to ravel all this matter out,
> That I essentially am not in madness,
> But mad in craft.

(181–88)

Nor does the speech stop here. Finally permitted to answer, she assures him she will keep his secret. But can she? And how will she, a new bride, effect this? Does she believe that Hamlet is not mad? In the text, Shakespeare raises these difficult questions. In the theater, actor-managers and directors resolve the difficulty through excision. Thus David Garrick ended this scene before Hamlet's comments on bedding. His earlier and more gentle couplet "I must be cruel only to be kind. / Thus bad begins and worse remains behind" (178–79) closes the scene. Nor was Garrick alone. Many others followed the same pattern, including Henry Irving in the late nineteenth century and Sothern and Marlowe at the beginning of the twentieth. Their audiences as well as those of John Barrymore and Forbes-Robertson were also denied the first four scenes of act 4. Explaining that his aim in shifting the scenes was "to allow more scope and freedom of movement of the characters," Forbes Robertson rationalized that since "Acts and Scenes are not marked in the Folios beyond the second Scene of the second Act, and not at all in the Quartoes," he was not bound by the text.[5] His changes, however, surely must have affected the portrait of Gertrude.

Those audiences never heard Hamlet draw the vow of secrecy from his mother:

> Be thou assur'd, if words be made of breath,
> And breath of life, I have no life to breathe
> What thou hast said to me.

(197–99)

Nor did they witness the emotional turmoil of her next scene, the challenge of Claudius's "What, Gertrude? How does Hamlet?" (IV.i.6) or the King's opening observation, a clue to Gertrude's intense state, "There's matter in these sighs, these profound heaves— / You must translate" (1–2). As a result, they missed watching her decision to hide from Claudius all that had transpired in the bedroom scene. Instead, these excisions transported the audience from Gertrude's closet to Ophelia's madness. No intervening scenes created a gap of time between Polonius's murder and his daughter's descent into insanity.

This altering of the text of the closet scene, modifying its intensity, continued into the mid and late twentieth century—in the productions of John Gielgud, John Houseman, and Richard Burton. While not accepting Garrick's pattern where the scene ends with the couplet preceding Hamlet's last orders to his mother, these versions continued to eliminate large chunks of text. As a result, the heroic Hamlet image has remained despite the absence of the soliloquy following the exit of Fortinbras's men. And Gertrude has won only limited sympathy. Shakespeare's more complex portrait of a woman with multiple and conflicting allegiances often fails to surface in the theater. Yet, the scene does mark the beginning of Gertrude's uncertainty about Claudius.

For the first time, she realizes she must choose between husband and son. Those omitted scenes highlight her dilemma and broaden the portrait of Hamlet. Keeping her promise to him, she assures the King that her son is mad. Ironically, news of Polonius's murder seems to confirm Hamlet's sanity: "It had been so with us had we been there" (IV.i.13), her husband counters. Although she insists, "'A weeps for what is done" (28), Claudius wonders. Nor do Hamlet's actions moments later, his saucy responses to Rosencrantz and Guildenstern, followed by lightly masked arrogance to the King, suggest a "weeping" Prince. The puns, challenges, and air of defiance reinforce Claudius's decision. Hamlet must to England—and to death.

Whereas the sequential arrangement of scenes immediately following the mother-son encounter continues to emphasize Gertrude's role, a more leisurely pace precedes her next entrance. Hamlet has gone; Polonius is dead and buried. The juxtaposed scenes take the audience from the excitement in the palace to the lonely fields of Denmark then back to the palace. The Queen has time to change her mind—to move from active to passive role once more. The request to admit the mad Ophelia at the opening of scene 5 sparks Gertrude's refusal as she attempts once more to evade responsibility before acceding: "I will not speak with her" (IV.v.1). Ophelia enters, asks for the "beauteous majesty of Denmark" (21), sings songs of sex, frustration, longing, and death that are seldom heard on stage and breaks the heart of her rebellious brother.

New glimpses of the Queen emerge. For the first time, the drama offers concrete evidence of her strength and popularity with the people. The private person—the woman conflicted by divided loyalties—recedes before the public person, a respected figure. Confronted by the angry Laertes who has just forced his way into the palace, Gertrude acts with composure, "Calmly, good Laertes" (117). The stage directions embedded in the text reveal that she uses more than mere words. "Let him go, Gertrude, do not fear our person" (123), the King protests. She has restrained Laertes, concerned for her husband who, not without a little irony, has capitalized on the moment by adding, "There's such divinity doth hedge a king / That treason can but peep to what it would" (124–25). Whereas the audience recognizes the irony of Claudius's lines, Gertrude does not. Uncertain of her allegiance in the first few acts, we now see the woman alone struggling between two opposing forces, a conflict she will eventually resolve in the last scene. At this point, however, she supports Claudius, influenced by his confidence in his kingship and perhaps also by his lament after Ophelia's first exit, "O Gertrude, Gertrude, / When sorrows come, they come not single spies, / But in battalions" (77–79). She has lied for Hamlet, sought to avoid the mad Ophelia, but now she acts. When Laertes demands, "Where is my father?" and the King responds with a single word, "Dead," Gertrude quickly intercedes, "But not by him" (129). Her line invites disclosure of Hamlet's responsibility for Polonius's death. Compassion for Claudius has led her, unwittingly, to provoke Laertes to murder her son. In this scene, stage directions defined her power, whereas these lines reveal her confusion and mixed allegiance.

Absent from the scenes of plotting, Gertrude next appears as messenger of Ophelia's death. "One woe doth tread upon another's heel / So fast they follow. Your sister's drown'd, Laertes" (IV.vii.163–64), the Queen movingly reports. In this set speech, Shakespeare links the two women whose lives had touched only briefly. Describing in detail the garlands, wreaths, and flowers the doomed young woman collected, and evoking the vision of her floating, "Her clothes spread wide, / And mermaid-like awhile they bore her up" (175-76), Gertrude reveals her own sorrow and sense of loss. Artists have drawn on this speech for illustrations; filmmakers have introduced it on the screen. The most famous of these paintings is Millais's nineteenth-century work, showing Ophelia, her garments buoying her up, floating on the water. The painting, in fact, became the source for Laurence Olivier's textual alteration of *Hamlet* (134). In the film, the vision of Ophelia floating on the water combined with a voice-over of Gertrude have replaced Shakespeare's text; the scene's ending has disappeared. Despite using a new medium, Olivier is following an earlier pattern, shortening Gertrude's speech and cutting the scene's ending. Evoking pity for the dead Ophelia, he, like earlier actor-managers and directors, shrinks the portrait of the Queen.

Did the speech offend because of its details, or was it too long and too moving to give to Gertrude? Did it unnecessarily expand her role? Surely it gives us insight into her emotional sensitivity as she describes how trapped Ophelia was by "her garments, heavy with their drink" that "Pull'd the poor wretch from her melodious lay / To muddy death" (181–83). But the lines have been excised by Olivier, Gertrude's reference to the "poor wretch" eliminated, and only the bare facts have been retained. Interrupting the plotting of her husband, who is spinning a web in which to ensnare both Laertes and Hamlet, she bursts in free of guile, wanting to share the tragedy, her honest reaction apparent in her lines. The cuts in her speech therefore seem inexplicable except as they indicate a skewed interest in retaining as many of Hamlet's lines as necessary to create the clearest single portrait, sacrificing the nuances in the definitions of the women.

Both this speech and the scene's close add to our understanding of the Queen who is silhouetted against the men who listen to her: Laertes and Claudius. The former fears showing emotion; the latter fears Laertes's wrath. Little moved by the death of Ophelia, callous Claudius explodes: "How much I had to do to calm his rage! / Now fear I this will give it start again" (192–93). While his anger may be directed at the situation, his lack of sympathy, of pity at the news of Ophelia's death, further distances husband from wife. Thus the close of the act refines their relationship, continuing to develop a schism between them. Conversely, the ending strengthens the link, albeit invisible, between the two women—and anticipates the Queen's final gesture of defiance to Claudius.

Sustaining the tone of her report of Ophelia's death, the Queen, at the graveside, wistfully speaks of the unfulfilled promise:

> Sweets to the sweet, farewell!
> I hop'd thou shouldst have been my Hamlet's wife.
> I thought thy bride-bed to have deck'd, sweet maid,
> And not have strew'd thy grave.
>
> (V.i.243–46)

The lines take us back to the moment in act 3 when both women relied on the judgments of father and husband, endorsing their scheme. Since then, the younger has lost her way, unable to fathom the mixed signals of the patriarchal world while the elder is still discovering the irreconcilables in her own split universe. When Hamlet jumps into the grave, affirming his love for Ophelia— "Why, I will fight with him upon this theme / Until my eyelids will no longer wag" (266–67)—the Queen picks up his words, "O my son, what theme?" (268). She then hears the answer denied Ophelia when father and King spied "unseen": "I lov'd Ophelia. Forty thousand brothers / Could not with all their quantity of love / Make up my sum" (269–71). Because of the intensity of his response, this section of text is never cut.

After the challenge of the closet scene, Gertrude changes. Her set speech on Ophelia's death, her response to Hamlet at the grave-side, and her final action during the duel show a development in her character, paralleling, in a minor key, the changes in Hamlet. Attempting to explain his wild behavior at the grave, she must prove him harmless, inventing her own rationale. In the closing scene, she has no lines until she seeks to wipe Hamlet's brow, then drinks to his fortune. For the last time, the King attempts to stop her. But the woman who reiterated his words, reshaping them for acceptability in act 1, the woman who sought to save him from Laertes in act 4 and began to see her own strength, the woman condemned by her son as a whore in act 3, perceives herself as an individual. It is not accidental that Gertrude responds to the King's directive, "Gertrude, do not drink," with "I will, my lord, I pray you pardon me" (V.ii.290–91). David Giles's 1971 television production shows her as a possible alcoholic, which suggests a decline in Gertrude rather than strength. For me, however, she exhibits a steady growth in her few speeches after Polonius's death.

In the first Quarto (Q 1) there is also an exchange at IV.vi between Horatio and the Queen that supports the idea of her emerging individuality. The section, not included in the Folio or in the conflated texts that are usually read, presents a positive woman of action. Horatio informs the Queen of having received a letter from Hamlet telling of the "subtle treason that the king had plotted." She responds, "Then I perceive there's treason in his lookes / That seem'd to sugar o'er his villanie" and plots with Horatio to keep her son's plans secret from the King.[6] Was the scene excised by the dramatist or by those who later put the Folio together? We don't know. We do, however, see that in one early form of the play, Gertrude clearly appears to be a woman of action. Moreover, when one considers the conflation of texts so generally accepted, the absence of this passage suggests that editors, like later adaptors of the play, seem to have found it more comfortable to keep that particular window on Gertrude's emerging character out of any full text. If hers remains a somewhat ambiguous portrait, the absence of that section helps contribute to that delineation.

At the beginning of the play, Shakespeare seems to develop her character as a woman with the potential for power who rejects that power in favor of a sexual relationship and acceptance of the rules governing marriage in a patriarchal society. She might even have read the handbooks of the time on the proper behavior of brides so closely does she conform to the pattern. Introduced as "imperial jointress" in the first act, she has, in fact, opted instead for the conventional role of wife, clearly answering Claudius with a simple uncontesting "I shall obey you," in act 3. She later finds herself protecting him from the angry mob. The closet scene, where she is pushed towards self-examination, separates these two dramatic moments. The playwright shows the full scope of a woman seeking, as women do, to maintain a balance among her varied roles. The play questions the viability of such multiple role-playing without self-knowledge.

The tendency to simplify this challenge to women is perhaps most blatantly exhibited in Garrick's notorious version of 1772. Aiming to expand Hamlet's role through the reintroduction of many of his lines as well as early sections of the text that had been consistently excised, Garrick jettisoned the graveyard scene and compressed most of the end of the play. From the only extant version, which appears to be incomplete, as well as from contemporaneous reports, we discover a Gertrude who retreats from reality (G. W. Stone, Jr., 890–921). The absence of the graveyard scene speeds the action after Ophelia's second mad exit. But it also eliminates the character development of Gertrude. Gone is her moving report of Ophelia's death, revealing the Queen's sympathy for the young woman. Nor do we hear the contrasting reactions of Claudius and Laertes. Instead, concentrating on Hamlet, the action hurries to the confrontation between him and Laertes. Without a grave to jump into they nevertheless challenge one another. The Prince's admission of love for Ophelia remains. But the Queen's role alters completely. Instead of drinking the poison cup and defying her husband, she goes mad—a survivor off-stage during the play's final moments. Ironically, the absent reporter of Ophelia's death comes to life in another role, as courier of news that the Queen lies in her bed in a trance. She is a weak woman overcome by her conflicting loyalties.

In contrast, Shakespeare's Gertrude, in the last scene, seems to know who she is and refuses to comply with Claudius's wish. She will function as mother and Queen. She will exert power over herself. But, like Hamlet's actions, hers come too late. Unlike Hamlet, who was directed by his emotional agony as well as the ghost's words, she has allowed herself to be directed by Claudius's words and thoughts as well as her own sexual drives. Gertrude's slow movement towards that final schism counters Ophelia's movement away from the easy joy of youth and celebration of self. She gradually adjusts to the laws of a patriarchal society where sexual politics leads to women's low self-esteem and, often, self-loathing.

Unlike Gertrude, Ophelia does not stumble towards self-understanding but loses herself. Her path is one of descent, her greatest strength appearing in her opening scene when she cautions her brother to take his own advice. Simone de Beauvoir writes of the agony for adolescent girls who must choose between self and "other"—between considering themselves primary or perceiving themselves as "other" in a patriarchal world where men and men's values dominate (314). Shakespeare dramatizes this as Ophelia struggles first with her brother then with her father. A young girl growing to maturity, she must deal with their cynicism and worldly wisdom as they destroy her confidence in her newly emerging self. Offering an elder brother's wisdom, Laertes cautions his sister about believing Hamlet:

> Perhaps he loves you now,
> And now no soil nor cautel doth besmirch
> The virtue of his will, but you must fear,
> His greatness weigh'd, his will is not his own.
>
> (I.iii.14–17)

First Laertes hints; then he becomes more explicit, warning her against the siren songs of a lover—and their destructiveness:

> Then weigh what loss your honor may sustain
> If with too credent ear you list his songs,

> *Or lose your heart, or your chaste treasure open*
> *To his unmaster'd importunity.*
>
> (29–32, emphasis added)

The full text emphasizes a young woman's sexual vulnerability. But excision of the italicized lines as well as many others, dating from the earliest extant prompts, those of the seventeenth century, and persisting into our own time, blurs that emphasis. Garrick, Kemble, Irving, Forbes-Robertson, Macready, Sothern-Marlowe, and Barrymore among others cut the lines. Often unheard too are other sexual warnings that permeate Laertes's speeches, such as:

> The canker galls the infants of the spring
> Too oft before their buttons be disclos'd,
> And in the morn and liquid dew of youth
> Contagious blastments are most imminent.
>
> (39–42)

Here he refers to "liquid dew of youth," defining the early stages of youth but combines the phrase with "contagious blastments." The *OED* defines "blastment" somewhat vaguely, referring the reader back to "blasting" where the definition is: "withering or shriveling up caused by unseen agency." Are we then to read this as "when people are young there is a contagiousness in this shriveling up?" Or might there be a sexual implication here where "liquid dew of youth" refers not only to the beginning of maturity but also to sexual consummation, and "contagious blastments" suggests blasting of her reputation?

In an article on the history of sexuality, Martha Vicinus observes that "the dominant paradigm for sexuality is overwhelmingly male and heterosexual." She describes it as an "energy-control (or hydraulic) model. [S]exuality is seen as an independent force or energy disciplined by personal and social constraints. Sex is always something to be released or controlled" (136). Laertes's varied definitions and warnings to Ophelia all derive from this perception although he masks them in poetic metaphors. Aware of the implications of Laertes's lines, directors tend to abbreviate them. Sexual resonances disappear. Only the simple classic warning remains, as Ophelia is cautioned to "keep you in the rear of your affection, / Out of the shot and danger of desire" (34–35). In context, however, the lines contribute to Ophelia's confusion about Hamlet's honesty and the sincerity of his affection for her.

The absence of sexual overtones does not mean the elimination of gender definitions. McClintic, for example, whose textual excisions followed the general pattern, nevertheless relied on stereotypical behavior in his staging. The promptbook tells us that Ophelia, sitting on a stool, sews on a piece of embroidery during her talk with Laertes. He, in turn, enters carrying a sword, belt, and cape. These he eventually dons—stage business to occupy him while giving her advice. He finishes dressing moments before his departure. A heavily Freudian interpretation, this production stressed Hamlet's Oedipus complex, showing him in the closet scene with Gertrude where they look more like lovers than mother and son. In one photograph, for example, both characters are on their knees facing one another, their lips almost touching, her gown, a low-cut evening robe pulled down off one shoulder (see illustration). In contrast, Hamlet's photos with Ophelia lack passion. Here gender definition in staging reflects a particular contemporary perspective on sexuality rather than a greater drive for textual accuracy. One stereotype of women may have replaced another, but the consistency in textual excisions remained.

In fact, as Carol Carlisle has pointed out, only when actresses playing the role sought to understand its underlying unity did any Ophelia criticism emerge.[7] Moreover, the role was considered so minor that when an actress of any stature chose to play the distraught young woman, critics were surprised. One such example was Julia Marlowe, who, with her husband E. H. Sothern, toured the United States with *Hamlet*. Their interpretation of several of Ophelia's scenes testifies to Julia Marlowe's influence on the readings of the play that emerged. Neither embroidery nor sword and cape invade the brother-sister scene. Instead, the major prop is a scroll—a letter from Hamlet. Promptbook notes describe Ophelia kissing it when Laertes enters. Observing her action, he refers to the scroll later when advising her.

This first Ophelia scene establishes character traits that will be challenged, leading to lack of confidence in her own judgment and eventual disintegration into madness. The scene suggests her faith in the power of honesty. Following her brother's reminder before his departure, "Farewell, Ophelia, and remember well / What I have said to you" (I.iii.84–85), she willingly promises, "'Tis in my memory lock'd, / And you yourself shall keep the key of it" (85–86). But honesty places this promise in jeopardy when Polonius insists she "unlock" that memory. Shakespeare then emphasizes the adjustment demanded of her through the swift succession of counselors giving her the same advice. In vigorous, unmasked language, Polonius dismisses her confidence in Hamlet's honesty. "Affection puh! You speak like a green girl, / Unsifted in such perilous circumstances" (101–3), he admonishes, then mocks his daughter's innocence, "Do not believe his [Hamlet's] vows, for they are brokers, / Not of that dye which their investments show, / But mere implorators of unholy suits, / . . . the better to beguile" (127–31). In the language of commerce, he introduces her to the real world as he perceives it. Survival depends on deception, not honesty. If her brother's language was circuitous, her father's is direct, providing her first basic lesson on the ugliness of sex. When she assures her father that Hamlet "hath given countenance to his speech . . . / With almost all the holy vows of heaven" (113–14), Polonius asserts:

> Ay, springes to catch woodcocks. I do know,
> When the blood burns, how prodigal the soul
> Lends the tongue vows. These blazes, daughter,
> Giving more light than heat, extinct in both,
> Even in their promise, as it is a-making,
> You must not take for fire.
>
> (115–20)

The father's own admission—"I do know, / When the blood burns" how easily one makes vows that won't be kept—adds a new dimension to their conversation.

Here, as so frequently in other plays, Shakespeare indicates the different weight men and women attach to vows.[8] Ophelia's father is expanding her education. She had believed in the sincerity of vows. He assures her of their worthlessness. When, later on, in the nunnery scene, Hamlet says, "We are arrant knaves, believe none of us" (III.i.128), he is reinforcing her father's earlier lesson. Polonius's quick confirmation of her brother's warning had led Ophelia to question her own value system, or at least to concede that she might have been wrong. "Do you believe his tenders?" (I.iii.103) Polonius had asked. "I do not know, my lord, what I should think" (104), she had responded, finally admitting at the scene's close that she would obey her father's directive neither to believe Hamlet nor spend time talking with him. But her father changes his mind. Once more she speaks to Hamlet, this time in the "nunnery" scene, and discovers that brother and father were right: men's vows of love are meaningless.

Shakespeare gives us only one glimpse of this young girl with a positive sense of self. After her first scene, she will be wrestling with the many conflicting voices that seem to establish, with such confidence, the proper path of behavior for a young woman in a patriarchal society. Bowing to male superiority, she attempts to revise her standards, jettisoning her own instinctive faith in the Prince's words. As a result, she obeys her father's orders, whatever they may be.

Through the sequential arrangement of scenes, the dramatist suggests the folly of Ophelia's decision. Prior to her entrance, Hamlet, in soliloquy and later in conversation with Horatio, appears to be a moral young man disturbed by the seeming irregularity of his mother's hasty marriage. Ophelia's confidence in the honesty of his vows therefore seems reasonable to the audience. In contrast, her brother's comments reveal a youth with stereotypical ideas about relationships between men and women. He wishes to protect her from her own frailty but also, as she hints, from advances by young men like himself who occasionally slip into libertine ways. His warning also anticipates, although only vaguely, his later inability to judge Hamlet or to question Claudius's scheme. Conventional attitudes towards men and women—towards the holders of power and the powerless—dominate his thinking. At this moment in the play, however, he is simply the older brother, giving advice.

Ophelia's next appearance comes at the close of a scene exposing Polonius's weaknesses as a father. The full scene follows Hamlet's meeting with the ghost and seems to promise a light interlude after the intensity of the ghost's disclosure. Opening with Polonius's instructions to his servant, it presents a father generously thinking of his son: "Give him this money and these notes, Reynaldo" (II.i.1). What a relaxed, innocuous beginning. Here is a father who sounds happy and supportive, making no demands on his son, thus differing from the ghost of the previous scene who could only be quieted by his son's assurance, "Rest, rest, perturbed spirit" (I.v.182), leading to the introspective despairing, "O cursed spite, / That ever I was born to set it right!" (188–89).

But this favorable impression of Polonius is short-lived. He next suggests that Reynaldo inquire about Laertes's behavior as well as spread false rumors about him: "put on him / What forgeries you please" (II.i.19–20). Although Polonius assures Reynaldo— "none so rank / As may dishonor him" (20–21)—the father does propose "drinking, fencing, swearing, quarreling, / Drabbing—you may go so far"(25–26). What kind of a father is this? Reynaldo himself wonders, protesting, with Polonius's own words: "My lord, that would dishonor him" (27). The scene then reveals Polonius's method of rationalization. Not retracting the instruction he has given, he merely modifies it to suggest that the son only occasionally indulges in such activity. But even this arouses Reynaldo's continued protest. Finally the father explains his reasons. They betray a man who believes in spying.

Only after this expanded portrait of Polonius, detailing his attitude towards his male child, does his female child, Ophelia, enter, describing a disturbed, distraught Prince. When, as usually occurs, the whole beginning of this scene is cut from stage productions, a tradition that dates back to the 1670 Smock Alley prompt, we lose the detailed development of a scheming father. Shoving Ophelia from center stage, the new sequence stresses Hamlet's anguish after his meeting with the ghost. Gone is the sharp juxtaposition of the two major forces in her life—a spying father and a lost lover. Instead we see only a kindly father, listening to his daughter's report of Hamlet and revising the earlier advice. Upset by what she has witnessed and concerned for the young Prince, she recounts the experience in detail:

> My lord, as I was sewing in my closet,
> Lord Hamlet, with his doublet all unbrac'd,
> No hat upon his head, his stockins fouled,
> Ungart'red, and down-gyved to his ankle,
> Pale as his shirt, his knees knocking each other,
> And with a look so piteous on purport
> As if he had been loosed out of hell
> To speak of horrors—he comes before me.
>
> (II.i.74–81)

Hesitant to interpret Hamlet's gestures, Ophelia merely reports, waiting for her father's conclusions. But this vivid account surely challenges the all-knowing father who had sneered at her early comments, "My lord, he hath importun'd me with love / In honorable fashion" (I.iii.110–11). Could Polonius have been wrong when he answered, "Ay, fashion you may call it. Go to, go to" (112)? The audience knows that Hamlet's choices are more complex—the pledge to the ghost probably motivating this farewell to Ophelia. But Polonius, who remembers the false vows made "when the blood burns," now thinks Hamlet's words may have been sincere. And Ophelia, having abdicated judgment on these matters, listens.

Believing love must surely be the cause of Hamlet's madness, Polonius apologizes to his daughter:

> I fear'd he did but trifle
> And meant to wrack thee, but beshrew my jealousy!
>
> (II.i.109–10)

Although a note in one edition interprets the last phrase, "beshrew my jealousy" as "curse my suspicions," the word *jealousy* also had its more familiar meaning in Shakespeare's time, as we know from lines in *Othello* and *King Lear*, for example.[9] Polonius's line may even hint at a brief admission of jealousy that his daughter's suitor would replace the older man in her affections.[10] Although such a father may fear the loss of his daughter's love, Polonius need not fear. His domination of her increases until, by the time we reach the nunnery scene, she considers his wishes above her own. Here, in II.i, believing the error his, he rationalizes:

> By heaven, it is as proper to our age
> To cast beyond ourselves in our opinions,
> As it is common for the younger sort
> To lack discretion.
>
> (111–14)

He manages to balance the sins of the elders with those of youth. If fathers are overcautious, blame it on the "younger sort," who lack discretion.

Polonius then decides they must immediately report Hamlet's behavior to the King. But the lines are curious; they give new insights into the councilor's motivation. Rather than concern for Ophelia, they imply concern for himself—the politician. Having discerned possible royal disapproval of a romance between the two young people, he would protect himself. Ophelia has now created a problem: "This must be known, which, being kept close, might move / More grief to hide, than hate to utter love" (115–16). Polonius is probably reacting to what he believes to be Claudius's wishes although he includes the Queen in his comment:

> What might you,
> Or my dear Majesty your queen here, think,

> If I had play'd the desk or table-book,
> Or given my heart winking, mute and dumb,
> Or look'd upon this love with idle sight,
> What might you think?
>
> (II.ii.134–39)

No, he assures them, he had told his daughter that "Lord Hamlet is a prince, out of thy star" (141). Based on her later lines, however, Gertrude does not disapprove but even encourages Ophelia—"I do wish / That your good beauties be the happy cause / Of Hamlet's wildness" (III.i.37–39). And at the graveside, we will hear the Queen mourn, "I hop'd thou shouldst have been my Hamlet's wife" (V.i.244). Despite his protests, Polonius is functioning here as the politician rather than the father.

Since the interaction between characters helps define them in drama, the characterization of him that emerges during his instructions to Reynaldo contributes to our understanding of his daughter. Concern for himself, lack of confidence in his son whose youth he envies, and loyalty to King dominate. Promptbooks, however, testify to a skewed portrait, eliminating Polonius's darker side and creating a weak, characterless, easily manipulated Ophelia. Not only is the entire Reynaldo half of the scene cut for the stage, but gone too are sections of the exchanges between father and daughter including the references to jealousy and to the cautions of age countering the indiscretions of youth. While it is true that in reading the play we find this excised material, it is also true that what we see in the theater influences our overall response. Reduced to Ophelia's description of the Prince and her father's "Come, go we to the King" (II.i.114), the scene on stage has two functions: to emphasize Hamlet's anguish, and to speed the action. Ophelia shrinks to a two-dimensional character: as the object of Hamlet's affection, she is the young woman who deceives him and who subsequently goes mad. But Shakespeare, although he gives Hamlet 31 percent of the speeches and Ophelia only 5 percent, nevertheless sketches in a young woman of some breadth who is trapped in a world more hostile than Juliet's with a father far less caring—a man concerned with his own fortunes first (Spevack, 3:812–91). He might indeed come from the pages of Lawrence Stone's history, a politically ambitious man with little sensitivity to his children (187–88). The portrait is unrelenting. And Ophelia's madness has its source in that portrait: not merely her father's death and Hamlet's rejection, but also Polonius's complex manipulation of her—his denial of her selfhood.

Arriving at the palace with her father, she listens while, bursting with confidence, he claims to know the reason for Hamlet's madness—Ophelia's rejection of his love. Countering the Queen's skepticism, Polonius unconcernedly reads aloud Hamlet's love letter to his daughter—even commenting on its "vile" phrases. He never attempts to understand her or sympathize with her as Capulet does in *Romeo and Juliet*.[11] In fact, the development of these two young women on the brink of maturity reveals Shakespeare's artistry in individualizing the women characters even while suggesting that they face many of the same challenges. Coming of age in a household where her advisers are men, Ophelia acquires their perceptions of sex. Juliet can wait joyously for the coming of night and Romeo. Ophelia can only wait with great trepidation for the proclamation of love or devotion from a man who, her advisors promise, will surely deceive her.

Illustrating his own understanding of sex and his disdain for love, Polonius uses language of animal entrapment to describe his plan for uncovering Hamlet's intentions: "I'll loose my daughter to him. / Be you and I behind an arras then, / Mark the encounter" (II.ii.162-64). Because Hamlet enters immediately after the King's brief answer, "We will try it" (167), the scene allows for varied staging, including Hamlet's earlier entrance and the possibility that he overhears their plan. In the 1936 Houseman production, the stage direction reads, "Hamlet cannot help hearing this" (Box 13).

If one were to diagram with two crossing diagonal lines Ophelia's movement downward from selfhood to madness and Gertrude's slow painful ascent from role-juggling to independence, the scene of planning the trap would anticipate the spot where the two emotional paths cross: "the nunnery scene." There, in the moments before the exchange between Ophelia and Hamlet, Gertrude's uncritical approval of the plan along with her failure to censure the deception matches Ophelia's easy acquiescence. Both women abdicate moral judgment.

For Ophelia, the nunnery scene marks her descent into a deception from which she will never recover even though when we next see her—at the play—she has not yet gone mad. This central scene defines her problem. Programmed by her father to act the coy girl returning a beloved's favors, she discovers herself trapped, destroyed by Hamlet's sudden query: "Where's your father?"

(III.i.129). Assailed earlier by Hamlet's sudden shifts of mood from "I did love you once" (114), to his violent explosion against her, "Get thee to a nunn'ry, why wouldst thou be a breeder of sinners?" (120–21), she is unprepared for this direct question of truth versus falsehood. With no one to help her and little time to think, Ophelia weighs her options and her allegiances. She faces a moral choice as well as an immediate threat. The proximity of her father and the King, eavesdropping on the conversation after having stage-managed it, threatens her. Betraying them, she would be lost. But by dishonestly answering Hamlet, she will also be lost, guilty of betraying both herself and him. Caught between two sets of loyalties, Ophelia responds as she believes she should: "At home, my lord" (130). Her value system crumbles. Loyalty to father and king has superseded all else, including loyalty to self. By destroying the foundation of her morality, her commitment to honesty, she has also destroyed herself. From there to the close of the scene, she must listen in confusion as Hamlet damns her:

> If thou dost marry, I'll give thee this plague for thy dowry:
> bethou as chaste as ice, as pure as snow, thou shalt not escape
> calumny.
>
> (134–36)

Her few subsequent comments address his emotional state rather than his words. In response to his "Let the doors be shut upon him [Polonius], that he may play the fool nowhere but in's own house. Farewell" (131–32), she exclaims "O help him, you sweet heavens!" (133). To his next outburst damning her to a nunnery a second time, she cries, "Heavenly powers, restore him!" (141), revealing anxiety over his state—and perhaps over her answer. A breakdown has occurred. In not answering his words, she reminds us of Emilia who, hearing Desdemona's despair at the loss of the handkerchief, fails to reveal any culpability but instead comments on Othello's emotional state by talking in general terms of men's lust.[12] Fear combined with loyalty motivates both women characters. The banter about beauty and honesty that marked the beginning of the scene between Ophelia and Hamlet has been replaced by passion, invective, and despair. Mourning Hamlet's decline as well as the loss of his love, Ophelia breaks down in the familiar set speech beginning, "O, what a noble mind is here o'erthrown" (150) only to be confronted at its close by Claudius's cynical comment, "Love? His affections do not that way tend" (165), and her father's rejoinder, "How now, Ophelia? / You need not tell us what Lord Hamlet said; / We heard it all" (181–83). No word of comfort from her father, though she sacrificed her love for the Prince to participate in the scheme of the elders. Her lie has meant nothing. To both father and king, she is invisible.

In the Sothern-Marlowe promptbook where we see a more sensitive Ophelia, as I mentioned earlier, she reluctantly takes the prayer book pushed into her hands by her father and, weeping during the early section of the meeting with Hamlet as if not wishing to be a part of it, is admonished from the side by her father. The extensive stage directions here allow us to visualize the interaction. At the beginning of the scene (III.i.43), Polonius thrusts the jewel casket in front of Ophelia. Countering her hesitation, he "taps the casket in a commanding way" so that she reluctantly accepts it. Further indicating her lack of enthusiasm for this encounter, she allows the prayer book to hang "from her girdle." Seeing this, Polonius lifts up the book, which she then "listlessly [takes] in her hand." At line 88, the stage directions continue. After detailing the actions of the King and Polonius as they place her on stage, she turns a final appealing glance toward her father when she sees Hamlet enter reading, "recoil[ing] from her task." But Polonius "points to Hamlet, . . . directs her to enter," then father and king "back out" leaving her alone to deal with the Prince. Noting that he is "deep in thought," she attempts to act casually as she "lifts the book from her girdle," and reads it while crossing the stage. This coincides with his lines beginning, "Soft you now, / The fair Ophelia" (87–88).

Stage directions even indicate her point of view as they attribute "an assumed indifference" to her first speech: "How does your honour . . ." leading him to adopt "a formal attitude" in his response, "I humbly thank you, etc." When he accepts the casket that she offers, "she gives a small sob." During the next several lines, he is about to take her in his arms then draws back, later flinging her from him. With a sob she "sinks to the floor." At this moment, Polonius opens the curtain and looks out. When she sees him, she "suddenly stops sobbing and rises to her knees." Unfortunately, at this moment Hamlet too sees Polonius. Here Ophelia's knowledge of the plan is explicitly defined in the stage directions.

Not all productions, however, adopt this interpretation or present her involvement in the scheme as clearly as did Marlowe and

After having glimpsed Polonius peeking out from behind the arras, Hamlet curses the distraught Ophelia in this early twentieth-century production with Julia Marlowe and E. H. Sothern. Courtesy of the Billy Rose Theatre Collection, New York Public Library.

Sothern. Henry Irving, for example, stressed Ophelia's innocence. He had Ellen Terry play the scene as if she were unaware of the "lawful espials" of Polonius and the King (Hughes, 54–55). To achieve this, Irving had Ophelia stand dutifully by while the two men spoke in asides. She heard nothing [Irving, 1878]. Of course, this skews her portrait, giving too little weight to the moral choice she must make in this scene—and underestimating its effect on her later madness. For Irving, Ophelia is presented as a dumb pawn; in Shakespeare's more complex portrait, she is a conflicted young woman of sensitivity and intelligence.

John Gielgud, writing about the staging of the scene, observed that it "has never really been explained to my satisfaction in any book I have read or performance I have seen" (Gilder, 56). Accepting as a textual given Ophelia's knowledge of her father's plot, Gielgud found the timing difficult to resolve. This may have reflected his own theatrical background as the grand-nephew of Ellen Terry, but it also may have been the result of his experience in the 1936–37 production when Guthrie McClintic changed the timing of the discovery of Polonius from immediately following the return of the jewels to the moment later in the scene preceding Hamlet's pointed question, "Where's your father?" Probably, the scene didn't act properly with the earlier stage direction (Vol. 1).

Although most directors, actor-managers, and critics believe that Hamlet spies the eavesdroppers and are primarily interested in the timing, Irving's kind of staging seemed to contradict the text. It aimed to present a simple Ophelia as a clear foil for a complex Hamlet, stressing Irving's role. Primarily, however, the scene emphasizes the irony and self-destructiveness that follow from Ophelia's conforming to her father's expectations.

Directorial perceptions of Ophelia also emerge in photographs. Certain accepted patterns, like the carrying of a prayer book, seem obligatory. Other features reflect the wish to imitate a famous actress in a role, as is apparent in the costume of Julie Harris in 1964 mimicking that of Ellen Terry in 1878. Both wore large crosses hanging from chains around their necks and dresses trimmed with pearls and a slight ruff at the collar (see illustrations).[13] Sometimes, however, a new insight is projected through costuming. John Houseman dressed Polonius and Ophelia in matching outfits, emphasizing the close tie between them while also showing its destructiveness through the ominous look of authority in the father's face and the fear in the daughter's (see illustration).[14] Probably one of

Resembling Ellen Terry who carried a prayer book and whose costume was decorated with pearls (see first illustration), Julie Harris prepares for the "nunnery scene" in the New York Shakespeare Festival *Hamlet* production of 1964. Courtesy of the Billy Rose Theatre Collection, New York Public Library.

Dressed in matching costumes, Polonius (Aubrey Mather) warns Ophelia (Pamela Stanley) to behave properly in her forthcoming scene with Hamlet in the Leslie Howard, John Houseman 1936 production. Courtesy of the Billy Rose Theatre Collection, New York Public Library.

the most effective stagings occurred in Maurice Evans's G. I. *Hamlet* (1945), where the set included a statuette of the Virgin before whom Ophelia was praying when Hamlet first saw her (see illustration).[15] Here, the irony and deception were bitterly stressed, for Ophelia answered "At home, my lord" in what was clearly a holy or religious atmosphere.

The impact of the nunnery scene on Ophelia's later behavior becomes immediately apparent at her next meeting with the Prince. No spark remains of the sister who had teased her brother in act 1. She seems lifeless, accepting Hamlet's sexual innuendos as a given, without protest. Is she reacting this way because she believes he is a man who has lost his mind, or because she has accepted this lackluster role as the price of maturity—of being a woman in a man's world? Have the lessons of father and brother been too clearly confirmed? Like Titania with Oberon near the end of *A Midsummer Night's Dream*, Ophelia no longer challenges the Prince's words. Unlike Titania, however, Ophelia does not belong to the world of fairies. Ultimately, such conflict with the self explodes within her. In this scene however, she fails to protest:

> *Ham.* Lady, shall I lie in your lap?
> *Oph.* No, my lord.
> *Ham.* I mean, my head upon your lap?
> *Oph.* Ay, my lord.
> *Ham.* Do you think I meant country matters?
> *Oph.* I think nothing, my lord.
> *Ham.* That's a fair thought to lie between maids' legs.
>
> (III.ii.112–19)

And so the exchange goes on; Ophelia fails to contradict him as she does her brother, for example, in her first scene. Frequently excised, the lines contrast sharply with Hamlet's letter to her that Polonius so crudely read aloud earlier in the play:

> Doubt thou the stars are fire,
> Doubt that the sun doth move,
> Doubt truth to be a liar,
> But never doubt I love.
>
> O dear Ophelia, I am ill at these numbers. I have not art to reckon my groans, but that I love thee best, O most best, believe it. Adieu.
> Thine evermore, most dear lady,
> whilst this machine is to him, Hamlet.
>
> (II.ii.116–24)

Emphasizing the irony of Ophelia's response to Hamlet's query, "Where's your father?" are the religious symbols in this photograph of Frances Reid and Maurice Evans from the "GI *Hamlet*," presented in 1945 in New York. Courtesy of the Billy Rose Theatre Collection, New York Public Library.

The word *groans* here describes Hamlet's lovelorn condition. A part of his vocabulary, it takes on a new meaning in the player scene, where, addressed to Ophelia, it has sexual connotations. "You are keen, my lord, you are keen" (III.ii.248), she observes, only to be rebuffed by, "It would cost you a groaning to take off mine edge" (249–50). The line is frequently cut from stage productions although the contrast in usage illustrates Hamlet's seeming change of attitude. Cynicism and bawdy language have replaced tenderness and deep regard whether in reaction to the nunnery scene or as a reflection of the new persona he is wearing for the scene. To Ophelia, however, his words are real, the true expression of his attitude. They also reflect the freedom with which men may speak to women in a patriarchal society and the easy acceptance women must pretend.

When next we see Ophelia, she is drifting, a mad woman in the palace, unattended and unwanted. At first barred from seeing the Queen, who futilely hopes to sustain the balance of her various roles and is troubled because "Each toy seems prologue to some great amiss" (IV.v.18), Ophelia eventually gains entrance. Unseeing, she asks for "the beauteous majesty of Denmark" (21) then sings songs of lost love, true-love, death, and burial. Some critics have interpreted the first song as a veiled reference to the Queen's two husbands since it asks, "How should I your true-love know / From another one?" (23–24) then continues with the lines "He is dead and gone, lady, / He is dead and gone" (29–30). Other critics have felt that the early lines refer to Ophelia's own lost love, Hamlet, and the later lines to her father. During this first mad appearance of Ophelia, she also sings a ballad of a maid who lost her virginity to her lover who then deserted her. Are we to believe that Shakespeare has endowed her with sufficient lucidity in her madness to create a specific song on her desertion by Hamlet? Or might the innuendo, the hint, the coupling of fairy tales and reality merge here? As theater, the contrast between the songs and the young woman who sings them intensifies the tragedy, offering an example of the dramatic counterpoint so often found in Shakespeare's plays.

Her mad appearance is divided into two sections: the first precedes her brother's rude entry threatening insurrection; her second follows it, and includes Laertes as a witness. In the earlier scene, her lines at leaving bridge the worlds of madness and sanity: "But I cannot choose but weep to think they would lay him i' th' cold ground. My brother shall know of it" (69–71). How ominously rational this sounds. But then, "Come, my coach! Good night, ladies, good night" (71–72). And she is gone, the King ordering, "Follow her close, give her good watch, I pray you" (74). Although her actions, words, and costume identify her as mad, a small element of rationality lingers. She speaks words "That carry but half sense" but nevertheless "move / The hearers" (7–9).

With her second entry, however, no doubt remains. Its starkness convinces the audience of her madness. Interrupting a confrontation between her brother and the royal couple attempting to calm him, her entrance drains all passion and anger from him. Here, the Folio text contains one of the few stage directions not embedded in the dialogue. "A noise within: 'Let her come in.'" With that Ophelia enters. This time, not only has she been allowed immediate access, but, without talking, she becomes the focus of attention, her madness obvious to all. Stunned, her brother tries but fails to awaken her mind: "O heat, dry up my brains; tears seven times salt / Burn out the sense and virtue of mine eye!" (154-55). Then in anger, he continues, "By heaven, thy madness shall be paid with weight / Till our scale turn the beam" (156–57). But the infinite tragedy of Ophelia mad gives his speech still another turn, even while she continues speechless on stage: "O rose of May, / Dear maid, kind sister, sweet Ophelia!" (158–59): flowers, love, virginity, sibling—Ophelia.

She finally speaks, singing still another song, more childlike than the earlier ones, with a chorus of verbal nonsense, "Hey non nonny, nonny, hey nonny" (165). She is one with Shakespeare's fools. If audiences had hoped, during the long period when she says nothing, that the sight of her brother and the sound of his voice would restore her wits, her song reveals the extensiveness of the damage. She is in another world. Interspersing oblique references to an old man who is dead with the distribution of flowers to the gathered group, she alternates speeches with Laertes. Critics have variously interpreted the meaning of the flowers. As Hubler notes, "the distribution of the flowers . . . has symbolic meaning, but the meaning is disputed" (139). Delius, in the nineteenth century, even speculated that "these flowers existed only in Ophelia's fantasy, and there was no distribution of real flowers to the persons present" (*Variorum* 1:346). This idea was adopted in the John Barrymore *Hamlet* in 1922 where "Ophelia doesn't carry flowers but offers imaginary flowers."[16] It was also used in the G.I. *Hamlet* where she carries a big picture book, her demeanor suggesting "that she

At the beginning of the mad scene, Ophelia (Frances Reid) points out the flowers she will distribute to Claudius (Thomas Gomez) and Gertrude (Lili Darvas). Courtesy of the Billy Rose Theatre Collection, New York Public Library.

reverted to her childhood"; she points out the herbs and flowers in the book when supposedly distributing the flowers (161) (see illustration). Psychological theories developed to cope with mental illness of men at the front in World War II may have influenced this interpretation.

In fact, both the interpretation of madness and the costuming of Ophelia have reflected different attitudes towards this illness. In Shakespeare's time and the beginning of the seventeenth century, characters from the madhouse were used in drama, sometimes to entertain, sometimes to frighten, and sometimes to provide a moral lesson as occurred in such plays as *The Duchess of Malfi* and *The Changeling*.[17] Later on, however, particularly as actresses sought to understand the role more fully, they examined contemporary models of madness. Ellen Terry, for example, visited a madhouse of the time, hoping to find a model for her Ophelia:

> Like all Ophelias before (and after) me, I went to the madhouse to study wits astray. I was disheartened at first. There was no beauty, no nature, no pity in most of the lunatics. Strange as it may sound, they were too *theatrical* to teach me anything. Then, just as I was going away, I noticed a young girl gazing at the wall. I went between her and the wall to see her face. It was quite vacant, but the body expressed that she was waiting, waiting. Suddenly she threw up her hands and sped across the room like a swallow. I never forgot it. She was very thin, very pathetic, very young, and the movement was as poignant as it was beautiful. (*Memoirs*, 122)

Terry's interpretation in the nineteenth century emphasized the poignant and pathetic. According to Nina Auerbach in her biography of the actress, Terry absorbed some of the qualities of Ophelia: "Ellen Terry became Ophelia—a role she did not like, in which she did not like herself" (237). To what extent such a transfer of character into personal life occurred becomes difficult to ascertain. Because of Irving's treatment of the text, stressing Ophelia's innocence of any knowledge of her father's whereabouts in the "nunnery" scene, Terry's Ophelia would, of course, have been more pathetic than Shakespeare's text suggests.

The search by an actress to understand this role is heard again in the twentieth century when Lillian Gish sought advice, in preparation for the 1936 production. Ideas about women, madness, and neurotic behavior had changed. Not only was Freud on the scene, but the stream of consciousness form of writing led people to search for motivation beneath the surface. In correspondence with Norman Hapgood, she must have expressed her concern. He wrote in response:

> In Nantucket, a few days ago, I was reading a copy of the *Ulysses* of James Joyce, with the result that I wish to call your attention to parts of it.

He then directed her to specific pages devoted to "the general task of living down into the subconscious world of Ophelia." Here Hapgood also mentioned supportive material on "Wilhelm Meister" and "Hamlet le Distrait." Finally, the writer concluded: "Ophelia, it seems to me, cannot be approached at all from the outside."

The influence of Freud was everywhere. Earlier, Heywood Broun had commended the Barrymore production, considering this Hamlet to be "as modern as the most recent disciple of Freud. . . . His [Hamlet's] tragedy lay in the fact that he did not have the courage of his complexes."

The introspective quest of character, however, did not eliminate the need to give physical definition to a role on stage. Gish's costume for the mad scenes was both striking and in many ways dated. She wore a dress resembling an evening gown of the time, 1936, then parted further from tradition by the choice of color (see illustration). Neither black, as Terry would have wished—since Ophelia is in mourning—nor white, the usual color, symbolizing innocence and virginity, but a bright yellow was the director's choice. According to Gish:

> McClintic's conception of Ophelia was strikingly original. Instead of a sweet, pathetic little girl he wanted a lewd Ophelia. I wore a costume of bright yellow, with a red stocking pulled over one arm and its partner tied around my neck. McClintic got the idea for the stocking on the arm as he was walking down Broadway one evening and saw a demented woman mumbling to herself. She was wearing stockings on her hands instead of gloves. (*Lillian Gish*, 335)

If Terry had to search a madhouse for her prototype, McClintic had merely to stroll on Broadway. A decade earlier, Arthur Hopkins had found inspiration in modern dance for Ophelia's awkward and stark appearance. His mad Ophelia, played by Rosalinde Fuller, wore a costume hanging in severe heavy folds, while she, standing with legs akimbo and arms strangely extended, projected

Dressed in a bright yellow gown with a red stocking pulled over one arm, Ophelia (Lillian Gish) turns to the Queen (Judith Anderson) and asks for "the beauteous majesty of Denmark" in Guthrie McClintic's 1936 *Hamlet*. Courtesy of the Billy Rose Theatre Collection, New York Public Library.

Stalking onto the stage, Rosalinde Fuller as Ophelia brings modern dance movements to the 1922 John Barrymore *Hamlet*, produced by Arthur Hopkins. Courtesy of the Billy Rose Theatre Collection, New York Public Library.

the chilling effect of madness (see illustration).[18] Whatever the costume, however, the role defines madness as Hamlet's does not.

Ophelia's real madness contrasts with his feigned madness, helping define his actions and arousing sympathy for her. Instead of being perceived as a weak vessel easily manipulated by her father, she becomes an obvious victim of pressures too difficult to absorb. The dramatization of her madness brings a sense of terror to the audience. Conflict about and denial of self-identity or ultimate loss of that identity have a high price. Although paths do exist where women may compromise by adopting a multiplicity of roles, as Gertrude does at the beginning of the play, the dramatist here suggests the cost of such options. No single self exists. Role-playing has replaced it. Inevitably, too, identification through another, or usually several others, rather than oneself must lead to inner conflict because the demands of those others diverge. They will tear one asunder. The conflict besetting Ophelia in the nunnery scene leads to a choice of father rather than self. Having forsaken self-identity, she then loses all when she loses her father, for she has adopted his perceptions of her and of women. Shakespeare's insight into the fragility of a young woman just coming into maturity who lacks the ability to withstand these pressures emerges in this succinct but complex portrait.

Whereas Gertrude's role spans the play, picking up tonal differences as Hamlet moves from one mood to another, Ophelia's role concentrates on a few moments, offering a brief glimpse at youth, romance, and dreams, and dramatizing the quickness with which they may be washed away. Despite the brevity of the role, promptbooks provide clear evidence of cutting. More important, the tampering with Polonius's lines distorts her portrait. Creating a genial, rather than arbitrary, strong, and oppressive father, actormanagers and directors may shape a councilor who contrasts with Claudius and provides a humorous foil for Hamlet. But such distortion affects our perceptions of Ophelia. Because she must not only illuminate the problems of a daughter with a strong, manipulative father but also the meaning of madness as it does not affect Hamlet, her role has a relevance beyond its length. Hamlet, struggling to find himself, ultimately does, whereas she, attempting to please, eventually succumbs to madness, her own value-system totally destroyed.

The Queen, on the other hand, eventually manages to gain some measure of self-knowledge. Perhaps in self-defense, she has stopped looking at "both sides," the suggestion Margaret Fuller made to women centuries later, and has sought to find her own answers based on her own moral standards. Particularly interesting in this work that so clearly concentrates on Hamlet is the way the dramatist examines the challenge of self-knowledge as it applies to women. Different obstacles surface—obstacles created by a social system that generalizes its expectations about women and sets parameters for their behavior. In the next chapter we see how a woman has internalized those expectations and sought to counter them by transferring her moral base as well as her ambition to someone else: her husband. In contrast, Gertrude never loses her sense of values although she seeks, at the drama's beginning, to play to perfection her many, and often conflicting, roles.

In their brief appearances, Ophelia and the Queen illustrate the destructiveness for women of adopting an alien set of values. The struggle to understand the world and those around them, as difficult as it may be for a young man, is intensified for a young woman who is expected to jettison any sense of her emerging self, and pretend it does not exist. And even for an older woman, whose roles are multiple, diverse expectations can prove crushing—they can even confuse someone as strong as Gertrude. In this play, Shakespeare explores some of the ways in which male dominance and patriarchal expectations can warp women's lives.

Sir Laurence Olivier and Vivien Leigh, a terrified Macbeth and his Lady in the banquet scene in the 1955 Glen Byam Shaw *Macbeth*. Angus McBean photograph, courtesy of the Harvard Theatre Collection, The Houghton Library.

CHAPTER FIVE

Dependent Identities

MACBETH

The Thane of Fife had a wife; where is she now?
V.i.42–43

Inhabiting separate worlds, Lady Macbeth, Lady Macduff, and the witches illuminate one another's concepts of morality and power, suggesting the complexity of these ideas in the play. Basically, morality refers to the ability to differentiate between right and wrong, while power refers to the distinction between domination and submission. But the lust for power in *Macbeth* and the confusion about what or whose moral standards to adopt complicate these easy definitions.[1]

The bearded women—the witches—who open the play, set the tone of evil and other-worldliness. "Fair is foul and foul is fair. / Hover through the fog and filthy air" (I.i.10–11) they chant, moments after having invoked the name of Macbeth. Insisting we suspend disbelief, Shakespeare immediately links their world with the "real world" of the tragedy, jumping in scene 2 to the bloody sergeant who reports Macbeth's exploits on the battlefield. A hero, Macbeth has had no problem recognizing good and evil. Fighting for the one, he vanquished the other, unseaming his enemy, Macdonwald, "from the nave to th' chops" and fixing "his head upon [the] battlements" (I.ii.22–23). But good and evil are less easily distinguishable for Macbeth in the next scene, when the three weird sisters return. His opening line, "So foul and fair a day I have not seen" (I.iii.38), mimicking their earlier refrain, anticipates the evil link between him and the witches.

Stage directors and actor-managers have long debated the sex of the witches and the manner of presenting them. In the seventeenth

155

century, William Davenant wrote a version of Shakespeare's play with singing, dancing witches. In the eighteenth century, David Garrick, promising to restore the original text, nevertheless retained the tradition of singing witches (Bell's edition, 1773). As Pedicord informs us,

> This entire scene is altered from Davenant and given a new musical setting by Garrick to enhance the Witches scene. Basis for the songs is found in Middleton's *The Witch*. (3:32)

A 1776 text, competing with Bell's, not only contains all of the witches' songs but also credits the composer, Mr. Leveridge, for "Musick in the second act, . . . 3rd act, Enter Hecate, spirits in the Clouds call; Act the Fourth, Musick at the Cauldron" (Bowen, 69–72). By the end of the century, the musical witches had multiplied. A "Chorus of Spirits, and Witches," composed of sixteen men and nineteen women, appears in the cast list for John Philip Kemble's 1803 text. Although based on Garrick's version, Kemble's also transfers the roles of Hecate and the speaking witches to male actors (A2).

While these interpretations were occurring on stage, critics confronted the question of how to accept the witches' prophecies in an age of enlightenment. Samuel Johnson, in his famous "Miscellaneous Observations on *The Tragedy of Macbeth*" (1745), speaks not only for his time, but for ours. Admitting first that any contemporary dramatist who would base the whole action of his tragedy on enchantment would "be banished from the theatre to the nursery" (7:3), Johnson distinguishes between the easy acceptance of witchcraft in Shakespeare's time and the skepticism in his own. The editor then slyly observes:

> The reality of witchcraft or enchantment, which, though not strictly the same, are confounded in this play, has in all ages and countries been credited by the common people, and in most by the learned themselves. (7:3)

So much for people being too sophisticated for "enchantment or witchcraft." Today, films are constantly taking us into the world of fantasy. Nevertheless, the problem of presenting the witches on stage remains. Since they open the play and set the tone of mystery and evil, they must be convincing and frightening without overstepping that thin line between evoking horror or eliciting laughter.

How should these characters be projected on stage? Should they appear as women or men? Or should they be gender neutral, if that is possible? Shakespeare calls them weird sisters. Banquo in first speaking to them describes them as women and uses the pronoun *her:*

> You seem to understand me,
> By each at once *her* choppy finger laying
> Upon her skinny lips. You should be women,
> And yet your beards forbid me to interpret
> That you are so.
>
> (43–47, emphasis added)

If we accept these descriptions in the text, we must not only decide how to clothe these characters on stage but also what their relevance is to the play's two human women.

Terry Eagleton, in 1986, dramatically applies the term *heroines* (2) to the witches, stressing their relevance to the play. While I disagree that they are "heroines," I do think that they figure in the complex triangle of the play's women. They relate especially to questions of power and moral values.

Who are these witches and where do they come from? As we know, Middleton's witches in *The Witch* provide some source for the eighteenth-century versions. Subsequent research goes further, theorizing that rather than borrowing from Shakespeare, Middleton's play may have been the source for some of the witch material (Bullough 7: 424; Muir xxxv–xxxviii). But Middleton's witches are comic; Shakespeare's are not. Most recently, Taylor and Jowett have theorized that "collaboration and adaptation were a normal part of the theatrical world" and that Heminges and Condell would not have excluded a work in which "Shakespeare wrote the lion's share" (225). Thus the witch material, while it may have been written by Middleton, may also have been part of the original play. Holinshed's *Chronicles* of Scotland furnish another, and historically more relevant, source although those witches are decidedly mortal women (Scotland, 149–50). When the daughter of one of them— described as a "soldier's concubine" in the *Chronicles*—betrays her mother to the army, the mother, caught in the act of witchcraft, is burned at the stake.

Although the witches, who were working their magic to bring about the death of the king, "were taught by evil spirits," they were "hired to worke the feat by the nobles of Murrey land," who were in rebellion against the king. In the margin of the *Chronicles* appears the comment: "The nobles of the countie set the witches on work" (Scotland, 150a). Thus, the mortal women, burned as witches, had been directed in their work by the men of the county and seemed to be pursuing a morally legitimate purpose.

In contrast, Shakespeare's witches appear out of nowhere and disappear into space defying mortality and morality:

> Say from whence
> You owe this strange intelligence, or why
> Upon this blasted heath you stop our way
> With such prophetic greetings? Speak, I charge you.
>
> (75–78)

In the Trevor Nunn 1976 videotape, Macbeth takes out a dagger, threatening them. In the Orson Welles 1948 film, Macbeth "splashes after the witches trying to find them, calling out to them in the mist" (3). The Bell edition (1773) has the three witches "rise from under the stage" (7) at the beginning of scene 3, then vanish at the close of the above speech (9). The Garrick changes, indicated in the promptbook, eliminate this and have the witches enter from the sides (Burnim, 110). Kemble divided the text. "Thunder and Lightning—Witches vanish" (10) followed the words "With such prophetic greetings?" Thus Macbeth's charge to the witches addressed empty space. Banquo's lines furnish the unsatisfactory answer to their identity:

> The earth hath bubbles, as the water has,
> And these are of them.
>
> (79–80)

Unlike Hamlet who doubts the ghost's identity—or Banquo, who moments later asks, "What, can the devil speak true?"—Macbeth not only wishes "Would they had stay'd!" (82) but too quickly accepts their words. "Your children shall be kings," he assures Banquo, who then responds with the words his companion longs to hear confirmed, "You shall be king" (86).

The witches know their man. Although they answer Banquo's query, "If you can look into the seeds of time, / . . . Speak then to me" (58–60), he is not their prey. Ambition does not drive him to adjust his moral values, as it does Macbeth. Banquo's quick description, "Good sir, why do you start, and seem to fear / Things that do sound so fair?" (51–52), suggests this adjustment. The witches' prediction, "All hail, Macbeth, that shalt be King hereafter!" (50), hits a nerve, probably reawakening a dream.

In this and the following scene we see Macbeth's blurred vision of the moral line between right and wrong several times. It appears first in his speech beginning "This supernatural soliciting / Cannot be ill; cannot be good," and continuing:

> If good, why do I yield to that suggestion
> Whose horrid image doth unfix my hair
> And make my seated heart knock at my ribs,
> Against the use of nature?
>
> (130–37)

We hear his confusion again at the announcement of Malcolm's elevation to Prince of Cumberland, immediate successor to the crown:

> that is a step
> On which I must fall down, or else o'erleap,
> For in my way it lies. Stars, hide your fires,
> Let not light see my black and deep desires;
> The eye wink at the hand; yet let that be
> Which the eye fears, when it is done, to see.
>
> (I.iv.48–53)

Macbeth's lines confirm the audience's fears of his susceptibility to the predictions. Despite Banquo's warning that sometimes "The instruments of darkness tell us truths, / Win us with honest trifles, to betray's / In deepest consequence" (iii.124–26), Macbeth doesn't listen. He slips in a moral quagmire. And the witches, having "wound up" their charm, work their spell.

After introducing Macbeth in the first four scenes and clearly exposing his vulnerability to the witches' predictions, Shakespeare shifts his focus in one of the great introductory scenes in the canon: Lady Macbeth's entrance reading the letter from her husband. Ellen Terry's interleaved manuscript notes to the 1888 Irving edition read, "It is wretched to be discovered on stage. She should be reading *at the back*, by the failing light—& then come forward to the firelight to see better" (opposite p. 21).[2] The letter presents several enigmas. Are we hearing only a section of it, or the whole? Does Macbeth tell her of the prophecy to Banquo or withhold this information to be certain of her support? The audience hears only news about Macbeth. Although later, in the sleepwalking scene, she refers specifically to Banquo's murder, we never know whether Lady Macbeth heard of the original prophecy before plotting Duncan's death.

The letter has an unctuous strain reminiscent of Claudius's opening entrance with Gertrude when he too refers to his wife as partner, calling her "Th' imperial jointress" (I.ii.9) of the state. Twice Macbeth speaks of their partnership, first calling her "my dearest partner of greatness," and then seductively transferring the prediction by referring to "what greatness is promis'd thee" (I.v.11-13). Is Lady Macbeth really a partner or is she primarily a helpmate—helping him to what he wants? Is she a subordinate with no real power of her own? As the play develops, she finds herself excluded from all decision making. Does this result from their momentary partnership in murder or belong to the larger pattern of their relationship?

At this moment in the play, she believes herself his partner and intends to help him attain the crown:

> Glamis thou art, and Cawdor, and shalt be
> What thou art promis'd.

> (15–16)

As the soliloquy continues, an inflated notion of her power over him combines with a misreading of his character. Describing his nature as "too full o' th' milk of human kindness / To catch the nearest way" (17–18), she tells us something his lines have not. His reactions neither to the witches nor to the news of Malcolm's elevation suggest a man "full" of human kindness. Nor does the description of his victory, with its brutality, indicate any tentativeness or hesitation. Nevertheless, her perception of their relationship—of her strength and his gentleness—ultimately determines her actions.

Tantalizing us with the contradiction "Wouldst not play false, / And yet wouldst wrongly win" (21–22), she reveals her own moral judgment with the word "wrongly." She then jettisons these values in favor of being the fully supportive wife:

> Hie thee hither,
> That I may pour my spirits in thine ear,
> And chastise with the valor of my tongue

All that impedes thee from the golden round,
Which fate and metaphysical aid doth seem
To have thee crown'd withal.

(25–30)

Later in the play, another woman evaluates her husband's actions. Her words are direct, free of ambiguity:

His flight was madness. . . .
Wisdom? to leave his wife, to leave his babes,
His mansion and his titles, in a place
From whence himself does fly?

(IV.ii.3–8)

Unlike Lady Macbeth, Lady Macduff is guided by her own sense of right and wrong, rejecting any excuses for Macduff's actions. If she exaggerates when telling her son "Your father's dead" (30), she is merely reinforcing her disapproval of his flight. Reason and a sense of moral responsibility should have dictated otherwise.

In an essay on "Manhood and Valor" in Shakespeare, Eugene Waith analyzes Macbeth's later hesitation about pursuing the murder: "His mental torment grows out of the conflict between the narrow concept of man as the courageous male and the more inclusive concept of man as a being whose moral nature distinguishes him from the beasts" (266). Just as the critic differentiates between the limited and broad concepts of manhood, so one may also distinguish between the limited and broad concepts of womanhood. The former derives from the expectations on woman as daughter, wife, and mother. Here obedience, subservience, and supportiveness of the ruling male are primary. When, however, one considers the broad concept of womanhood, it parallels that of man, defined primarily as "a being whose moral nature distinguishes [her] from the beasts." Lady Macbeth's mental torment, apparent in the sleepwalking scene (act 5), grows out of this conflict between the varied meanings of womanhood.

By including Lady Macduff, the play insists on examining the sources for a woman's moral decisions. Although her brief scene comes late in the text, it allows us to see a woman of unwavering conviction. Unfortunately, because of its brutality, the scene is frequently excised from the stage, denying audiences this graphic contrast between the two mortal women: the one who supports her husband, though he would "wrongly" win, and the other who censures her husband's decision to flee, leaving his family in mortal danger.

Shortly after committing herself to the narrow definition of womanhood, Lady Macbeth gains an opportunity to test it. News arrives of Duncan's forthcoming visit. Inspired by her sense of power as the source of Macbeth's strength, she recklessly prays:

> Come, you spirits
> That tend on mortal thoughts, unsex me here,
> And fill me from the crown to the toe topful
> Of direst cruelty!
>
> (40–42)

Her chilling vow seems to challenge the witches' exclusive right to the title "instruments of darkness" (iii.124). And yet, she differs from them. They need no vows; they make no sacrifices; nor do they have any concern for moral values. Rather, they speak in riddles and double meanings, playing a waiting game where the victim traps himself. Lady Macbeth, on the other hand, vows by those things she, as a mortal, holds dear: her role as a wife—"unsex me here"—and as a mother—"Come to my woman's breasts, / And take my milk for gall" (47–48). Capturing the intensity, humanity, and recklessness of Lady Macbeth's oath-taking, Trevor Nunn's videotape dramatizes the terror she feels. Suddenly and terrifyingly, she touches earth—as if touching an electric shock— pulls back, then touches it again and holds her hand there while calling on the "spirits / That tend on mortal thoughts" (40).

Lady Macbeth's lines belong to a familiar pattern of mortal action in Shakespeare's plays—that of oath-taking.[3] Oaths reveal character. Frequently the dramatist questions the sincerity of the oaths and the too-easy manner of the oath-takers, a weakness more usual with his male than his female characters. Men tend to swear by their honor; if in love, by the moon; and sometimes by their lives. Women choose somewhat different touchstones for their vows. In *All's Well That Ends Well*, for example, Helena's reputation as a maid, her virginity, her chaste good name, and, only at the last, her life are offered as forfeit should she fail to cure the King. She convinces him of her earnestness. In contrast, *Love's Labour's Lost* illustrates the futility of oath-taking and the frequency of men's oath-breaking. In *Romeo and Juliet*, Romeo's hastiness and intensity and the transience of love are questioned by Juliet who cautions against vowing by "th' inconstant moon." At the opening of *King*

Lear Lear's vows, triggered by passion and vanity, initiate the process of his tragic fall. In *Macbeth*, Lady Macbeth's equally passionate vows, made on things she holds sacred, also anticipate her tragic and inevitable fall. Her aims, like Lear's, are flawed and, unlike his, reflect an evil intent.

Growing out of a woman's experience, these vows, despite their negative and therefore unnatural twist, frighten us, and, as W. Moelwyn Merchant suggests, sexually affront us. Unfortunately, skewed analyses of Lady Macbeth's actions frequently result.[4] Kenneth Muir, for example, in his introduction to the Arden edition, after conceding human qualities to her, nevertheless concludes:

> It is true that Lady Macbeth is not naturally depraved or conscienceless (any more than Satan was): but she deliberately chooses evil, her choice *being more deliberate than her husband's.* Macbeth speaks of ambition being his only spur; but he would never have overcome *his reluctance to commit murder without the chastisement of his wife's tongue.* She, not metaphorically or symbolically, but in deadly earnest, invokes the powers of darkness to take possession of her. (lxix, emphasis added)

Unlike his usually careful scholarship, Muir's analysis here seems culturally determined rather than textually shaped. Value judgments abound, first in his reference to the "choice of evil"; second, in his conclusion that Macbeth would never have murdered to reach the crown; and third, in the evaluation of language's relative power. Why does Muir believe Shakespeare's use of metaphoric or symbolic language indicates a character's wavering commitment? Or, conversely, why does he assume that direct language indicates the earnest speaker? The critic offers no parallel examples from other plays to bolster this theory. Usually language reflects the nature of the speaker or illuminates the interaction between characters on stage. But Muir's analysis, by placing the major responsibility for the crime with Lady Macbeth, transports us back to the Garden of Eden and the story of Eve.

Preparing for this role, Ellen Terry, in her notes, offers more perceptive comments on the speakers and their language:

> He can't face things and *talk* of 'em, but he can *do* them. *She* can talk and plan but *shd* not be able *to do,* so easily. So when she meets the King, she shd not be so like "the innocent flower." (opp. p. 24)

The actress understood not only the limitations on the two characters but also the difference between speaking and doing. In contrast, the editor went beyond the text to arrive at a value judgment based on the fact that he found Lady Macbeth's words repulsive. Merchant too, despite recognizing the antipathy they would arouse—leading to distortions in criticism—fell victim to their power. Acknowledging parallels between her vows and Macbeth's "Stars, hide your fires," the critic called the latter an "embarrassed dislocation in moral judgment" (76)—in other words, a momentary lapse. No such excuse modifies his judgment of Lady Macbeth.

Her first meeting with Macbeth, following her soliloquy, suggests how well husband and wife understand one another and how similar their aïms are. "Thy letters have transported me beyond / This ignorant present, and I feel now / The future in the instant" (56-58), she warmly welcomes. When he announces the news she has already received, "Duncan comes here tonight" (59), there is an obvious subtext: the desire for Duncan's death. Each, individually, has confided this idea to the audience—one by expressing "dark thoughts," and the other, more openly, by avowing that their guest's visit to the castle will be "fatal." Thus her query, "And when goes hence?" (a59) continues that other, unspoken dialogue between them as Macbeth responds with the too-studied, too-careful line: not merely "Tomorrow," but "Tomorrow, as he purposes" (60). They seem to speak the same language. Unfortunately, Lady Macbeth then breaks the pattern: "O, never / Shall sun that morrow see!" (60–61). What he had kept below the surface she forces into the light. Only her description of her husband's face betrays his complicity.

Having allowed her to take the verbal lead, he may now attribute all initiative to her. The bloody thoughts that earlier did "unfix" his hair will now be expressed through her words; Macbeth will seem to fight them. By the time the scene closes, the audience knows that Lady Macbeth will be functioning not as the moral restraint on Macbeth but rather as his partner, encouraging him to murder. Her last long speech in the scene, outlining their future actions, indicates a willing, cooperative, even creative coconspirator, who warns:

> Your face, my Thane, is as a book where men
> May read strange matters. To beguile the time,
> Look like the time. . . .
> . . . Look like th' innocent flower,
> But be the serpent under 't.

(62–67)

Macbeth's reply to her proposal of murder is ambiguous and brief. "We will speak further" (72). Although he shows only a limited moral concern here, Lady Macbeth's vehement language and extraordinary vows have marked her as the more vicious of the two. Audience sympathy moves toward Macbeth and against his wife.

This first appearance of husband and wife together establishes the nature of their relationship and suggests their roles in the unfolding action. Because the scene offers a momentary contrast between the two characters—a contrast which seems to escalate in their next few scenes together—it challenges the actor-manager or director whose interpretation must grow out of the whole text. He must not forget Macbeth's first reactions to the witches' prophecy or accept as suddenly true Lady Macbeth's comment on her husband's warmth and humanity. In fact the director must resist the temptation to romanticize Macbeth, and, worse still, demonize his Lady. Here, knowledge of future action must be assimilated into the portrait. As I will demonstrate, the dramatist rounds out the characterization of a lost and tortured human—clearly differentiated from the witches—who moves in a mortal world. The sleepwalking scene logically develops from those first encounters between husband and wife. For the play to work effectively on stage, it must therefore be perceived as a whole, full of conflicts and contradictions rather than as a simple story of the workings of an inhuman and unhuman, immoral and power-hungry wife.

The portrayals of Lady Macbeth on stage have varied, ranging from fierce virago to sexual temptress to supportive wife. Documenting these changes in her exhaustive study *Shakespeare from the Greenroom*, Carol Carlisle concludes:

> Is she "masculine"—imposing of figure and domineering of manner? Or is she "feminine"—either a wily temptress or a devoted wife, but in any case, graceful and charming? At some points the answers to these questions overlap; for, regardless of the truism about "the female of the species," the more feminine Lady Macbeth has been made on the stage, the less fiendlike she has usually seemed. (395)

Because theater builds on the dynamic interaction between characters, the portrayal of Macbeth often determines that of Lady Macbeth. Her behavior varies to complement his. Henry Irving, we are told, altered his interpretation between his earliest (1875) and last (1888) productions, shifting from a more heroic to a harsher portrait as the actor became convinced that Macbeth was a "moral coward" and a "bloody minded, hypocritical" villain (Hughes, 73). Inevitably, this affected Ellen Terry's acting of Lady Macbeth. Sometimes, however, the definition of Macbeth is less decisive or consistent than Irving's. This, too, may influence an actress's approach.

In our own century, Laurence Olivier's Macbeth (1955) was projected as a sympathetic character at the start whose wife, despite good intentions, failed to understand him. Glen Byam Shaw comments in the promptbook: "She thinks that she understands him well, and she does, to a very considerable degree, but the strange, imaginative, Celtic side of his nature she doesn't understand" (60). Where does the text offer this split between her understanding him "well" and not understanding his "strange, imaginative, Celtic" nature? Rather, this romanticizing reflects the director's conception of a hero of breadth who has a wife of limited sensitivity.

For the actress playing the role, such a directive not only confines, but also confuses. Strongly committed to helping her husband at the opening of scene 5, a sympathetic woman bent on supporting his drive for the crown, and recklessly—foolishly—unafraid of moral consequences, she must simultaneously understand and not understand. The subtext to the director's analysis seems to be, "although she understands Macbeth, he, not she, is a sympathetic character." Vivien Leigh received bad reviews in this production (Cottrell, 262). But one wonders how any actress could have succeeded, handicapped by such conflicting directions.

Ultimately the major test in resolving interpretation of these roles occurs when she and Macbeth are once more alone together (I.vii) after their initial meeting. The encounter, however, does not happen immediately. Rather, it is preceded by his long, self-incriminating soliloquy. Debating whether or not to murder Duncan, Macbeth intermingles references to pity and hospitality towards a kinsman with darker thoughts, setting the tone:

> I have no spur
> To prick the sides of my intent, but only
> Vaulting ambition, which o'erleaps itself,
> And falls on th' other—

> (I.vii.25–28)

Again ambition, "vaulting ambition"—the same ambition that had silently protested Malcolm's promotion to Prince of Cumberland— spurs him on. Even the language and imagery build on that earlier speech: "that is a step / On which I must fall down, or else o'erleap" (I.iv.48–49). Vaulting, or jumping, now intensifies the concept of o'erleaping, providing the image of an "ambition" that cannot be contained within its normal limits.

Only Lady Macbeth's entrance interrupts any further soul searching. What other thoughts he may have had or where they may have led, we do not know. Insisting on ambiguity here by leaving Macbeth unresolved in his decision, Shakespeare shifts the focus from husband to wife. Before he can speak, she urges him to the murder, questions his manhood, and speaks of plucking the nipple from "the babe that milks me" (55), dashing out its brains. Because of the repugnance of the images presented by Lady Macbeth, critics tend to forget, or overlook, her husband's earlier words. Bernard McElroy, for example, notes that in contrast with Lady Macbeth, who speaks of the golden round with "sanguine anticipation" (220), Macbeth is "not really ambitious" and "scarcely mentions the crown" (219). That opening soliloquy has been forgotten.

On stage, Macbeth's soliloquy frequently fails. J. S. Knowles, writing in the nineteenth century, offers a partial explanation. He found actors unable to express the "perturbation" in the lines:

> The manner in which this soliloquy is generally delivered reminds me of the seaman who is accustomed to the gale, and sits cool and collected at the helm, though at every yard there yawns a grave before him. I would have it an entirely different thing. Macbeth is no such seaman. There should be infinite discomfiture and confusion in it. It should be delivered by fits and starts. (*New Variorum*, 93)

Nearly a hundred years earlier, John Philip Kemble's delivery of this soliloquy was described in equally unflattering terms. Comparing it with the acting of Sarah Siddons, Kemble's sister, the author writes on the interleaf of an 1808 text: "Kemble speaks this as if he had never seen his sister—like a speech to be recited—none of that hesitation or working of the mind which in Mrs. Siddons seems to inspire the words as the natural expression of emotion" (opp. p. 22). Why was the speech so ineffective? One suspects that the answer lay in the conflict between the words of the text and the attempt of the performer to present an attractive Macbeth. According to Joseph Donohue, Kemble's performance conformed to the interpretation of most eighteenth-century criticism. It made "the central character a virtuous man seduced by false prophets, a scheming wife, and his own ambition into a crime revolting to his nature"(71). That approach often reappears today. However the soliloquy confirms the similarities rather than differences between husband and wife.

As we know, Shakespeare uses soliloquies for a variety of purposes—sometimes to include us in a character's secret, as occurs with Juliet, sometimes to heighten our awareness of a character's scheming and evil intention, as in the case of Iago or Richard III. Here, the soliloquy illuminates another aspect of character— Macbeth's method for evading moral responsibility. His speech stands in direct contrast with his response to his wife. Once she enters, his self-questioning ceases; his inner conflict ends. Freed from the burden of answering himself, he may then debate with her. All the arguments favoring murder become hers—and reprehensible. He may listen and disagree. However, ambition, nourished by the witches' first successful prediction, has already betrayed him in his soliloquy. She is therefore merely encouraging him in the direction he was going:

> Was the hope drunk
> Wherein you dress'd yourself? Hath it slept since?
> And wakes it now to look so green and pale
> At what it did so freely?
>
> (35–38)

Her metaphor is confusing. Is she asking if he drank hope, dressing himself in it? Or does the word *drunk* refer to the state of being drunk? "Did you dress yourself in drunken hope and are you now frightened?" As critics have observed, the metaphor is mixed. But the words *drunk, green, pale,* and *slept* are suggestive enough as a character slur, urging him to act.

Continuing, she asks:

> Art thou afeard
> To be the same in thine own act and valor
> As thou art in desire?
>
> (39–41)

Here, she seeks to encourage him to those acts and "valor" which will support his dreams; but the dreams are rotten and morally insupportable. Her later decline into madness will illustrate the emptiness of such a role—the loss of a sense of self, and in this case, the carelessness about maintaining a moral base. The human spirit—as opposed to the spirit of the fiend—cannot function merely as a spur for someone else. Although one critic writes of Lady Macbeth's "incredible mixture of insinuation and bullying" (Ramsey, 289), her statement reveals the confidence of a woman who believes her husband invulnerable.

"Gender-neutral" (Schweickart) criticism seems impossible here. Samuel Johnson, for example, considers Macbeth's response—"I dare do all that may become a man; / Who dares [do] more is none" (46–47)—as the line and a half that "ought to bestow immortality on the author, though all his other productions had been lost" (8:767). He believes that with these words Macbeth destroys the sophism of his wife's argument. Johnson continues: "Courage is the distinguishing virtue of a soldier, and the reproach of cowardice cannot be borne by any man from a woman, without great impatience" (8:767). At this point Johnson's own perceptions of women impinge on textual interpretation.

More recently, D. W. Harding finds in the exchange two different interpretations of the word *manliness.* He writes: "The nature of manliness . . . is a question running all through the play, manliness as lived by the man and manliness as seen in the distorting fantasy of the woman" (245). Glen Byam Shaw's description of Macbeth as a man of imagination, positively and sympathetically portrayed, has shifted to Harding's description of Lady Macbeth as a woman of "fantasy"—but unfortunately a psychotic "distorting fantasy." The words are loaded: the critic contrasts "fantasy" not merely with experiential knowledge—in other words, a creation of imagination—but with a fantasy that alters, reshapes, and skews in unnatural, warped ways.

Criticism of this scene tends to emphasize Macbeth's righteous stance expressed in his early response to his wife, "We will proceed no further in this business" (31). As a result, she has been cited as the chief instigator. However, his protest too quickly fades. Rather than a moralist, he resembles the pragmatist who may on occasion gamble against the odds, as he does when going into battle, disdaining "Fortune" (I.ii.17). More often, such a character tends to weigh his chances. With stakes much higher and success less certain in this scene, the pragmatist prevails: "If we should fail?" (59) No sudden deviation in character occurs. Rather, a consistency exists with the hero who was first described by the wounded messenger.

Both Macbeth's question and Lady Macbeth's answer "We fail?," punctuated in the Folio with a question mark, are theatrical cruxes.

Since punctuation remains problematic in the Folio, that question mark need not dictate Lady Macbeth's attitude. It hasn't. Editors have not always adopted it, and actresses, seeking to endow the words with meaning, have ranged in their interpretations. Helen Faucit spoke it as a declarative sentence permeated by a sense of fatalistic adjustment: "If we fail, then we fail," but then changed it "at once into words of encouragement" (Carlisle, "Helen," 216). Occasionally a hysterical tone persists "We fail? How could we possibly?" At other times the voice is positive and optimistic. According to Anna Jameson, Mrs. Siddons gave it three successive intonations from "contemptuous interrogation" to "indignant astonishment" to a "dark fatalism" as if saying "If we fail, why then we fail, and all is over" (*New Variorum*, 109).

Continuing beyond these two words, however, Lady Macbeth offers a concrete plan: drugging the men of Duncan's chamber then blaming them for the murder. Without hesitation, Macbeth, applauds her. Their debate had been superficial. "Bring forth men-children only!" he exclaims, reinforcing her own self-devaluation—her awareness of the subordinate place of girl children—as he acclaims her genius with his highest praise, "For thy undaunted mettle should compose / Nothing but males" (I.vii.72–74). How ironic. She has suddenly, if temporarily, been accepted in the male world but only as a breeder of males.

Such acceptance does not last long, as Shakespeare demonstrates in the discovery scene. Unfortunately, a pattern of excision marks her absence there, skewing the emphasis and denying audiences the opportunity to watch a complex interaction of characters with Lady Macbeth playing a brief, but significant role.

Before that scene, however, the distinction again arises between her and the witches. Although called weird sisters, they have a sense neither of family nor of human concern. Lady Macbeth, on the other hand, recollects her father. Murder is more difficult than she had thought. "Had he not resembled / My father as he slept, I had done't" (II.ii.12–13), she apologizes. The moral code—buried, warped, forgotten—halts her from committing murder; her husband follows the drawn dagger. Immersing her hands in blood will prove enough to haunt her later on. In contrast, the witches, moving to a crescendo in the scene where they invoke the apparitions, have no trouble with blood-stained hands or hearts.

After the murder is discovered, Shakespeare begins to unfold Lady Macbeth's tragedy—the futility of her attempt to move into

the male world, and, having adopted her husband's moral standards, her ever-increasing isolation even from him. The first intima-
tions of this exclusion appear in act 2, scene 3, which opens with
the drunken Porter scene. As critics have frequently noted, this
section in its sharp contrast with what has preceded and its anticipation of what is to follow adds comic relief, reminding the audience of the gatekeeper in hell.[5] The diversion is brief. Macduff
enters, berates the Porter for inefficiency and drunkenness, then
leaves to awaken Duncan. "O horror, horror, horror! (64) . . . Murther and treason!(74)" shouts the shocked Macduff, ordering the
alarm bell to be rung. Lady Macbeth strides concernedly on stage,
"What's the business, / That such a hideous trumpet calls to
parley / The sleepers of the house?" (81–83). Macduff's gender
determined response greets her:

> O gentle Lady,
> 'Tis not for you to hear what I can speak:
> The repetition in a woman's ear
> Would murther as it fell.
>
> (83–86)

Although his lines imply he would shield her from the knowledge,
ironically contradicting what we, the audience, have witnessed as
her audaciousness and scorn of male weakness, Macduff quickly
forgets this concern when Banquo enters.

Suggesting how irrelevant she is to the world of the play, Macduff
blurts out, "Our royal master's murther'd!" (87). It is almost as if
she were invisible. Lady Macbeth's flawed response to the news
of Duncan's death follows. An all too brief, "Woe, alas" (87), precedes her unsympathetic, and unnatural, "What, in our house?"
(II.iii.88) provoking Banquo's reproof, "Too cruel anywhere" (88).
This brief dismissive comment contrasts with his warm, brotherly
greeting to Macduff, "Dear Duff, I prithee contradict thyself, /
And say it is not so" (I.vii.89–90). The quick shift in language and
tone intensifies the suggestion that Banquo suspects Macbeth, if
not his Lady.

When, however, she is omitted from this scene, as often occurs,
the "Dear Duff" too disappears. Interpreted as merely a clue to
the actor to shift address from Lady Macbeth to Macduff, the "Dear
Duff" also implies fraternity and friendship. Without her, the sequence changes. Cleansed of emotional relationships, it offers only
factual material. The lines "Our royal master's murther'd!" are

followed immediately by "I prithee contradict thyself / And say it is not so." Something subtle is lost in such an excision—the close relationships in this male world and its exclusion of women.

Having just heard the personalizing of relationships between Banquo and Macduff and perhaps aware of her own blunder, Lady Macbeth wonders if her husband too will falter. With Macbeth's entrance at this moment, returning from the murder chamber, he begins, "Had I but died an hour before this chance, / I had liv'd a blessed time" (91–92). His words promise an equally foolish mistake as her reaction to the news of the murder, "What, in our house?"

Lady Macbeth listens. Should she say something? Macbeth not only continues with this double-edged set piece, but then admits having murdered the grooms, already identified by Lennox as apparently guilty. Immediately, Macduff reacts: "Wherefore did you so?" Macbeth tries to explain, "Who can be wise, amaz'd, temp'rate, and furious, / Loyal, and neutral, in a moment?" (108–9) He then describes the dead Duncan, whose "silver skin" was "lace'd with his golden blood" (112). What a strange, mixed image. And how audience attention must be riveted on Lady Macbeth while listening to her husband's words:

> Who could refrain,
> That had a heart to love, and in that heart
> Courage, to make's love known?
>
> (116–18)

"Help me hence, ho!" (118), she cries at once. "Look to the Lady," Macduff orders. But no one does. Other matters concern them. Not until the line is eventually repeated is she carried off. What a remarkable bit of stagecraft, and how it emphasizes her unimportance and the peripheral place of women in this world. Theatrically, the sequence of speeches demands constant shifts of attention from the audience. Their focus must move from Macbeth to Lady Macbeth to Macduff, then across the stage perhaps to Malcolm and Donalbain (who, in asides, whisper their suspicions of everyone), and finally insistently back to Lady Macbeth. The dual response— her immediate request for help and Malcolm's aside to his brother protesting their need for silence despite the magnitude of their loss—testifies to the weakness of Macbeth's speech. Shakespeare's dramaturgy here, particularly the repetition of "Look to the Lady," suggests how integral she is to this section of the play—and how gender defined, despite that earlier vow, "Unsex me here" (I.v.41).

How then do we interpret the faint? Is it real or feigned? If feigned, it indicates fear of discovery and presents a manipulative way to interrupt the flow of conversation. If the faint is real, it can indicate extreme relief after the intensity of what she has just gone through—the murders, then the verbal blunders—as Furness suggested in a letter to Ellen Terry:

> My dear Miss Terry remember she is *very feminine.* remember too she *really faints*—aghast at the wonderful story Mac makes of the murder— all is told—*well*—and they are safe she thinks and *then faints.*[6]

Whether this comment influenced Terry or merely reaffirmed her own perception of the scene is uncertain. However, in her own copy of the text, she not only double and triple underlines the words "very" and "feminine," but later, on the interleaf facing Macbeth's line regretting his murder of the grooms, she writes:

> She is not (in truth) horrified by this news.—'*Anything, Anything* to be safe.' Strung up, past pitch, she gives in at the *end* of his speech— when she finds he is safely through his story and *then* [at "Help me hence"] *she faints* really. Strung up at first she relaxes when all seems safe and they swallow her husband's masterly excuse. (opp. p. 37)

Some critics believe the faint is a ploy to shift attention away from Macbeth; others perceive here Lady Macbeth's emotional release, not from satisfaction, but exhaustion—a prelude, however brief, to the illness which will finally overcome her. Offering a range of readings, *The Variorum* includes a delightful debate on the subject of the faint (161–64).

On stage, however, actor-managers and directors must resolve the ambiguity. They have. For over a hundred years Lady Macbeth remained absent from the scene. The many printed acting texts of the eighteenth and most of the nineteenth centuries testify to the universality of this excision.[7] Kemble's version, drawing heavily on Garrick's, set the pattern.[8] Historically, however, she disappeared even before Garrick's time (T. Davies, II.95). Having restored much of the original, Garrick failed to reinstate her into this scene. Thomas Davies offers the rationale. London audiences would have laughed, even with such a capable actress as Mrs. Pritchard in the role. He writes:

The players have long since removed Lady Macbeth from this scene. . . .—Many years since, I have been informed, an experiment was hazarded, whether the spectators would bear Lady Macbeth's surprize and fainting; but, however characteristical such behaviour might be, persons of a certain class were so merry upon the occasion, that it was not thought proper to venture the Lady's appearance any more. (II.95–96)

Why did the scene arouse laughter, and what should this tell us about the kind of character that Lady Macbeth had already become on stage? Had the acting been reasonable—frightening, but unfiendlike—audiences should not have been tempted to laugh. However, because of the interaction of characters on stage, the development of one must integrate with that of others. The role of Lady Macbeth hinged on the interpretation of Macbeth. Despite his obvious ambition before she even enters the play, the searing quality of some of her lines and the fact that his is the major "tragic" role led to her being categorized as a stereotypical villain. One critic has even called her "the fourth 'witch'" (Proser, 57) despite her mortality, humanity, and decline into sleepwalking at the close—hardly a characteristic of a witch. For the performance to succeed, therefore, this human quality must be projected along with that of a woman who has sacrificed her moral values to her primary belief in her role as wife only to discover, ironically, her isolation in a male world.

When finally, in the nineteenth century, she reappeared in the scene, it was in a new guise. The dual "Look to the Lady"—the sign of her irrelevance—had disappeared. Instead, she became the focal point of the action. Manuscript notes in a promptbook describe Mme. Ristori's version of this scene.[9] At the line "What's the business," she enters in her nightdress (opp. p. 28), then at "Help me hence" is immediately attended to after Banquo's "Look to the Lady" (opp. p. 29). The writer of this material notes:

With *Ristori,* Macduff & Banquo are C[enter.] A little behind Malcolm enters and gets R[ight] C[enter]. Macduff after *"wherefore did you"* whispers to Banquo C[enter] and watches THE GUILTY PAIR very narrowly. Banquo doing the same. Lady M. appears very anxious that her husband should not betray them and encourages him with her looks as much as possible, she being L[eft], he R[ight] in a line and Macduff C[enter] in rear enables her to let only her husband see her countenance. *"This was a great success"* At "his love known" Lady M.

"Help me hence ho" (she faints). Banquo "Look to the Lady." . . . this was the end of Act 2. ("THE GUILTY PAIR," emphasis added; *Mac* 9, opp. p. 29)

Two developments appear here: first, the reference to people suspecting the "guilty pair," and second, the absence of the repetition of "Look to the Lady." Nothing in the text indicates that the men in the play suspected Lady Macbeth, as the doctor's astonished reaction to her sleepwalking later testifies. Macbeth, on the other hand, immediately aroused suspicion, particularly Banquo's, but also Macduff's, and certainly the young princes', who swiftly fled. Moreover, by ending the act here, rather than at the exit of the fleeing princes, the focus remains on Lady Macbeth. While this was an unorthodox production, by the end of the century Henry Irving had more positively established the tradition of keeping Lady Macbeth in the scene. Like Ristori, Irving, too, retained only one "Look to the Lady," and she was attended to immediately.

Thus her reintroduction skewed the text: she was suspected at once. Glen Byam Shaw, for example, comments on her actions indicating immediate response to the line and elaborate concern for the lady. The director links her actions to Macbeth's speech:

He almost takes a ghastly pleasure in describing the horror of the scene in full detail. His wife cannot stand the strain & she loses consciousness. Immediately, the focus, if not suspicion, centre on her. *Her husband goes to her at once* & as she recovers they are face to face with the knowledge of their guilt & surrounded by those strained, white faces peering at them out of the darkness. (emphasis added; Shaw, 103)

Here she has been elevated to "centre" stage rather than remaining insignificantly in the shadows, the delicate, overlooked, unimportant bystander of the text.

Nor is this pattern of focusing on Lady Macbeth without precedent once she is returned to this scene. For example, in a 1911 prompt for a Sothern-Marlowe production, at her "Help me hence, ho!" appears the direction *"falls"* (21). Immediately after, at Macduff's "Look to the Lady," appears *"Carry Lady Mac out."* The specific instruction appears on the facing interleaf:

Two men catch Lady Mac—as she faints—they take her arms.—One man takes her feet—two of the ladies gather in front of her. They take her up stairs Left and off.

As a result, of course, the second "Look to the Lady" is cut. But if the repetition was intentional, such immediate attention to Lady Macbeth alters the larger picture of her unimportance in this male world.

Only occasionally has the faint been played as a repetitious action receiving little attention. In the Trevor Nunn production, Lady Macbeth faints twice in this scene (RSC prompt, 1977). The taped version shows her falling into Macbeth's arms greatly upset by what he is saying and concerned for his mental stability. Throughout, the strong erotic relationship between them appears as the extra motivation for the act of murder.

Theatrically the repetition of the lines has still another purpose— to illuminate from two different angles the almost obvious guilt of Macbeth. Momentarily freezing time, the dramatist allows us to hear the comments of Malcolm and Donalbain, "Why do we hold our tongues, / That most may claim this argument for ours?" (119–20), answered by "What should be spoken here, where our fate, / Hid in an auger-hole, may rush and seize us?" (121–22) And then the moment passes. The simultaneous reactions of Lady Macbeth and the sons have been registered on the audience. To stress the passage of time, the dramatist assigns the repeated lines not to Macduff, who first spoke them, but to Banquo. He then continues, lacing his speech with innuendo. Opening with a subordinate clause, "And when we have our naked frailties hid, / That suffer in exposure" (II.iii.126–27), it includes the personal denial "In the great hand of God I stand, and thence / Against the undivulg'd pretense I fight / Of treasonous malice" (130–32). For Macbeth these lines have a clear message. But Garrick's, Kemble's, and all those nineteenth-century acting texts that followed their versions, cut that opening subordinate clause referring to "naked frailties," thus eliminating one dynamic element in the play: Macbeth's constant sense of vulnerablility to Banquo.

Rich in action and sudden shifts, the scene offers insights into Lady Macbeth and the role of women in the *Macbeth* world. With her absent, a single plot thread replaces the interweaving strands of suspicion and friendship. In the long-popular, abbreviated version, audiences were seeing a quick shift from the aftermath of the murder to its discovery. Lady Macbeth's absence eliminated the preparation for her later decline. No longer did she divert attention from Macbeth's admission to having killed the two men in Duncan's chamber. Nor did audiences hear her blunder, "in our house," foreshadowing her later inability to cope.

In those versions, the scene opens with Macduff's query "Was it so late, friend, ere you went to bed?" (II.iii.24) and closes with Macbeth's suggestion that they all "put on manly readiness and meet i' th' hall together." Eliminated are the Porter's soliloquy at the opening and the conversation between Malcolm and Donalbain at the close. The audience hears neither their suspicions of all present nor their plans to flee. Some promptbooks allow them to learn of their father's murder by "those of his chamber, as it seem'd" (101); other productions shunt them offstage even earlier. After Macduff's question on first arriving, a one-line reply—usually by Seyton, not the Porter—suffices, followed by Macbeth's entry. He exchanges a few words with Macduff who then exits to awaken the King. Lennox's comments on the "unruly night" are retained, probably because they include the sense of premonition, and allow some moments to elapse before Macduff returns, exclaiming, "O horror! horror! horror!" (64). Not Lady Macbeth but Banquo responds to the ringing of the alarm. Nor is there any gender-defined hesitation about divulging the news, "Our royal master's murder'd." Macbeth's speech beginning "Had I but died an hour before this chance, / I had liv'd a blessed time" remains; however another textual jump occurs as Banquo's "Fears and scruples shake us" leads almost immediately to the scene's close, Macbeth's "Let's briefly put on manly readiness, and meet i' th' hall together" (133–34).

Although Lady Macbeth's presence in the scene is brief, it suggestively indicates her invisibility. Altering the text, however, has several direct results. Her excision shifts the emphasis from suspicion of all present to a stress on manliness. On the other hand, making her the focus of guilt—as occurs when she is returned to the scene but given a single faint—blurs the irony of her involvement. Both readings seem to contradict the subtlety of her brief appearance here, a pattern repeated when she next comes on stage for an even shorter moment, but one again worth examining.

Occurring two scenes later, Lady Macbeth's presence offers significant insight into her development in the play. Time has elapsed. Macbeth has been crowned, and she is queen. In an ominous opening soliloquy, Banquo reflects:

> Thou hast it now, King, Cawdor, Glamis, all,
> As the weird women promis'd, and I fear
> Thou play'dst most foully for't.

$$(III.i.1–3)$$

These thoughts abruptly end when King and Queen enter, turning all their attention to this former partner in battle. Lady Macbeth has one two-and-a-half line speech establishing her role as cohost with Macbeth. Their lines mesh in a perfect, harmonious unity beginning with his half line to Banquo "Here's our chief guest"(i.11), and completed by her:

> If he had been forgotten,
> It had been as a gap in our great feast,
> And all-thing unbecoming.

(III.i.11–13)

Echoes of Gertrude and Claudius welcoming Rosencrantz and Guildenstern resonate in these lines. Later in the scene another parallel arises as each king dismisses his queen (along with the others) to develop a plot: in Macbeth's case, of murder; in Claudius's, of spying and deception. However, the women's roles take different directions. Gertrude's subservience to Claudius reaches its nadir in her scene, whereas Lady Macbeth is still at the beginning of her descent.[10] Ultimately Gertrude starts the climb up to find her own voice; no such hope exists for Lady Macbeth. To find her own voice, she must first recognize her singleness—aloneness—then accept moral responsibility for her acts. Gertrude acknowledges the "black and grained" spots on her soul (III.iv.90). Lady Macbeth has transgressed further. When she recognizes a moral responsibility for her actions, she retreats into madness.[11]

Her brief appearance in this scene with Banquo, however, allows a momentary pause, further reinforcing for the audience her exclusion from the male world of power. Linked to Macbeth through their joint roles as accomplices, she still believes she shares his life. But this scene, opening with their appearance of unity and amity, and closing with his independent action—instructions to Banquo's murderers—questions that premise. When she is removed from the scene as she was during much of the eighteenth and nineteenth centuries, the contrast between the roles of husband and wife was further weakened and the irony of her involvement in the murder lost.[12]

With no intermediate scenes, audience exposure to Lady Macbeth jumped from the image of a woman with bloodied hands to a woman weighed down with remorse. A morality message was implicit. But Shakespeare's staccatolike rhythm of her fleeting appearance and reappearance blurs such a theme. Rather, in brief incisive strokes, he develops the portrait of a woman alone, whose momentary union with her husband in murder has not altered this condition. Even linked to a man of power, she still inhabits a separate world.[13]

Complementing her absence from these scenes are excisions in Macbeth's lines that soften his character.[14] In his first conversation with Banquo's murderers, for example, Macbeth reveals his scorn for people, his manipulativeness, and the intensity of his name-calling. Historically, however, many of these lines never reach the stage. Cut in promptbooks is his vituperative:

> Ay, in the catalogue ye go for men,
> As hounds and greyhounds, mungrels, spaniels, curs,
> Shoughs, water-rugs, and demi-wolves are clipt
> All by the name of dogs.
>
> (III.i.91–94)

Frequently reduced to a brief exchange between Macbeth and the murderers, the interview includes the more general query—"Are you so gospell'd, / To pray for this good man . . . / Whose heavy hand hath bow'd you to the grave?" (87–89)—and their reply. As a result, the portrait emerges of a man trapped by circumstances; the actor may then build a more sympathetic character, as Garrick, Irving, Kemble, Lacy, Kean, Forbes-Robertson, Olivier, and many others have done.

Excisions also created ambiguity surrounding Lady Macbeth's involvement in Banquo's murder despite the text's lines clearly acquiting her:

> Let your remembrance apply to Banquo,
> Present him eminence both with eye and tongue:
> Unsafe the while, that we
> Must lave our honors in these flattering streams,
> And make our faces vizards to our hearts
> Disguising what they are.
>
> (ii.30–35)

Reminding her of her duties to Banquo, Macbeth fails to mention his earlier conversation with the murderers and his plot on Banquo's life. Illustrating his easy deception of his wife, the speech clears her of prior knowledge of the murder. But these lines along with her concerned response, "you must leave this" (35), presenting a woman who still believes she can live with the deed she has committed, generally disappear from the stage.[15] In their exchange, Shakespeare indicates that although Macbeth pursues the path of escalation of crime and Lady Macbeth believes she can put the single act behind her, neither can forget. By excising this section, actor-managers and directors blur the comparison while casting further suspicion on Lady Macbeth.[16]

The tendency to stress her criminality frequently occurs perhaps because of hostility to strong women, especially those who seem to cast off their natural roles as defined by the larger society outside the theater. Orson Welles in his (1948) film, for example, not only deleted Lady Macbeth's attempts to comfort and cheer her husband, but then transferred his line "Thou know'st that Banquo and his Fleance lives" (37) to the Queen herself. Although Welles's film obviously changes the text's intent by shifting responsibility for Banquo's murder to Lady Macbeth, the creation of this monstrous queen reflected contemporary attitudes.

The film appeared shortly after the word *momism* crept into our language. Coined by Philip Wylie in *Generation of Vipers* (1942), it defined strong mothers who destroyed their sons so that they eventually became weak men. But it also extended the definition to domineering wives who treated their husbands like dependent sons. Wylie wrote: "The mealy look of men today is the result of momism and so is the pinched and baffled fury in the eyes of womankind" (197). Welles's Macbeth is a warm, sympathetic character until almost the end of the film. His Lady Macbeth is a shrew rather than the tragic character she is in Shakespeare's play.

This particular scene, where Macbeth directs her remembrance to Banquo, reveals her growing tragedy. Asking a servant to tell the King she "would attend his leisure / For a few words" (3–4), she betrays a tentativeness and uncertainty unrecognizable in the woman of act 1. She has felt her exclusion from Macbeth's life. Alone, she then expresses her spiritual emptiness in a brief soliloquy:

> Nought's had, all's spent,
> Where our desire is got without content;
> 'Tis safer to be that which we destroy
> Than by destruction dwell in doubtful joy.

(III.ii.4–7)

Characteristically, the speech includes an extreme statement. Speculating about changing places with the murdered Duncan, Lady Macbeth is taking the first tentative step towards madness; she has misjudged the effect of her deed on her own sense of morality. More important, however, she has lost her husband's companionship. If she had based her encouragement of him on her belief in their shared reign, their closeness, she is now experiencing the unexpected—separation.

At the conscious and verbal levels, her acceptance—"What's done, is done" (12)—coupled with her attempt to comfort Macbeth, further throw her back into the traditional role of woman. His long speech beginning "We have scorch'd the snake, not kill'd it" (13) contrasts with her resignation. This woman who spoke of dashing the brains of an infant, suggesting a totally unconcerned, unnurturing, unwomanly woman, immediately exhibits concern for her husband,

> How now, my lord, why do you keep alone,
> Of sorriest fancies your companions making,
> Using those thoughts which should indeed have died
> With them they think on?
>
> (8–11).

The audience, however, has not seen a man who has kept alone, morose—but one who has baited murderers and offered them rewards. Just as earlier she had misread her own strength and her husband's "milk of human kindness," she once again misreads him. She, not he, has been alone. While he may have contributed to that separateness, it is built into the play and reflects the male-dominated culture in which women find themselves. Her lines to Macbeth then continue the theme. "What's done is done."

Anticipating the next murder, however, he teases her, promising "A deed of dreadful note" (44), but refusing to share the information. "Be innocent of the knowledge, dearest chuck, / Till thou applaud the deed" (45–46). Terms of endearment interweave with references to the bloody deed. He expects her approval. Although at the end of the play we discover, in the sleepwalking scene, that she eventually shared the knowlege, here she is clearly innocent, listening in amazement as he hints of bloody deeds:

> Come, seeling night,
> Scarf up the tender eye of pitiful day,

And with thy bloody and invisible hand
Cancel and tear to pieces that great bond
Which keeps me pale!

(46–50)

The scene's close reiterates the debate: can things "bad begun make strong themselves by ill" (55) as Macbeth claims, or should "things without all remedy / . . . be without regard" (11–12) as she proposes? In other words, are there demands on the murderers that they cannot elude, or is it possible to pretend the murder never occurred and just live on?

The distinction between Lady Macbeth and the witches sharpens. They will never rationalize or become despondent as she does here. Rather, as Macbeth falls further and further into their trap, they become exultantly triumphant. For Lady Macbeth, however, remorse, unknown to the witches, begins. In the 1911 Sothern-Marlowe promptbook appears the comment "Macbeth plays scene in half hysterical manner—repressed, agitated, half wild. Lady Macbeth trying to quiet him, but herself terrified and distraught" (opp. p. 28). She observes her husband's terror, "Gentle my Lord, sleek o'er your rugged looks" (27), and his sleeplessness, in vain trying to calm him while upset and confused herself.

The constant redefinition of the portrait of Macbeth continues in acting versions. Having stripped the text of his crude talk to the murderers and later his instructions to his wife to entertain Banquo, actor-managers next trimmed act 3, scene 3, omitting the third murderer and his role as watchdog of the other two. Those signs of Macbeth's paranoid oversuspiciousness, a prelude to his murder of Lady Macduff, disappear. Instead, Kemble's text (1803) and the many based on it, for example, open with the poetic reference to the sky and time of day, "The west yet glimmers with some streaks of day" (III.iii.5). Other acting versions even eliminate the entire scene.[17] Objecting to this practice, one nineteenth-century observer, commenting on the interleave of a Charles Kean text, wrote:

This scene is very important as it indicates the new monarch's disordered brain the very scene before the occurrence.[18]

The writer then complains that "Though the scene preceding the banquet is one of preparation,—[it is] grossly marred in the theatre generally" (*Mac* 9, opp. 37). Nevertheless, excision continued. Irving cut the scene from his 1888 production, Forbes-Robertson retained it in 1898, while Sothern and Marlowe at the beginning of the twentieth century crossed it out. Although total exclusion of the scene may be partially due to a wish to avoid an extra stage set, it may also reflect a desire to protect the audience from further on-stage murder and to leave undramatized the brutality of Macbeth's first single act of murder initiated without Lady Macbeth's involvement.

The banquet scene (III.iv) dramatizes that lack of knowledge. Lady Macbeth is "innocent of the knowledge" of Banquo's murder. Here she must react to a series of extraordinary situations when her husband confronts Banquo's ghost. Unlike the witches, who will be directing the apparitions that Macbeth sees later on, Lady Macbeth knows nothing of the future. All she knows and sees is her husband exploding against nothing—a ghost visible neither to her nor to her guests. She must face these men. She must explain, entertain, and distract them from her husband. She must, in fact, act the supremely gifted hostess, as well as wife and mother-figure chiding Macbeth to be a man.

Her first test occurs in the scene's opening moments when the blood spattered murderers appear at the banquet. What unlikely guests! Always on the lookout, Lady Macbeth must now shield her husband's opening actions from the keen observation of the royal guests. In the Sothern-Marlowe book appears the stage direction:

> [D]uring Macbeth's scene with murderers Lady Macbeth crosses back and forth front of table keeping guests occupied. She steals stealthy glances at Macbeth—now and then. (opp. p. 30)

How is Macbeth to act at this moment? What is the placement of the table? Where do the murderers enter to converse with Macbeth? And later, how are the ghost's appearance and disappearance staged? One promptbook reports that "Charles Kean destroyed this scene by speaking to the murderers in precisely the same voice as to his guests" (*Mac* 9, opp. p. 38). Margaret Webster, in the production with Judith Anderson and Maurice Evans (1941) gave the role of third murderer to Seyton, a practice followed by Glen Byam Shaw (1955), who then had Seyton, with blood on his face, report the murder. Through this transference of roles, having a familiar character rather than the scruffy "murderers" report the deed at the banquet, Shaw minimized the necessity for Lady Macbeth to create a diversion at the scene's opening.

Nevertheless, when Banquo's ghost appears, she must draw on all her improvisational skills. Compared with her actions in the earlier scenes after the murder, she must now face far greater challenges. "My Lord is often thus. . . . The fit is momentary" (52–54), she explains the first time, hoping that this will be a passing outburst. Simultaneously she must work to bring him back to the present, relying on the same line she has used earlier, "Are you a man?" (57). But this time the challenge doesn't work because to Macbeth Banquo's ghost remains tauntingly in view. Moreover, unlike the vision of the dagger where the audience heard only Macbeth's description of what he imagined, here the audience usually sees Banquo's ghost. Although Kemble unsuccessfully attempted to eliminate the ghost, leaving an empty chair, and one commentator argued for the potential effectiveness of this device, the text indicates the ghost's presence on stage.[19] In addition, because he is bloody, having been made a corpse only moments earlier and now seemingly returned from the dead, the sight shakes the audience, intensifying their horror at the scene.[20]

Macbeth's reaction dramatizes that horror, placing a tremendous burden on his wife. Having known nothing of the plot to murder Banquo, she little understands what Macbeth sees, but believes he has gone mad (see illustration). Like Ophelia reacting to Hamlet's outburst in the nunnery scene, and like Gertrude appalled at his sudden vision of his father's ghost, Lady Macbeth sees nothing. Only the audience shares Macbeth's vision and can understand his retort to her question "Are you a man?" "Ay, and a bold one, that dare look on that / Which might appall the devil" (58–59).

Again her concept of manliness and scorn of womanliness converge. His answer arouses her anger and leads to her revealing her own deeply ingrained self-denigration:

> O, these flaws and starts
> (Impostors to true fear) would well become
> A woman's story at a winter's fire,
> Authoriz'd by her grandam.

> (62–65)

What misogyny is embodied in these lines! "Flaws and starts" are merely "impostors" pretending to be signs of fear, characteristics of a woman, perhaps, but not of a man. The lines might also support those who contend that the faint was feigned, a woman's way of reacting seized upon by Lady Macbeth to fool the men. When she finally breaks down, it is not through "flaws and starts" but, despite strong control, in her sleep. Womanliness to her means lack of courage and foolish, unrealistic responses to a challenge. Once more, the dramatization speaks to the same concerns as does Kate Millett on the ways in which a minority, or powerless group, will assimilate into its thinking the attitudes and prejudices of the majority.

Quite consistently Lady Macbeth has sought to identify with her husband and in that process to lose any sense of self. De Beauvoir describes this in writing of woman as Other and man as Subject:

> [I]t is still a world that belongs to men—they have no doubt of it at all and women have scarcely any. To decline to be the Other, to refuse to be a party to the deal—this would be for women to renounce all the advantages conferred upon them by their alliance wih the superior caste. (p. xx)

Lady Macbeth knows this. But there are risks too—even while

> Man-the-sovereign will provide woman-the-liege with material protection and will undertake the moral justification of her existence; thus she can evade at once both economic risk and the metaphysical risk of liberty in which ends and aims must be contrived without assistance. (pp. xx–xxi)

Ultimately, the problems that liberty presents for anyone are those between self-determination and easy acceptance of a form of slavery—between the "ethical urge" to affirm one's "subjective existence" and the willingness to "become a thing" (de Beauvoir, xxi). This conflict surfaces for Lady Macbeth.[21] Here, in the banquet scene, she must face the prospect of making her own decisions and taking risks. These decisions would have economic, political, and of course mortal consequences should her husband's guilt be discovered.

No matter how she wills it, her experiences differ from his, and her moral standard has been shaped by other forces. When, still facing Banquo's ghost, Macbeth rages, "Behold! look! lo! how say you?" (68), Lady Macbeth must act. George J. Bell describes Mrs.

Siddons's responses at this moment: "Her anxiety makes you creep with apprehension—uncertain how to act. Her emotion keeps you breathless" (opp. p. 44). On the interleaf of her copy, Ellen Terry wrote: "'I wonder she don't go mad.' Sweetly but with a ghastly mouth—the mouth tells all—the pain and the effort and the madness" (opp. p. 48). At the ghost's disappearance, Macbeth, unwilling to admit defeat, again refers to Banquo, saluting him with a toast. The ghost reappears. Lady Macbeth must invent—but this time, her husband's speech is more extensive, and more self-revelatory: "Take any shape but that, and my firm nerves / Shall never tremble. Or be alive again" (101–2). Lady Macbeth can chance no more, especially after Rosse's query, "What sights, my lord?"(115). Again she improvises: "Question enrages him" (117) and dismisses the court. Nevertheless, by the scene's close, she is exhausted and broken. The stage direction in the Sothern-Marlowe prompt reads:

> Lady Macbeth draws away from Mac—crouching at his feet—He sits in abject despair—dazed-looking and into space. Lady Mac begins to cry aloud. She throws her arms across Macbeth's lap, buries her head in them—her body wraked with sobs and moans as curtains close. (opp. p. 33)

Emotionally worn, she has not only tried to protect him, but has listened as he rejected her advice. The chasm between her and the witches has widened. "How say'st thou, that Macduff denies his person / At our great bidding?" (127–28), he asks. Replying with a question, "Did you send to him, sir?" (128) she implies that his oversuspiciousness will lead to the treacherous mental condition she has just witnessed. In this short speech, her language has shifted in form and tone, marking a change in their relationship. The declarative sentence, so characteristic of her earlier speeches, has been replaced by the interrogative, while the "sir" emphasizes the distance between them and her sense of being his inferior—a woman in a man's world. He both answers her and rejects the advice suggested by her question:

> I hear it by the way; but I will send.
> There's not a one of them but in his house
> I keep a servant fee'd.

Without a break, he continues:

> I will to-morrow
> (And betimes I will) to the weird sisters.

More shall they speak; for now I am bent to know,
By the worst means, the worst.

(129–34)

Although claiming he wants to know the worst, he expects supportive advice from the witches in contrast with the negative criticism he hears in his wife's question. She would help him adjust to his new role without pursuing further crime, but her comforting leads him elsewhere.

This is the last time we see Lady Macbeth sane. Ironically, her closing line—"You lack the season of all natures, sleep" (140)—stresses her role as nurturer, concerned for her husband's welfare, and as wife, suggesting bed, sleep, and sexual closeness. She has never been "unsexed."

Thomas Davies reports Mrs. Pritchard's performance in the role:

> Mrs. Pritchard shewed admirable art in endeavouring to hide Macbeth's frenzy from the observation of the guests, by drawing their attention to conviviality. She smiled on one, whispered to another, and distantly saluted a third; in short she practised every possible artifice to hide the transaction that passed between her husband and the vision his disturbed imagination had raised. Her reproving and angry looks, which glanced towards Macbeth, at the same time were mixed with marks of inward vexation and uneasiness. When, at last, as if unable to support her feelings any longer, she rose from her seat, and seized his arm, and, with a half-whisper of terror, said, "Are you a Man!" she assumed a look of such anger, indignation, and contempt, as cannot be surpassed. (II.105–6)

Unfortunately, the review fails to indicate the limitations of that acting text. Lady Macbeth had disappeared from both the "discovery" scene and the joint invitation to Banquo—in other words the scene where Macbeth gives orders to the murderers. Nor did Mrs. Pritchard's Lady hear Macbeth's directive "Let your remembrance apply to Banquo" (III.ii.30) since it was excised.[22] Reduced, the role moved immediately from conspirator—encouraging her husband to murder—to disconsolate wife—distanced from that husband—the brief, intermittent steps in her character development omitted.

When she actually disappears from the text, as she does at this point, Shakespeare interposes other women characters to contrast with and illuminate the enclosing male world. Lady Macduff, also mortal and alone, contributes dramatic commentary on the wife who uncritically supports her husband's ventures. Suggesting the differences among women in a patriarchal society, she raises questions about the meaning of individuality. The witches, functioning in groups, emphasize the schism between mortal and nonmortal. Lacking conscience and delighting in strange incantations, they hold the power of ambiguous prophecy.

Sequentially, their scene, an interlude with witches who exude confidence, immediately contrasts with the emotional close of the banquet. Whether the director follows the text to the Hecate scene, or bows to critical skepticism about its authenticity and jumps ahead to the apparitions scene that opens act 4, the witches' exuberance contrasts with Lady Macbeth's insecurity and mental exhaustion.[23] Audiences cannot miss the direct comparison. The Hecate scene allows for music, dancing witches, and the theatrical whisking off of Hecate in a chariot—a great release from the tensions of the banquet. The apparitions scene too provides a contrast, in this case ironic, between the banquet just concluded and the one in preparation for Macbeth's arrival. Chanting their magic formulas, these hags—weird, or weyward, sisters—throw toad, fillet of fenny snake, eye of newt, and toe of frog, among other goodies, into the boiling cauldron.

How do these otherworldly women affect our responses to Lady Macbeth? Do they isolate her or illuminate her more human and therefore more fallible qualities? Peter Stallybrass observes that "witchcraft in *Macbeth* . . . is not simply a reflection of a pre-given order of things: rather, it is a particular working upon, and legitimation of the hegemony of patriarchy" (190). Stallybrass is referring to the inclusion of witches in the play and their function in relation to Macbeth. In addition, the witches also relate to Lady Macbeth and the theatrical transformation of characters from text to stage. When the witches become dancing, singing choruses, losing their fiendlike qualities, they reflect societal attitudes of actor-managers and directors. The "hegemony of patriarchy" then manifests itself in productions isolating Lady Macbeth as the play's most terrifying female.

Unconcerned about the textual skewing that might result, however, or perhaps convinced of Lady Macbeth's total viciousness, these actor-managers not only developed the tradition of dancing, singing witches but also found approval from audiences and editors. A note in Bell's edition (1773), for example, lauds ending the third act with musical witches, believing this gives "the piece much more spirit and propriety, than the form in which *Shakespeare* left

Concentrating on Macbeth and the witches in the lower section of the page, this eighteenth-century book illustration captures the eeriness of the apparitions scene as the immense upper space is filled with a snake, a bat, and flying trees against a dark background while the moon seems to belong to the real world beyond.
Courtesy of the Folger Shakespeare Library.

it" (44). It had become an extravanganza with a symphony accompanying Hecate "whilst . . . [she] place[d] herself in the machine"
before announcing "Now I go, and now I fly" (45) to a huge troop of
dancing witches. The comment at the bottom of the page applauds:

> The Third Act, though rather laboured, and made up of unnatural
> circumstances, is, when well performed, extremely entertaining; and
> the witches conclude it, both respecting what they speak and sing,
> excellently. (45)

The Folio's "Song within: 'come away, come away' etc." provided
the rationale for inserting additional songs. Not until Irving's earlier
(1875) production did they temporarily disappear. However, Irving
sought success as well as authenticity. By 1888 he had reversed
himself, explaining in his Preface:

> When this tragedy was represented at the Lyceum in 1875, Locke's
> music was omitted altogether, including his setting of the two songs,
> "Come away," and "Black Spirits and White." The introduction of
> this music into Shakespeare's tragedy has been the subject of much
> animadversion from critics any time during the last hundred years or
> more; but as far as regards the two songs mentioned, we find these
> clearly indicated in the First Folio edition of Shakespeare's works
> (1623). (5)

Skepticism about the scene's authenticity remains, however, even
while directors recognize its theatrical value in counterbalancing
the close of the banquet. Among those in the twentieth century,
Margaret Webster (1941) and Glen Byam Shaw (1955), for example,
excise the Hecate scene but retain the emotional contrast by following the tradition of jumping ahead to the next witch scene (IV.i).
Responding to a theatrical demand, such excision minimizes the
play's growing darkness. The brief intervening scene between Lennox and a lord records the rumblings in the land as Macbeth's
popularity wanes (III.vi).[24] On the other hand, directors like Peter
Hall have been more reluctant to discard Hecate, finding the scene's
structural validity too great to overlook:

> I don't take the view that the Hecate scenes are corrupt, or that Hecate
> should not be played. She gives metaphorical presence to God, or
> rather, anti-God. This is essential to the dramatic action, like the later
> Shakespearian masque world, the arrival of Jupiter or Diana. What
> happens is that the real old women release supernatural evil through

the actions of Macbeth; they have put into his mind something which is already there, and this becomes totally visible in the play. (242)

In this interview with John Russell Brown, Hall not only confirms Irving's argument for the scene's authenticity but also questions its removal simply because of the difficulty in staging and interpretation (243). Finding the verse "odd and mesmeric," Hall believes it was "deliberately primitive, drawing on folk tradition of riddles, spells, incantations, nursery rhymes" (243). For this director, Hecate removes the "static nature" in "the development of the characters of the witches" (244). Hall then continues, offering a metaphysical analysis:

> Whereas when Hecate is played the supernatural releases in Macbeth what he already wants, what he knows already; and he releases cosmic evil in the world which is given metaphorical shape in the presence of Hecate who provides this coven of mad old women with a baccanalia they have never dreamt of. (244)

Obviously Hall's witches would have a different theatrical presence than those of the eighteenth and nineteenth centuries.

Despite questions of the Hecate scenes' authenticity, the witches and their prophecies are integral to *Macbeth*. Although some critics consider the scenes more effective in the study than in the theater (Bradley, 284), the apparitions scene (IV.i) when well staged, can be eerie and frightening, presenting a doomed, trapped Macbeth. Irrational, demanding, and bewitched, he is so caught up in the reality of the experience that after the witches vanish he turns to the entering Lennox and asks, "Saw you the weird sisters?" (IV.i.136). But they are visible only to Macbeth, who then receives the news that Macduff has fled to England. Again coincidence confirms the truth of the prediction. Macbeth orders:

> Seize upon Fife, give to th' edge o' th' sword
> His wife, his babes, and all unfortunate souls
> That trace him in his line.
>
> (151–53)

His irrational fears of Macduff, expressed near the close of the banquet scene, have acquired reality. Lady Macduff will die.

And thus another woman enters the play. Functioning as a voice of reasonableness, in contrast with Macbeth's irrationality in the previous scene, and a voice of independence, in contrast with Lady Macbeth's moral confusion, Lady Macduff also exemplifies the woman who questions her husband's actions. To some in the audience she may have evoked thoughts of independent women in contemporary culture, who questioned existing male patterns of behavior. Protesting her husband's flight, she debates its wisdom. The crescendo reached at the close of the previous scene falls away before the peace and calm and normalcy of Lady Macduff's castle.

The scene opens with an exchange between Lady Macduff and Rosse, who has brought her news of her husband's flight. "What had he done, to make him fly the land?" (IV.ii.1), she asks, wondering what crime he might have committed. Refusing to answer directly, Rosse offers a palliative instead, "You must have patience" (2). It fails to satisfy her. This directive to women often serves as a litmus test in Shakespeare's plays, directing our sympathies. Although patience may have been extolled as a virtue in the Renaissance for both men and women, "patience" as recommended for women in several plays seems to translate into passivity and inaction. Octavia, for example, in *Antony and Cleopatra*, advised by Caesar to "Be ever known to patience" (*Ant.*, III.vi.98), follows his advice. We as audience then dismiss her, dismayed by her lack of initiative. Again, in *Much Ado About Nothing*, Hero, in contrast with Beatrice, tends to accept male decisions. Audiences prefer the outspoken Beatrice. On the other hand, Shakespeare does prescribe patience in the case of Lear, for example, where it contrasts with irascibility and hotheadedness.

The women characters who most win our sympathy and respect insist on reasoning for themselves. Lady Macduff belongs in this group. In a play where a wife's major concern has been to help her husband reach his goal, Lady Macduff questions her husband's value system, unwilling to accept his power of reasoning over her own. When Rosse insists, "You know not / Whether it was his wisdom or his fear" (IV.ii.4–5), she creates the metaphor of the birds in the nest, protected by the parent, then accuses:

> All is the fear, and nothing is the love;
> As little is the wisdom, where the flight
> So runs against all reason.

(12–14)

She perceives flight as characterizing both fear and lack of reason when it endangers family, no matter what the ultimate goal may be. Goals do not excuse morally insupportable immediate actions. After arguing with Rosse, she then turns to her son: "Sirrah, your father's dead, / And what will you do now? How will you live?" (30–31) beginning a stychomythic pattern of debate between them. Although we know and the son believes that his father is not dead, the speech underlines the positiveness of her conviction. Ultimately, this scene not only illustrates Macbeth's growing bloodthirstiness, since it ends in the murder of Lady Macduff and her children, but it also presents a strong woman of independent mind and moral principles who offers a sophisticated contrast with the play's other women.

Just as Emilia and Iago provide a marital pattern against which Desdemona and Othello may be more sharply drawn, in this play Lady Macduff illustrates those qualities that highlight Lady Macbeth's deficiencies.[25] An innocent victim of the spiraling immorality of which Lady Macbeth was equally guilty with Macbeth, Lady Macduff is not, however, an innocent, naive, unknowing woman. Nor need an innocent victim of murder be a naive "innocent," as the Holocaust and all mass murders by tyrants have illustrated over history. In presenting Lady Macduff in theatrical context, therefore, the director must resist the stereotypes surrounding "victim" and "woman," while exploring the nuances of the text.

Unfortunately, the scene has frequently been excised either for its bloodiness or lack of drama. The Dramatic Censor's comment offers a clue to the general early reaction:

> Here Shakespeare, as if the vigorous exertion of his faculties, in the preceding scene, required relaxation, has given us a most trifling superfluous dialogue, between Lady Macduff, Rosse, and her son, merely that another murder may be committed, on the stage too. We heartily concur in, and approve of, striking out the greatest part of it. (1773, p. 51)

But the scene is much more than a trifling dialogue and an excuse for on-stage murders. It tells us a good deal about concepts of manliness and womanliness, and even more, the sense of self that a woman, as a well as a man, must have. Throughout, Lady Macduff, by thinking for herself, is aware that she fails to conform. Alone with her children after Rosse's departure, she next receives a hasty message to fly. In her response to the warning, her speech analyzes the rewards of doing good.[26] Having protested "I have done no harm," she then comments:

> But I remember now
> I am in this earthly world—where to do harm
> Is often laudable, to do good sometime
> Accounted dangerous folly. Why then, alas,
> Do I put up that womanly defense,
> To say I have done no harm?
>
> (74–79)

This is not the speech of an innocent, naive woman, who believes virtue is rewarded and sin condemned, as the Shaw prompt-book suggests:

> Lady Macduff is a *simple sweet* woman, she *cannot understand* how her husband could possibly leave her and his children without even saying "Goodbye" & go to a foreign country. Ross tries to calm her & explain, but it is no good. Her *instinct* as a mother tells her that her family is in great danger. (p. 174, emphasis added)

Rather than examining Lady Macduff's lines closely, Shaw "instinctively" reacts to a woman who contrasts with Lady Macbeth, drawing on a stereotype. In other words, if a woman is a conspirator in murder—a "wicked" woman—her opposite must fulfill all the societal definitions of a "good" woman, not least among these is that women react by instinct rather than reason. Twice in that brief description we find the disparagement of a woman's mental ability, first in the description that she is incapable of "understanding" and later in the reference to instinct.

In the particular section cited above, Lady Macduff also speaks of "womanliness," recognizing that such a defense will be of little value to her. Here Shakespeare presents a direct contrast with Lady Macbeth who, to protect her husband from himself, almost fainted—either a purposefully womanly action or an unconscious one. Lady Macduff rejects such devices. Her lines are reminiscent of Hermione's who, when accused, says,

> I am not prone to weeping, as our sex
> Commonly are, the want of which vain dew
> Perchance shall dry your pities; but I have
> That honorable grief lodg'd here which burns
> Worse than tears drown.
>
> (*The Winter's Tale*, II.i.108–12)

Hermione will not stoop to weeping although aware of its effectiveness in evoking sympathy. She expects reason and reasonableness to move her husband. Because of her role in the play, criticism has seldom considered her a character without understanding and lacking in the ability to reason, but has applied other stereotypes, frequently removing her from the human realm.[27]

Although Lady Macduff's plight differs from Hermione's and her role is far more brief, even here Shakespeare's characterization goes beyond the simple portrait. Unfortunately, audiences have seldom seen Lady Macduff; even fewer have witnessed her murder. The 1773 Bell text, for example, although retaining the opening conversation between Lady Macduff and Rosse, excises the exchange between mother and son [beginning "Sirrah, your father's dead" (IV.ii.30)—including their debate about traitors—] and closes the scene with the messenger's warning to fly [and her response beginning "Whither should I fly?"] (73). It ends before the murderers enter. Indeed, throughout most of the eighteenth and nineteenth centuries and even into the beginning of the twentieth, the practice of cutting went further. Some acting versions excised the entire scene.[28] Not until well into the twentieth century was Lady Macduff restored to stage versions.[29]

Occasionally, however, she was victim to the other distortion that occurred: adding text so that Lady Macbeth and Lady Macduff come face to face. Both Davenant, in the seventeenth century, and Welles, in the twentieth, saw a close relationship between the two women. Davenant presents them as direct opposites—one conspiratorial, the other open, honest, and supportive of her husband, thus violating the portrait of Lady Macduff in Shakespeare's play.

In contrast to William Davenant, Orson Welles presents a more complicated relationship between the women. Particularly in the scene immediately preceding the murder of Lady Macduff and her children, Welles suggests a contrast for Lady Macbeth between "what is" (her own guilt) and "what might have been" (the innocent delight of a mother in her son). Visiting Lady Macduff in her quarters, Lady Macbeth listens smilingly to her guest's young son, then participates in the debate on traitors, Welles giving her some of Lady Macduff's lines. This incongruous distortion of the text has its roots in an earlier scene when Lady Macduff bids a warm farewell to Macduff before he hastily departs on horseback immediately after Duncan's murder, leaving her behind at Macbeth's castle. Little remains to suggest a woman who totally disapproves of her husband's flight, questioning his wisdom. Finally, as Welles develops the scene, a direct correlation exists between the murders of Lady Macduff with her children and Lady Macbeth's later illness and suicide.

The more common treatment of the Lady Macduff scene in the theater, however, is excision. Examining the skewed text that results offers additional insights into Lady Macduff's role within the play. First of all, her absence alters audience response to the Malcolm-Macduff confrontation that immediately follows. In the full text, audiences or readers share information still unknown to the characters on stage and therefore anxiously watch Macduff and listen, wondering how he will react to the news. Malcolm's question therefore has particular poignancy and relevance:

> Why in that rawness left you wife and child,
> Those precious motives, those strong knots of love,
> Without leave-taking? I pray you,
> Let not my jealousies be your dishonors,
> But mine own safeties.
>
> (IV.iii.26–30)

Repeating in a slightly different form the question asked by Lady Macduff, Malcolm meets a similar indirect answer:

> Bleed, bleed, poor country!
> Great tyranny, lay thou thy basis sure,
> For goodness dare not check thee.
>
> (31–33)

Macduff disappoints us. Because of what we have seen, we expect more. But perhaps Shakespeare is intentionally creating a flawed hero so as to raise questions about moral actions, particularly questions of degree, since he is comparing Macbeth and Macduff as well as their wives, who never meet. Lady Macduff's earlier query resonates in Malcolm's words, contributing to that comparison. When, as has frequently occurred, actor-managers and directors excise this exchange, attempting to present an unambiguously noble hero, the text's subtleties are lost.[30] These scenes suggest the variable standards men and women apply when making decisions and illustrate the questionable morality of choosing politics over family.[31]

With the Lady Macduff scene cut, however, comparisons are lost and the dynamics of sequential scenes altered. In the reconfigured sequence where the Malcolm scene immediately follows Macbeth's vow to surprise Macduff's castle and murder "His wife, his babes, and all unfortunate souls / That trace him in his line" (IV.i.152–53), the political becomes primary. Not having seen the murders or known about them, the audience has no mixed feelings about Macduff and his desertion of family. Rather than reacting ambiguously to him because he's comfortably alive in England while his wife and children have just been murdered in Scotland, audiences sympathize with him, delighted at his skill in eluding capture. Of course, the suspense that Shakespeare injects into the play, differing from the source material where Macduff knows of the murders before going to Malcolm, affects audience involvement in the outcome.

For over a hundred years, therefore, the contrast between Macbeth's superstitious irrationality and Lady Macduff's rationalism was replaced by the image of antityranny rising up against the tyrant.[32] "Let us seek out some desolate shade, and there / Weep our sad bosoms empty" (IV.iii.1–2), Malcolm begins. The calm and peace of these words—their desolation—contrast with the intensity and fury of Macbeth's scene with the witches in this altered sequence. Such a version of the play then has primarily to do with men, witches, and one evil, demonic woman. But Shakespeare's work does not.

Women, their lives, their responses, their value systems are an integral part of the drama. By the late nineteenth century, critics were beginning to realize the flaw in stage productions resulting from the excision of Lady Macduff. Countering the comments of the Dramatic Censor a century earlier, many of those critics quoted in the *New Variorum* note the distorted reactions that result. Fletcher, for example, observes:

> It mars the whole spirit and moral of the play, to take anything from that depth and liveliness of interest which the dramatist has attached to the characters and fortunes of Macduff and his Lady. (267)

The critic feels that recounting the deaths does not do justice to the portraits Shakespeare develops through dialogue in the previous scene. Worse, the excision weakens audience hostility to Macbeth, presenting a "false notion" of the dramatist's aim in creating "this most gratuitously criminal of his heroes." Fletcher calls this a "narrowing" of the theatrical space and "weakening of . . . interest" in the virtuous characters meant "to move" audience sympathies. Bodenstedt, another commentator, observes that the scene's absence diminishes "the force of Macduff's cry of agony" and, later, of "Lady Macbeth's heart-piercing question in the sleep-walking scene" (267–68).

The excision of Lady Macduff also further isolates the Queen and eliminates the repetition of a pattern of loneliness characterizing women's existence in that society. Finally, it is not simply the actual murders themselves that move us so deeply but the fact that Lady Macduff—a mere sketch, but one drawn with expert lines—provides an inkling of the potential for a strong, independent woman. Reporting the deaths cannot match this.

By presenting her murder on stage after creating that intimate portrait of mother and child, Shakespeare raises questions about Macduff, human priorities, and war. His unconcern about his family and his rationalizations forgiving Malcolm's gross vices arouse ambivalent responses. Although disgust with Malcolm begins Macduff's redemption for the audience, the intensity of his reaction to the murders wins us. We hear his repeated queries about his wife and children. His famous lines, "What, all my pretty chickens, and their dam, / At one fell swoop?" (IV.iii.218–19) with its echoes of Lady Macduff's earlier bird analogy suggest a subtext of unity and empathy between husband and wife. Finally, his reaction to the directive "Dispute it like a man" (220) with "But I must also feel it as a man" (221) provides a clear contrast with Macbeth, as criticism has generally noted in its analysis of manliness in this scene. Less frequently noted has been the ease with which that "unmanliness" has been converted to an acceptable reaction when he asserts:

> O, I could play the woman with mine eyes,
> And braggart with my tongue! But, gentle heavens,
> Cut short all intermission. Front to front
> Bring thou this fiend of Scotland and myself;
> Within my sword's length set him; if he scape,
> Heaven forgive him too!
>
> (230–35)

Although we have heard Lady Macduff reject a "womanly defence," which includes tears, Macduff relies on a stereotype before converting his mourning to anger and a passion for revenge.

If Shakespeare questions the accepted definitions for manliness and womanliness in the major characters, he also extends this skepticism to Malcolm. Multiple excisions occur in the exchanges between him and Macduff, altering the portrait of the young prince and reshaping him into a more traditional male hero. Thus his line "I am yet / Unknown to woman"(125–26) always disappears from the stage along with the list of most of his vices. Although the concept of the purity of a prince may have been the ideal in the Renaissance, the line seems to tarnish the image of the ideal hero in the theater.[33] Glen Byam Shaw, for example, believed the script dictated an effete man. Despite the protest of the actor playing the role, the excision's universality suggests that Shaw's point of view has generally prevailed.[34] With Malcolm's self-denigrating admissions of vice gone, Macduff's many rationalizations excusing the young prince become unnecessary. A purer Macduff emerges as directors opt for easy contrasts of black and white, good and bad, rather than the shades of grey this play explores: the varying standards of morality for men and women and the limits on those standards for human action.

In the next scene, a somnambulant Lady Macbeth reveals those limits, exposing a tortured mind. Vivid visual images introduce the Queen long before she appears; an anxious Gentlewoman and a skeptical Doctor, having waited two nights in vain to see Lady Macbeth sleepwalking, engage in conversation. The woman reports:

> I have seen her rise from her bed, throw her night-gown upon her, unlock her closet, take forth paper, fold it, write upon't, read it, afterwards seal it, and again return to bed; yet all this while in a most fast sleep. (V.i.4–8)

Observing that such conduct would seem to indicate "A great perturbation in nature"(9), the Doctor would know more, "What, at any time, have you heard her say?" (12–13). But the woman refuses to answer. She will report what she has seen, not what she has heard. This he, and by extension, the audience, must discover for themselves. Compared with the ambiguity surrounding Lady Macbeth's faint, this scene is hedged with specificity.

Suddenly she appears: "Lo you, here she comes!" (19), announces the Gentlewoman. We know we will see the Queen in a nightgown with eyes open but mind asleep. Nevertheless, the woman confirms it. When the Doctor ventures, "her eyes are open," the woman quickly responds, "Ay, but their sense are shut" (24–25). Rubbing her hands but still not speaking, Lady Macbeth seems to be performing in dumb show. "What is it she does now?"(26) asks the

Doctor. The audience must have no question about the nature of the action. Nor must the performer be uncertain about what to do. Little is left for the director to change, only the manner of interpretation—but not the fact of the action. "Look, how she rubs her hands" (26–27), the Doctor continues. "It is an accustom'd action" (28), his informant volunteers, "I have known her continue in this a quarter of an hour" (29–30).

When finally she speaks, she begins as if in midsentence, "Yet here's a spot," followed by the more explicit and tortuous, "Out, damn'd spot! out, I say!"(31, 35). Her crimes then spill forth. References to bloodstained hands intermingle with incriminating self-revelation, horrifying the Doctor. Speaking in staccatolike sentences, she blurts out all those perturbations of nature that fight within her. "Will these hands ne'er be clean?" (43). And again, "Here's the smell of blood still. All the perfumes of Arabia will not sweeten this little hand" (50–51). Stage directions by the two observers give form and substance to Lady Macbeth's words, "Oh, oh, oh!"(52). "What a sigh is there!"(53) notes the astonished Doctor, sympathy beginning to overcome his earlier reaction. As critics have often noted, Lady Macbeth's constant reference to her hands, to their diminutive size, and her wish for perfume, are peculiarly feminine. But intermingled are lines reminding us of her ambition for power for her husband: "What need we fear who knows it, when none can call our pow'r to accompt?" (37–39). Through the joint venture of wife with husband she would erase the self-hatred she feels as a woman.

Nevertheless, the womanliness she would deny bursts forth in her sleepwalking and so too does her sense of woman's non-personhood. Expressed earlier as scorn, it emerges here in a cry of anguish through language stressing woman's anonymity. "The Thane of Fife had a wife; where is she now?" (42–43), Lady Macbeth cries out in that haunting line in rhyme. Critics may argue that it implicates Lady Macbeth in the murder. More pertinently, it illuminates her perception of women. For, while she refers to Duncan as "the old man" and "Banquo" by his name, she refers to Lady Macduff by function. She is merely "a wife," the indefinite article reaffirming Lady Macbeth's belief in women's non-importance in this man's world. Ironically, it is through language that the two women, carefully kept in separate spheres, are finally joined and compared. Lady Macbeth's query might also be one about herself. "The Thane of Cawdor had a wife; where is she now?" Striving to function only as wife, she has lost her moral bearings but is alive. Lady Macduff, on the other hand, lost her life, but her standards of human action remained intact. Moreover, she also provides a point of comparison not only for Lady Macbeth but also for Macduff, whom Shakespeare is presenting as an imperfect hero, but a hero nonetheless, to counter the infamy of a tyrant.

Although Lady Macbeth and the play's other women never appear again, they pervade its closing scenes in haunting ways.[35] Lady Macduff's death further motivates her husband to war. Macbeth's concern for his wife's illness juxtaposed against belief in the witches' predictions drive him, illuminating his state of mind. The forest moves and the skills of a doctor fail to cure that "dearest partner of greatness" (I.v.12). Finally, when the antagonists first meet, echoes of Lady Macbeth's "The Thane of Fife had a wife; where is she now?" reverberate in Macbeth's refusal to fight Macduff, admitting, "my soul is too much charg'd / With blood of thine already" (V.viii.5–6).

Brief scenes move us back and forth between the camps, much as they do in *Antony and Cleopatra*, one camp showing us men on the march, the other a man wrestling with defeat. Scene 2 with Malcolm's forces mentions Macduff's passion for revenge for his wife's death while also advancing the theme of infection and its cure. Like the later conversation between the Doctor and Macbeth, this one too contains inverted construction that has challenged commentators. The specific reference occurs in a speech by Cathness, a nobleman of Scotland fighting with Malcolm's forces:

> Well, march we on
> To give obedience where 'tis truly ow'd.
> Meet we the med'cine of the sickly weal,
> And with him pour we, in our country's purge,
> Each drop of us.
>
> (V.ii.25–29)

The word *med'cine* creates the problem since, as Muir notes in his edition, "Shakespeare usually uses it in the sense of drug" (149). Here, however, it seems to mean "doctor" just as it does in *All's Well That Ends Well* where Lafeu in speaking of Helena's gifts says, "I have seen a medicine / That's able to breathe life into a stone" (II.i.72–73) and then continues clearly attaching the word to the skills of a person, a doctor. In the speech above by Cathness, the reference to "him" (28) refers to Malcolm. Thus the general meaning is that we will meet Malcolm, who will function as a doctor. Joining him in battle, we will pour our blood to purge the country of its sickness. I stress the ambiguity here because in the next example it has a more far-reaching effect on our understanding of Macbeth's reaction to his wife's death.

The critical passages occur when the Doctor discusses Lady Macbeth's illness with her husband (V.iii). However, Shakespeare sets the background earlier, during the sleepwalking scene, where the outline of the Doctor's character emerges. Watching Lady Macbeth, he reacts with a range of responses from astonishment, "Do you mark that?" (V.i.41) to a reprimand mixed with a sense of fear, "Go to, go to; you have known what you should not" (46–47), to sympathy, "The heart is sorely charg'd" (53–54), to a longing to escape this place and charge, "This disease is beyond my practice" (59)—and yet, reacting like a doctor—to a wish to project optimism, "yet I have known those which have walk'd in their sleep who have died holily in their beds" (59–61), and finally to compassion, "God, God, forgive us all!" (75), a line frequently excised.

Having heard what he should not, he must respond in scene 3 to questions about his patient asked by her husband, a tyrannical figure, and—obvious to the Doctor now—a murderer. Once again the dramatist reveals a knowledge of the psychology of people. Doctors generalize; doctors speak in platitudes; doctors try to promise without promising. Such are the answers Macbeth receives to his questions about his wife. "How does your patient, Doctor?" (iii.37), he asks amid preparations for battle, his two major concerns alternating in his mind. Carefully the Doctor responds:

> Not so sick, my Lord,
> As she is troubled with thick-coming fancies,
> That keep her from her rest.
>
> (37–39)

No need to be more specific. In the immediately following speech, Macbeth, expanding on the Doctor's analysis, begs for help:

> Cure [her] of that.
> Canst thou not minister to a mind diseas'd,
> Pluck from the memory a rooted sorrow,
> Raze out the written troubles of the brain,
> And with some sweet oblivious antidote

Cleanse the stuff'd bosom of that perilous stuff
Which weighs upon the heart?

(39–45)

A concerned husband amplifies his request. He knows the haunting thoughts that remain for both his wife and himself, and therefore can draw on that knowledge. This speech, however, addresses the question of a "mind diseased." And here Lady Macbeth is the subject.

Wisely and carefully, the Doctor generalizes, "Therein the patient / Must minister to *himself*" (45–46, emphasis added), using the generic "he." Macbeth's "that" (39) in the above speech refers back to those "thick-coming fancies" (38) and ahead to the rest of the speech. He is asking the Doctor to "Pluck from the memory a rooted sorrow" that the King knows troubles his wife. Although he too has inner demons, he still feels capable of combatting them. His wife, however, has fallen. The ambiguous word is "himself," which is sometimes interpreted as gender specific, applying only to Macbeth. Such a reading, however, seems to skew the text, altering the focus away from Lady Macbeth and, despite the intensity of the language, suggesting Macbeth's indifference to his wife's condition.

On stage, interpretations of the Doctor in this scene have varied from Shaw's, describing the Doctor as "fawning" and "timid," provoking "scorn from Macbeth and from us" (156) to notes in a Tyrone Power promptbook attributing insight to the Doctor and creating in him a stern voice of moral judgment. At the words, "That keep her from her rest," the writer observes:

He's looking straight into Macbeth's eyes, & the King regards him curiously, a query is in his mind "Does this man know,—he has attended her during her entire illness, those long hours of fever and restlessness when the body and the tongue spoke." . . . The physician is brave & truthful, and no doubt as good a physician as he was a man. (*Mac* 34)

As well as revealing the intensity and passion of Macbeth's plea for help for his wife, this exchange also acts as a prelude to the announcement of Lady Macbeth's death. The hopelessness and incurability of her illness are implicit in the Doctor's reply and will help explain Macbeth's tone of resignation when he later receives news of her death. Failing to connect that speech with this scene has led some critics to consider Macbeth an unfeeling husband. In context, the Doctor's previous observation of Lady Macbeth, the audience's exposure to her illness, and, therefore, surely Macbeth's awareness of it, all argue for her being the primary subject of a conversation between a doctor and the husband of his patient. Linking the sleepwalking scene with that reporting her death, the Doctor's comments thus forebodingly anticipate the future.

Macbeth's reaction to the Doctor's equivocal, and in Lady Macbeth's case useless, answer is a violent "Throw physic to the dogs, I'll none of it" (47). In fury and disgust, he changes the subject, commenting that the Thanes fly from him. But then, unwilling to think that nothing can be done for his wife, he begins again:

> If thou couldst, Doctor, cast
> The water of my land, find her disease,
> And purge it to a sound and pristine health,
> I would applaud thee to the very echo,
> That should applaud again.
>
> (50–54)

Applying the lines to Lady Macbeth, they appear to mean, "If you could, Doctor, look through the waters of my land for a cure, find my wife's disease [the words *cast* and *find* functioning as two verbs in series], and purge that disease out of her, bringing her to health." Although some critics, intent on tracing Macbeth's development, and far less interested in Lady Macbeth, have suggested that he is really thinking about himself here and asking for help in curing his kingdom of its ills, contextually, the lines seem to pursue his original intention, the hope for a cure for Lady Macbeth. For many, the word *cast* and the phrase *cast the water of my land* present the problem. However, a glance at the *OED* reveals pages on the varied meanings of *cast*.[36] Macbeth's anger had led him to change the subject temporarily to his other major concern, war, before returning again to Lady Macbeth. While it is true that earlier in the scene he spoke desolately of what he had lost, "honor, love, obedience, troops of friends, / I must not look to have" (25–26), and despaired "I have liv'd long enough" (22), he has also showed no interest in other people's ideas about how to win a war. "Bring me no more reports / . . . The mind I sway by, and the heart I bear, / Shall never sag with doubt, nor shake with fear" (1, 9–10), he warned the messenger. It seems unlikely, therefore, that he, a military leader, would consider asking a doctor to bring peace to his land.[37]

In many ways, the speech beginning "Throw physic to the dogs" illustrates Shakespeare's technique for showing a troubled mind, exploited later on in Leontes's speeches in *The Winter's Tale.* In staccatolike fashion, Macbeth moves from subject to subject pouring out his many conflicting and seemingly disorganized thoughts. He progresses from that intense response to the Doctor to the order "put mine armour on"; to the simple commentary "Doctor, the Thanes fly from me"; back to the subject of his wife; to the order to pull off some article of clothing. And then, thinking of the battle about to occur and caught in the medical reference to his wife, he combines the two as he wonders what "rhubarb, cyme or what purgative drug" could rid him of the English.

References to the witches, too, enter the conversation. No longer thought of in secret, they now offer Macbeth his single hope. Remembering their elusive promise of invulnerability, he boasts:

> Till Birnan wood remove to Dunsinane
> I cannot taint with fear. What's the boy Malcolm?
> Was he not born of woman? The spirits that know
> All mortal consequences have pronounc'd me thus:
> "Fear not, Macbeth, no man that's born of woman
> Shall e'er have power upon thee."
>
> (2–7)

At this moment the scene seems to alternate between the mortal wife and the otherworldly "all knowing" weird sisters, whose prophecies permit him to combat the reality that surrounds him— the frightened messenger and the flight of the Thanes. But for that other reality, his wife's illness, he can find no answers, no easy bromides. The Doctor's diagnosis offers neither hope nor solace; and to the witches, the Queen is irrelevant. Mortal, she will not survive as they do. Rather, the scene crystallizes the differences between them, reminding Macbeth of the fallible human world he too inhabits.

Above the din of the drums as soldiers are preparing for war, above the sounds of shouting, Macbeth hears a noise, not an imagined noise, but the cry of women. Again explicit stage directions arise from the text as he describes the quality of that sound: "The time has been, my senses would have cool'd / To hear a night-shriek" (v.10–11). Continuing, his lines take us back to act 1, when he wondered why his hair stood on end. Here in act 5, he recollects only that in those earlier times, "my fell of hair / Would at a dismal treatise rouse and stir / As life were in't" (11–13). And then he receives the not-unexpected news: "The Queen, my Lord, is dead" (16). Macbeth considers the options in his famous speech:

> She should have died hereafter;
> There would have been a time for such a word.
> To-morrow, and to-morrow, and to-morrow,
> Creeps in this petty pace from day to day,
> To the last syllable of recorded time;
> And all our yesterdays have lighted fools
> The way to dusty death.
>
>   (17–23)

Although critics have debated the exact meaning of "hereafter," no one questions the mood conveyed: that of weariness and desolation and of the endlessness of living with the sin of murder. Lady Macbeth's death reinforces his sense of his own mortality. Another time, perhaps even another life, would have been better. Compared with Macduff's highly emotional reaction to news of his wife's murder, Macbeth's response seems cool, distant, and resigned. But how different the circumstances. Unlike Lady Macduff, murdered with all her faculties intact, murdered in cold blood, her children with her, and her husband absent, Lady Macbeth's husband is present and has been concerned, frustrated at the futility of seeking a cure, and aware that if it lies only in the patient's ability to cure herself, then no cure exists, morally, but death for complicity in murder.

When finally Macbeth and Macduff come face to face, thoughts of the women once more impinge on the play: the witches through the ironic fullfillment of their prophecy, and Lady Macduff through the men's recollections of her—one seeking revenge, the other intent on avoiding yet another murder, humanized perhaps by his wife's death. Like a symphony, the women's roles create a pattern throughout the play. The shrill high sounds of the witches introduce the first musical phrase as it develops weaving in and out and reaching intense power before eventually becoming dimmer and dimmer. It forms the frame or overarching melodic line. Lady Macbeth's music enters later, richer, fuller, reaching a crescendo, then stuttering in staccatolike phrases to a close in a wailing minor key. Finally, the briefest span of all, the theme of Lady Macduff, a momentary brightness and singing melodic line enclosed by the other two, all against a background of jarring sounds, passion, and conflict.

Lady Macbeth never gains a sense of self. In the world of *Macbeth* men wield control. Although in the early scenes, she speaks taunt-ingly, she holds no power. Her references to manhood suggest her perception of manliness as equaling power, and conversely of womanliness as equaling powerlessness because clearly the gender holding the power is male. Lady Macduff's brief role further em-phasizes women's powerlessness, even while questioning male wisdom and morality. Thus sexual politics permeates this tragedy.

How does a woman achieve transcendence in a patriarchal soci-ety? Obviously not by limiting her role to that of "accomplice" because, as de Beauvoir suggests, by doing so, a woman doesn't identify, but rather abdicates the right to individuality.[38] On the other hand, Lady Macduff, who, on the surface, appears to have adopted the role of "Other," as wife and mother, rejects the compla-cent acquiescence to this role, challenging the voices of patriarchy, even while acknowledging her powerlessness. In their triumph at the close, the witches, female-identified fiends, reveal the other-worldly possibility for power, in contrast with Lady Macbeth. But because of production history, and more especially the easy acceptance of stereotypical behavior defining women, the witches have frequently functioned as entr' acte entertainment while Lady Macbeth alone has drawn critical condemnation. Perhaps the an-swer lies in a world where men do not impinge. Shakespeare suggests that the closest women come to inhabiting such a world is through an absence of male "keepers"—brothers, husbands, fa-thers. In *Twelfth Night* he creates such a world, but only for a moment, questioning whether it can actually exist.

PART FOUR

Economic World

Helen Hayes as Cesario/Viola listens skeptically as Malvolio, played by Maurice Evans, pompously delivers his message. Their costumes wonderfully define their roles in this 1940 production in New York. Photo from the author's collection from the Artcraft Archives.

CHAPTER SIX

Challenging Conventions

TWELFTH NIGHT

"But if she cannot love you, sir?"
"I cannot be so answer'd."

II.iv.87–88

Endowed with wealth, their lives graced by neither fathers, brothers, husbands, nor lovers, the two major women characters of *Twelfth Night* briefly challenge patterns of patriarchy. Not revolutionaries, but merely young women grasping at suddenly available freedom, each would taste independence in her own way. One retreats behind the garb of mourning for her dead brother while the other, also turning to her supposedly dead brother—her twin—for support, retreats into his persona, adopting his clothes and his pose. Although at the play's end, neither woman achieves her goal, defeated by contemporary conventions surrounding love and matrimony, the dramatist, here, raises questions about women, wealth, power, and conformity, and teases his audience with contradictory evidence.

Shakespeare takes the contemporary debate about women's attire, for example, holds it lightly in his hand, turns it like a multifaceted prism, reflecting and refracting the light, then puts it down, revealing the larger issue that it illuminates: women's independence.[1] With humor and insight, he asks how important is conformity in dress in defining an acceptable woman? Is the woman in breeches really a monster as some of the tracts of the period proclaim because the blurring of fashion could lead to "confusion . . . something that can't be accommodated, a monster" (Shepherd, 1–2)? Or is she related to the tradition of the warrior woman who, like Britomart in Spenser's *Faerie Queene*, fights for virtuous ends

211

(Shepherd, 67)? Denying these extremes and laughing at the debate, the dramatist offers another answer in *Twelfth Night.* In the mode of the modern social scientist, he presents a case and a control, revealing that whether dressed in her own garments—those proper to her sex—or in the borrowed clothes of the other sex, a single woman when young and wealthy faces problems in a patriarchal society, especially if she dares to fall in love and opt for marriage.

Although the play's two major women characters, Viola and Olivia, often have been presented on stage as exact opposites because one wears skirts, the other, breeches, the dramatist has carefully sculpted their roles as parallels—not the wealthy, self-confident, or arrogant Countess in skirts compared with the poor, clever, girl-disguised-as-a-page in breeches, but two bright, literate, young women, each with a sense of herself, each in her own way trying to cope, and each believing she has power. Economic independence and the absence of male authority figures in their families seem to promise self-sovereignty. The play explores the options each woman chooses, the resulting interaction between the two women, and the impact of sexual drives and patriarchal mores on their lives.

And here their difference in attire leads the women into unexpected situations and deflects them on their road to freedom. Disguised as the youth Cesario, Viola wins the heart of the independent Olivia but also, in this disguise, loses her heart to the Duke Orsino. Clothes, rather than freeing her, confine her to silence. In contrast, the woman in skirts forthrightly expresses her desire, overtly pursuing the "youth" Cesario.

As a result, Olivia suffers both in criticism and staging. Since patriarchal values favor the compliant woman over the aggressive one, Viola's breeches, ironically, appear far less threatening than Olivia's decision-making and husband-wooing. By endowing the young women with so many similar attributes with the potential for independence, the dramatist not only explores the limits on that independence for women, but also illuminates what is acceptable and unacceptable in women's behavior.

Even in the twentieth century, acceptable behavior for a young woman has been linked with her loss of independence. According to Simone de Beauvoir, women's "erotic urges" in a male-dominated society cause the problem. She writes of the decision women reach at maturity after having struggled during adolescence with the choice between self as primary and self as "Other." Using the term *subject* to refer to a person's perception of herself as central, or primary, de Beauvoir writes: "For the young woman, . . . there is a contradiction. . . . A conflict breaks out between her original claim to be subject, active, free," and the pressure of "her erotic urges" which dictates that she "accept herself as passive object" (314).[2] In *Twelfth Night* Shakespeare lightly dramatizes the shift in goals for both women. Because this is a comedy, the painfulness of the dilemma is not stressed as it is, for example, in a tragedy such as *Romeo and Juliet,* where Juliet has not yet recognized the necessity to "accept herself as passive object" and struggles to retain her self-sovereignty even while expressing her "erotic urges."[3] Here, in the comedy, Viola says merely, "O time, thou must untangle this, not I, / It is too hard a knot for me t' untie" (II.ii.40–41). But the dramatist's choice of opposite-sex twins, the weakness of Viola's argument for donning disguise, the basic social equality between the two women, and the subsequent hasty desire of each to discard the protective pose she has chosen suggest the applicability of de Beauvoir's comment.

The difference, however, in the ways the two women react to their "erotic urges" explains their "acceptability" in the eyes of critics, directors, and audiences. Unlike Viola, Olivia refuses to perceive herself as "Other," seeking instead to solve her problems by aggressively taking charge. After having claimed fealty to her dead brother's memory and adopting a vow of seven years of mourning, a period meant to discourage all the suitors who do not appeal to her, she then changes her mind about marriage when an attractive young "male" arrives at her door. Still retaining that sense of self as "subject, active, free," she nevertheless pursues Cesario, the disguised Viola. Thus in some ways, Olivia resembles Helena of *All's Well That Ends Well.* But Shakespeare has not only endowed Olivia with freedom, wealth, and power, he has also created an alternative double to her in Viola. Unlike Viola, however, Olivia refuses to leave everything for time "to untangle." Thus, while partially illustrating de Beauvoir's thesis—of the effect of "erotic urges" on women's decision-making—Olivia fails to conform to the properly acceptable behavior for a woman.

Behavior is ultimately more important for society than appearance: the debate on women's dress withers before that larger issue of woman's forwardness. Stage productions and criticism of *Twelfth Night* attack Olivia's violation of conformity in a variety of ways. First, they blur or ignore the many similarities between the women, magnifying Viola's role as a servant, and excising lines indicating her wealth and class. Thus, she becomes the "poor servant girl" as contrasted with the wealthy, aggressive Countess. In criticism, a blatant example of bias appears in William Winter's introduction to Augustin Daly's large souvenir promptbook of the 1893 production of the play. Winter writes that "Viola is Shakespeare's ideal of the patient idolatry and devoted, silent self-sacrifice of perfect love" (5). In contrast, Olivia draws the following comment:

> The poet has emphasized his meaning, furthermore, by the expedient of contrast between the two women. Olivia—self-absorbed, ostentatious in her mourning, acquisitive and voracious in her love, self-willed in her conduct, conventional in her character, physically very beautiful but spiritually insignificant—while she is precisely the sort of woman for whom men go wild, serves but to throw the immeasurable superiority of Viola into stronger relief. (6)

This hardly defines the Olivia whom we meet in the play—the young woman who graciously speaks of Orsino's virtues although she "cannot love him" (I.v.257); who good-naturedly accepts the criticism of her fool; and who even apologizes to the disguised Viola.

Although extreme in its language, Winter's reaction is not isolated. It had both predecessors and successors. Mrs. Inchbald's edition (1808), for example, faults Olivia for another aspect of her behavior, citing the "impudence of women in placing their affections, their happiness, on men younger than themselves" (4). For Inchbald the text itself warns against this in the Duke's words to Viola:

> Let stil the woman take
> An elder than herself; so wears she to him
> So sways she level in her husband's heart, & C
>
> (4–5)

Unfortunately, the editor lifts the speech out of context—a humorous context. The lines occur during a conversation between Duke Orsino and Cesario. Attempting to express herself as a man, Viola describes the person she loves (the Duke) as one "About your years, my lord" (II.iv.28). This leads to his swift reply that Cesario should choose a woman younger than "himself." The humor of the exchange is apparently lost on the indignant editor who even censures

Olivia's treatment of her glum steward, the egocentric, puritanical Malvolio. He, like the Duke, has dreams of marrying her. Misreading his role in the play, Inchbald recommends him:

> It might nevertheless be asked by a partizan (sic) of Malvolio's, whether this credulous steward was much deceived, in imputing a degraded taste, in the sentiments of love, to his fair Lady Olivia as she actually did fall in love with a domestic; and one who, from his extreme youth, was perhaps a greater reproach to her discretion, than had she cast a tender regard upon her old and faithful servant. (4)

Prejudice against a strong woman who fails to conform to accepted societal patterns leads the editor astray. She forgets that Cesario is not a youthful domestic but a young woman whose background very much resembles Olivia's, as the dramatist subtly informs us.

Using a sophisticated theatrical methodology, Shakespeare introduces each woman in a different way—playing upon potential audience bias even while revealing the similarities between the women. Shipwrecked in a foreign land, Viola strides ashore, speaks in her own voice, paints a picture of her misfortunes, and quickly decides how to deal with them. During her first appearance, in scene 2, she also reveals her background. In contrast, hearsay precedes Olivia's entrance. In scene after scene a variety of characters evaluate her decision to mourn her brother's death for seven years. Some of these characters also raise questions about the proper behavior for a young countess. Through this technique, the dramatist employs a series of incomplete vignettes by others to suggest the obstacles confronting her.

Critics and actor-managers—or directors—often fall into the trap. They accept the hearsay about Olivia then find the lovesick Duke Orsino—whom we meet in the opening scene—just as irrational as the woman he so passionately wants to marry but who emphatically rejects him. Herschel Baker, for example, calls them "a pair of high-born lovers [who] indulge a set of attitudes untested by experience" (xxiv) and writes of "Orsino's egomania" and "Olivia's silly posture of bereavement" (xxx). Geoffrey Bullough, too, observes that "by the end of the first scene we know by Olivia's oath to spend seven years grieving indoors that she is akin to [the Duke] in sensibility" (2:278). Actually, we never see Olivia weeping or miserable; the closest she comes to discussing her mourning is in her opening scene when her clown berates her, and she responds by commending his cleverness. Hearsay, primarily, reveals her

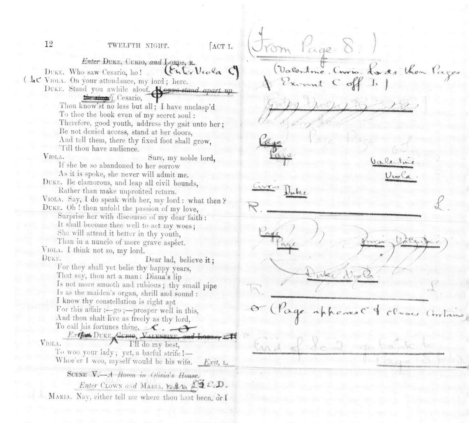

Promptbook page from the 1878 production of *Twelfth Night* arranged by Miss Neilson for Ellen Tree in the role of Viola. "From Page 8" at the top of the interleaf facing page 12 indicates that the Viola scene with the Duke had been moved to an early moment in the play. The bottom of the interleaf marks the close of the insert, "End of Sc. 2, go back to page 8 for Sc. 3." Courtesy of the Folger Shakespeare Library.

"silly posture of bereavement." On the other hand, Orsino exhibits his foolishness through his own actions and words in the play's opening scene although many of his lines are frequently cut from productions to make him seem less silly.[4]

That opening scene appears to have a purpose—to establish the world of Illyria, a mythic, ancient, unavailable world. Again we witness the dramatist's skill. For while he offers realistic reasons to suggest the kinds of options available to women who might freely move in society as equals of men, he quickly withdraws those options by creating this world. Though not inhabited by otherworldly creatures, this land of Illyria derives its magic from the sequential arrangement of scenes, keynoted by Orsino at the start. Unlike Hippolyta and Theseus, who provide a frame through which we, the audience, move into the enchanted wood on a mid-summer's night, or the weird sisters who set the mood for *Macbeth*, here the lovesick Duke sets the distinctive tone and establishes the particularities of place.

The opening scene not only immerses us in that unrecognizable and slightly skewed world of Illyria but also provides the first glimpse of Olivia through the eyes of the Duke. In love with love as well as the Countess, he seeks solace in music. "That strain again," the Duke commands, noting, "it had a dying fall" (I.i.4). And then abruptly, three lines later, "Enough, no more, / 'Tis not so sweet now as it was before" (7–8). He stops the instrumentalist then continues, his lines a mockery of the Petrarchan sonneteer's lyric to his love. Although the comedy later ranges between low, raucous farce and sophisticated verbal jousting, this opening scene carries the audience to that mythical land where both women seek to understand the meaning of freedom.

Recounting how he lost his heart, including a pun on the word *hart*, the Duke speaks in labored metaphors.[5] Languishing in adoration of Olivia, he offers a portrait of the lover according to the most exaggerated sonnet conventions:

> O, when mine eyes did see Olivia first,
> Methought she purg'd the air of pestilence!
> That instant was I turn'd into a hart,
> And my desires, like fell and cruel hounds,
> E'er since pursue me.
>
> (I.i.18–22)

Poor Orsino, transformed into a hart, has been pursued by his desires. Enhancing the otherworldly quality of this scene, Shakespeare dubs the courier "Valentine." He, too, contributes to the portrait of Olivia by admitting his failure to deliver Orsino's message. Denied an audience, Valentine reports on Olivia:

> The element itself, till seven years' heat,
> Shall not behold her face at ample view;
>
> (25–26)

Since the message was conveyed by Olivia's "handmaid," whom we later discover to be Maria, a woman with a tendency to trickery and a love of giving instructions, we cannot be certain whether Valentine's language and delivery characterize the speech patterns in Illyria, or whether they belong specifically to Valentine, Maria, or Olivia. The message has been sifted through two messengers; thus we are twice-removed from Olivia. Valentine continues his report:

> . . . like a cloistress she will veiled walk,
> And water once a day her chamber round
> With eye-offending brine;
>
> (27–29)

Once again an overblown metaphor colors the speech as the reporter describes a woman constantly weeping, a condition never to be witnessed by the audience. Shakespeare has begun the portrait that he will develop in each succeeding scene. Here, indeed, we might agree with Baker's evaluation, until we meet the young Countess.

In this dual portrait—of Orsino as well as Olivia—our sympathies hardly go out to the fatuous Duke even while we wonder what sort of woman would make such a vow. Shakespeare's audience may have recognized the satire on the Renaissance courtier— as we do not; however, Orsino's method of wooing proved as unconvincing to the young Countess as it does to us today. As for her seven-year vow, while it seems an extreme measure, it certainly should have discouraged this persistent wooer. Like the women of *Love's Labour's Lost* and Queen Elizabeth herself, Olivia chooses to postpone marriage. Unlike the women of the earlier play, whose one-year wait may imply later acceptance, Olivia's drastic seven-year postponement should prove sufficiently discouraging to send all her suitors elsewhere.

Ironically, at this early moment in the play, Orsino admires her decision even while wondering how she will respond when she does fall in love:

> O, she that hath a heart of that fine frame

To pay this debt of love but to a brother,
How will she love when the rich golden shaft
Hath kill'd the flock of all affections else
That live in her.

                                        (32–36)

Despite the awkwardness of this metaphor, as critics have noted, Orsino's shaft hits the mark. Olivia will soon offer love, gifts, and marriage to Viola disguised as the Duke's page, Cesario.

"This is Illyria." Inkwash for outdoor stage set for 1878 production. Classic tree on the left, a fountain, the sea, and distant hills in the center, and the outlines of buildings on the right define the space. Folger Promptbook *TN* 18. Courtesy of the Folger Shakespeare Library.

Lyrical, musical, with a touch of melancholy as well as humor, this first scene, with its shimmering surface, quickly dissolves before the next in which we hear the simplicity and directness of Viola's language. Differing in style and tone from Orsino, she tramps ashore and immediately questions the sea captain who has rescued her from shipwreck: "What country, friends, is this?" (I.ii.1) "This is Illyria, lady" (2), he replies. This is the land where she is unknown, where the Duke Orsino rules, and the young Countess Olivia rejects his advances. This is the land where Viola, herself, will seek new identity. In language revealing her skill with words and sensitivity to puns, she continues: "And what should I do in Illyria? / My brother he is in Elysium" (3–4). Even while she captures the resonances in language between "Illyria" and "Elysium"—between life and death—she attempts to sum up her own situation at this moment. We may be in the distant land of Illyria, but we are listening to a realistic young woman with practical wisdom, an ear for words, and a sense of the ludicrous in contrasting Illyria with Elysium.

This short exchange reveals a good deal about her: her concern for her brother, her obvious upper-class background and education through her reference to "Elysium," and her positive attitude: "Perchance he is not drown'd—what think you, sailors?" (5). In five lines, she poses three questions. And when the captain suggests that her brother may also have survived—tied "To a strong mast that liv'd upon the sea," (11–14)—Viola answers with the directness already evident:

> For saying so, there's gold.
>
> (18)

This first impetuous offer of gold springs from her reaction to his words of hope. She will reward his reassurance with money, a learned pattern, indicating her upper-class background. Later, a second, more considered promise grows from her resolve to conceal her true, female identity and pose as a eunuch. "I'll pay thee bounteously" (52), she vows.

Viola's social status emerges again when, in seeking to convince the captain to recommend her (in her disguise) to the Duke, she lists her musical skills.

> ... For I can sing
> And speak to him in many sorts of music
> That will allow me very worth his service.
>
> (57–59)

Critics have noted that she never does sing in the play. They therefore cite this as one of the many inconsistencies that tend to thwart audience expectations. M. M. Mahood writes in an otherwise perceptive analysis: "A further puzzle created by the second scene is that it leads us to expect Viola will sing to the Duke, but she never does so" (17). Nor is Mahood alone. Others, including

W. W. Greg in his bibliographical and textual study _The Shakespeare First Folio,_ had earlier seemed to establish this expectation as a fact:

> It is almost certain from the insistence on Viola's musical accomplishments at I.ii.57–58 that she was meant to be a singer, and from the awkward opening of II.iv that the song "Come away, come away death" has been transferred from her to Feste. (297)

More likely the insistence on musical training was meant to strengthen her class identification. As Warnicke points out, at this time upper-class young women frequently received a limited musical education (117 and passim). Nor would such an education qualify Viola as a professional—the role of Feste in this play. Rather she is providing one of her several "job qualifications" even if she does not use them once she is employed.

Scene 2 must be understood as Shakespeare's swift, frank introduction of Viola—one that will not be repeated. Rather than anticipating specific later actions, it sketches in her upper-class background. Not only her offers of money and reference to Elysium, but her indication of a musical education, would have been familiar clues to contemporary audiences. In addition, despite its ambiguity, her quick response to the captain's mention of Orsino, "I have heard my father name him" (I.ii.28), followed by the delightful specific, "He was a bachelor then" (29)—leading audiences to believe that the Duke and her father knew one another (never actually confirmed in the text)—seems to reinforce the class connection.[6] Not until the play's closing moments does she refer to her earlier life again, except in momentary lapses, such as her lines:

> My father had a daughter lov'd a man
> As it might be perhaps, were I a woman,
> I should your lordship.
>
> (II.iv.107–9)

Or it surfaces in her boast of her parentage to Olivia: "Above my fortunes, yet my state is well: / I am a gentleman" (I.v.278–79). In that instance, however, the gender shift masks her identity. But at this point in the play, scene 2 prepares the audience for the combat of wits that will ensue between the two women of similar backgrounds when they finally confront one another three scenes later.

Yet societal values and accepted stereotypes about women blur those similarities and stress the women's differences. As I pointed out earlier, hostility to the young woman who would defy conventions creeps into the criticism just as sympathy for Viola, who suffers in silence, develops. Like the critics, editors and actor-managers, too, prefer to sharpen the contrast between this ship-wrecked young woman soon to masquerade in breeches and the wealthy young Countess Olivia who exercises nonconformist attitudes towards men.

To strengthen the difference between the women, staged versions help reshape Viola by excising her line "For saying so, there's gold" (I.ii.18) and deemphasizing her class through costuming. The excision has persisted from the eighteenth century into the twentieth. The Bell edition (1773), for example, which claims to record the play "As Performed at the Theatres-Royal," jettisons Viola's offer of gold to the captain, suggesting what audiences saw at Drury Lane and Covent Garden after 1741.[7] Mrs. Inchbald (1808), as we have seen, refers to Olivia's falling in love "with a domestic" (4–5) and John Philip Kemble, whose acting version, first published in 1810, becomes the standard for theatrical productions for close to a century, also excises the reference to gold.[8] By the end of the nineteenth century, Henry Irving creates his own version, one which stresses his role of Malvolio. Nevertheless, Irving adopts many of Kemble's excisions, including Viola's offer of a reward.[9] In the twentieth century, Herbert Beerbohm Tree, among others, also excises the line, perhaps thinking it unseemly for a young woman to be so comfortable with money. More likely, Tree is following a tradition both in text and attitude towards Viola.

As well as introducing her, scene 2 further develops the portrait of Olivia through hearsay. The captain narrates and Viola listens. A down-to-earth and non-involved spectator, he responds to Viola's query about Orsino's bachelorhood with uncertainty, assuring her only that a month earlier, before the captain left, Orsino was seeking Olivia's hand:

> And then 'twas fresh in murmur (as you know
> What great ones do, the less will prattle of)
> That he did seek the love of fair Olivia.

(I.ii.32–34)

In scene 1, Orsino had provided the emotional background; in scene 2, the captain fills in many of the publicly known details about the young woman. A "virtuous maid," the phrase identifying her youth and unmarried status, she is also:

> ... the daughter of a count
> That died some twelvemonth since, then leaving her
> In the protection of his son, her brother,
> Who shortly also died;
>
> (36–39)

Alone and wealthy, Olivia has much in common with the young woman listening. Malcolmson makes a similar point although she leaves Viola's exact status in doubt: "The scene does not explicitly define Viola's status as either noble or gentle; rather, her rank is veiled from us just as Viola veils it from the people she will meet. . . . [W]e, and the characters, will know her through her role-playing and her 'intent'" (37). Although staging tends to obscure Viola's status, I believe that the dramatist offers sufficient clues both in her speeches and her actions to indicate her upper-class background.

As the captain continues, he also helps identify Illyria's social system, one that places an unmarried woman under the governance of a male in the family.[10] Finally, the captain speaks of the Countess's actions now that her brother's protection has ceased. In deference to the love she bore him: "They say, she hath abjur'd the company / And sight of men" (40–41). Omitting any reference to the seven-year limit on the mourning period, relayed by Orsino's messenger in scene 1, the captain's "they say" confirms his general reliance on hearsay and his distance from Olivia. When, therefore, Viola resolves to serve this countess, the captain quickly discourages her:

> That were hard to compass,
> Because she will admit no kind of suit,
> No, not the Duke's.
>
> (44–46)

Obviously, if the Duke has failed, Viola should not even consider such an option. Accepting the captain's advice, she quickly shifts her objective and decides on wearing breeches: "I'll serve this duke; / Thou shalt present me as a eunuch to him" (55–56).

Critics have questioned the ease with which Viola changes her mind, considering her later persistence and success in meeting Olivia. As Ruth Nevo observes, although Viola, upon hearing of Olivia's loss, exclaims, "O that I served that lady," she "does not fly to the Countess Olivia for succour, woman to woman, despite her sympathy for a fellow-mourner. Instead she chooses to be adventurously epicene in the Duke's entourage" (205). Nevo believes that Viola makes a sacrifice here by asking to be presented as a eunuch, a rational explanation for her high voice and feminine appearance. More importantly, the young woman's transformation permits her to enjoy the freedom of action allowed her twin brother, and formerly denied her because of her sex. The speed of her decision also leads C. L. Barber to comment that "the shipwreck is made the occasion for Viola to exhibit an undaunted, aristocratic mastery of adversity—she settles what she shall do next almost as though picking out a costume for a masquerade" (241). He is less concerned with the reason for her choice than with her free and easy manner, her language in making the decision. Unlike these modern critics, Samuel Johnson expresses disdain for Viola's actions and considers this a plot weakness:

> Viola seems to have formed a very deep design with very little premeditation: she is thrown by shipwreck on an unknown coast, hears that the prince is a batchelor, and resolves to supplant the lady whom he courts. (7:312)

The play, however, refutes this theory, as we discover later on when Viola, having fallen in love with the Duke, bemoans the limitations placed on her by disguise then courts the Countess for him.

Differing from Johnson, most actor-managers and directors, as well as critics, favor Viola over Olivia. To focus more sharply on the disguised young woman, these men often transpose the first and second scenes. Again Kemble's influential version dominates. It opens with noise, thunder, and lightning, heralding Viola's arrival on the shores of Illyria. Beerbohm Tree, in 1901, dramatizes Viola's weakness on arrival although the text offers no such suggestion. Sailors bring her ashore "as if insensible. She is put reclining on the steps. Wet dress. Sailors with chest and bundles." Winthrop Ames, in 1906, also has the sailors "supporting a woman, then carrying in a child" (a character added for pathos, I suspect). Augustin Daly, the famous American manager at the end of the nineteenth century, goes even further. He opens the play with the arrival of Viola's brother on the shores of Illyria, eliminating all suspense as to whether or not her twin has survived.

Despite Daly's more radical alteration of sequence, it was only a temporary aberration whereas Kemble's pattern has persisted. As recently as the summer of 1986, New York audiences were treated to a Kemble format under the aegis of Joseph Papp, the production opening with Viola's arrival in Illyria. Possibly the drive for realism and interest in plot development contributed to the decision to open with the second scene. More likely, however, the increased emphasis on the heroic Viola in contrast to the foolish Olivia was responsible.

Unfortunately, that transposition sacrifices the airy, wistful tone of the first scene with all its implications and resonances—a scene as important to the play as the three witches who open *Macbeth* or the ghost on the ramparts who chills the air with foreboding in *Hamlet.* In Shakespeare's sequence, Orsino's impassioned pleas and posing in the first scene add credibility to Olivia's decision whereas when the play opens with scene 2, she sounds arbitrary and unreasonable since the sea captain warns Viola of the impossibility of meeting this woman.

Shakespeare's scene sequence (as Clifford Leech observed) has its own specific validity and dictates a pattern of relationships (36–37). The patterns in the plays usually affect and often heighten the impact of the work on the audience. Shakespeare's method resembles that of the painter who establishes positive and negative areas of a painting, each helping to illuminate the other while through both he weaves color, line, and design that unify the whole. In *Twelfth Night,* Orsino's opening scene provides the background (or negative) area—of fantasy—against which Viola's realistic approach proves refreshing. Woven through both is the slowly developing character of Olivia.

Scene 3 intensifies the portrait of the Countess. This time the dramatist takes us closer to her world, introducing us to the ebullient and varied characters who inhabit her home. There, the multidimensional, and skewed, characterization continues to grow as others' words fill in the blank spaces of the sketch first begun by Orsino. The robustious, roaring, frequently drunk Sir Toby, identified in the cast list as "uncle to Olivia," introduces us to the comic characters even while he stews, "What a plague means my niece to take the death of her brother thus? I am sure care's an enemy to life" (I.iii.1–3). Maria, the serving woman, rather than answering, sharply reprimands, "Your cousin, my lady, takes great exceptions to your ill hours" (5–6), bearing witness to a more dynamic Olivia than thus far promised by either Orsino or the sea captain. With these two speeches, Shakespeare has catapulted us into Olivia's household and established the firmness of the mistress's control. She has accepted the obligations of her position. A life of mourning has led neither to a retreat from reality nor to an abdication of responsibility, merely an affirmation of the single life.

Challenges to that single life, however, seem endless. Suitors spring up everywhere. Even Sir Toby has a candidate—his drinking companion, the foolish Sir Andrew Aguecheek, a gull easily separated from his money. Nevertheless, Sir Andrew, skeptical of his chances, would withdraw from the field, admitting, "Your niece will not be seen, or if she be, it's four to one she'll none of me. The Count himself here hard by woos her" (I.iii.106–8). For the third time, we hear of the Count's persistent wooing. Anxious to prevent the departure of his wealthy drinking mate, Sir Toby confidently insists, "She'll none o' th' Count. She'll not match above her degree, neither in estate, years, nor wit" (109-10). Although his motive is suspect, Sir Toby, while he ultimately will prove wrong about the "degree" of Olivia's intelligence, or wit, is correct about her rejection of the Count and probably about her youthful age. Sir Andrew does not contradict him.

Interestingly, critics, too, have wrestled with the question of her age while directors have indicated their opinion through dress, make-up, and stage movement. They usually decide in favor of seniority, thus emphasizing the ways in which an older woman can be bested by a younger, more conventional one. The hostility to the older, aggressive woman on stage remains; she is a subject for laughter and audience mockery. And here the language of the text may inadvertently contribute to this misreading, for whereas Olivia is acting herself, a young single woman, Viola, playing a man's role, is described as "not yet old enough for a man, nor young enough for a boy" (I.v.156–57). Leo Salingar in 1958, for example, considers the Countess, "psychologically an elder sister to Viola"(125).[11] Although not censorious, as was Mrs. Inchbald in 1808, Salingar resembles Inchbald in stressing an age differential betweeen the two women. However nowhere, neither in the language nor actions, does the text indicate an Olivia chronologically older or more psychologically mature than Viola. On the contrary, perhaps because of her disguise and the challenges it poses, Viola reveals keen insights into both her condition and Olivia's, insights unavailable to the deceived Countess.

In fact, Sir Toby's comment supports the notion that the two young women were approximately of the same age, thus reinforcing the similarities introduced at the start. Only later, when trapped in a comic relationship and engaged in wit combats built on disguise does confusion arise as to their respective ages. This, however, may result from costuming and staging. For example, an illustration of an older Olivia actually appears in the pages of costume designs in an Augustin Daly souvenir promptbook. Her face looks a bit pinched as well as haughty, in contrast with the illustration for Viola, who, with blonde, curly hair worn in a version of a wide pageboy, has an innocent, inquiring, friendly look on her face and stands in a deferential pose.[12] Although both illustrations seem to have provided the basis for the women's costumes, they must also reflect perceptions of the characters in the nineteenth century.[13]

Occasionally, of course, some independent thinking occurs and we read in a promptbook, "Olivia's youth should be emphasized in every way possible to make her love affair with so callow a strippling as Viola convincing" (Ames prompt, facing I.v. 294–95). The comment is sparked by Olivia's soliloquy at the close of the scene where she first meets Viola. Again in a 1988 production at Stratford, Ontario, Olivia's youthfulness was stressed when she giggled with delight at discovering this new young "man," then subsequently discarded her black dress for a pink one.

As the play moves towards this moment when the two women meet, their divergent introductions continue: Olivia's through hearsay, Viola's through direct presentation. In scene 4 Orsino describes his passionate love for the incomparable Olivia, meanwhile confessing to his new page, the disguised Viola, "I have unclasp'd / To thee the book even of my secret soul" (I.iv.13–14). Incredibly, she has won her way into his confidence in a mere three days. Despite her brief period of service, Orsino is revealing all his innermost thoughts to her. The ease with which she accomplishes this suggests that she had no trouble being accepted in an aristocratic household because she could draw on the mores of her upper-class background to adjust to her new situation. But Viola has lost her heart to him even as he is entrusting her with his most precious errand, the wooing of Olivia. Shakespeare thus presents the first challenge to a wealthy young woman who would gain freedom from her sexual identity by donning male attire. Breeches have their drawbacks; but so do skirts, as Olivia too will soon discover.

When she finally sweeps onto the stage in scene 5, in all her grandeur or loneliness, certainty or uncertainty, age or youth, arrogance or self-confidence, she has been thoroughly characterized by the conflicting impressions passed on by others. John Russell Brown writes of the silences in the play—the moments when words are not spoken but audience attention is riveted to a character (28). Surely audiences are waiting to see just what she looks like, how she carries herself, and how she behaves. But the tendency to tamper with the text again changes the portrait. Just as the transposition of the play's first two scenes combined with the omission of many of the Duke's foolish self-pitying lines alter audiences' perceptions of him, and excision of Viola's reference to gold masks her upper-class background, so standard cuts in scene 5—some going back to the early nineteenth century—affect our first impression of Olivia.

Although the scene opens with twenty-five lines of teasing conversation between Maria and the Clown—lines preparing the audience for the Countess's annoyance with him—they seldom reach the stage. Henry Irving, John Philip Kemble, Augustin Daly, and Herbert Beerbohm Tree, among others, chopped off some or all of the exchange.[14] As a result, Olivia usually sounds arbitrary and arrogant at her entrance. To the Clown's "God bless thee, lady!" (I.v.36–37), she replies, "Take the fool away" (38). Nor does his "Do you not hear, fellows? Take away the lady," (39–40) amuse her. Olivia angrily charges, "Go to, y' are a dry fool; I'll no more of you. Besides, you grow dishonest" (41–42). In the conversation usually omitted, however, Shakespeare provides an explanation for this behavior. Officiously acting as her mistress's surrogate, Maria reprimands the Clown for his several absences. In their exchange lies the rational basis for Olivia's opening speeches, particularly her anger at the Clown. The excision contributes to a one-sided and distorted impression of her.

In fact, in the full text, she proves a tolerant manager of this conglomerate household. We glimpse her reasonable governance particularly when she allows the Fool his famous argument against mourning for her brother. "I think his soul is in hell, madonna" (68), he begins, quickly contradicted by her, "I know his soul is in heaven, fool" (69), leading to his conclusion, "The more fool, madonna, to mourn for your brother's soul, being in heaven" (70–71). The reasoning wins her admiration. "What think you of this fool, Malvolio? doth he not mend?" (73–74), she laughingly concedes. But her steward, a somber man with a great sense of self-importance, is not amused. Olivia then criticizes him, offering astute character analysis in her reprimand: "O, you are sick of self-love, Malvolio, and taste with a distemper'd appetite. To be generous, guiltless, and of free disposition, is to take those things for bird-bolts that you deem cannon-bullets" (90–93). Shakespeare has endowed her with a directness of language that matches Viola's. But in some promptbooks, such as those based on the Daly edition (p. 16, *TN* 21; p. 22, *TN* 10), the second sentence, with its analogy to "bird-bolts" and "cannon-bullets," has been excised. As written, the full text reveals Olivia's strengths. During the brief time that she is on stage, she appears neither unintelligent, intolerant, nor humorless. Nor does she exhibit any extremes of grief.

Rather, the young Countess appears well qualified for the battle of wits that will follow between her and Viola—two women who have, in their own ways, built their independent personas on the death (or seeming death) of their brothers, one through mourning, the other through disguise. The equality of their verbal gifts emerges at their first meeting. Sent to woo Olivia for Orsino, Viola combines flattery with insolence. "Most radiant, exquisite, and unmatchable beauty—I pray you tell me if this be the lady of the house. . . . I would be loath to cast away my speech; for besides that it is excellently well penn'd, I have taken great pains to con it" (I.v.170–74), she complains. When Olivia answers only "Whence came you, sir?" (177), Viola persists in her emphasis on the prepared speech being spoken to the properly identified Olivia: "I can say little more than I have studied, and that question's out of my part" (178–79).

Seeming to be aware of what Viola is doing, Olivia queries next, "Are you a comedian?" (182). To this Viola somewhat saucily responds, "No, my profound heart; and yet (by the very fangs of malice I swear) I am not that I play" (183–84). Why the expression "by the very fangs of malice"? What is its relevance? Does it have an underlying message or reveal her envy of Olivia? For surely, a suitor would not be using the "fangs of malice" to support an argument. Rather while the phrase may suggest an arrogance and a pose of self-confidence on Viola's part, it may also reflect her attempt to simulate male assertiveness first by swearing and then by calling up this strange phrase, perhaps a substitute for "by the devil." In closing, she repeats her request, "Are you the lady of the house?" (184–85). Finally Olivia gives an almost direct answer—although still equivocating—"If I do not usurp myself, I am" (186). But Viola responds in kind. "Most certain, if you are she, you do usurp yourself" (187–88). And then once more she refers to her memorized speech "in praise" of Olivia, the suggestion being that not Olivia herself, but the conventions of love are responsible for this praise.

This short exchange is usually reduced on the stage. Since drama is built on the interaction between characters—in other words, since dialogue helps define personality—the omissions alter the portraits of the women. The section leading to Olivia's question "Are you a comedian?" and Viola's mixed answer with its "fangs of malice" are frequently excised. What remains is Olivia's simple "If I do not usurp myself, I am."[15] Nor do audiences usually hear Olivia's sardonic admonition to Viola to "Come to what is important in't. I forgive you the praise" (192–93), indicating her sense of humor and awareness of the verbal battle under way. In the subsequent conversation, the cuts in Olivia's lines are rather curious. "Speak your office" (207) is all that remains of a speech that includes "Sure you have some hideous matter to deliver, when the courtesy of it is so fearful" (206–7). Eliminated too is the contretemps touched off by Viola's "I hold the olive in my hand" (209–10)—an offer she finds difficult to sustain after Olivia's simple observation "Yet you began rudely" (212). Viola immediately takes up the challenge, "The rudeness that hath appear'd in me have I learn'd from my entertainment" (214–15).

Their verbal combat continues, intensified by Viola's request that Olivia raise her veil although as the Countess notes, "You are now out of your text" (232). Nevertheless, she agrees to "draw the curtain, and show . . . the picture" (233), challenging, "Is't not well done?" (235) A too-quick response springs from the woman in breeches, "Excellently done, if God did all" (236). Just as sharply, however, Olivia retorts, "'Tis in grain, sir, 'twill endure wind and weather"(237–38). But much of this verbal jousting disappears from the stage, and Viola's speech begins instead with the flattering, "'Tis beauty truly blent" (239).

Consider too, the exchange triggered by Olivia's wonderful speech outlining the "divers schedules" of her beauty:

> It shall be inventoried, and every particle and utensil labell'd to my will: as, *item*, two lips, indifferent red; *item*, two grey eyes, with lids to them; *item*, one neck, one chin, and so forth. Were you sent hither to praise me?
>
> (I.v.245–49)

Undaunted, the page Cesario/Viola disapprovingly comments: "I see what you are; you are too proud; / But if you were the devil, you are fair" (250–51). And then, as if remembering her mission, she jumps from critical direct address to her major subject, "My lord and master loves you" (252). Promptbooks, reflecting stage productions, tend to retain only the last line, omitting Olivia's "schedule" of her beauty as well as Viola's accusation of pride. Thus the text, mocking the ideal of courtly love, emphasizes pertness and honesty over flattery. These excisions rob the portrait of Viola of irony and reduce Olivia to a stolid, unimaginative woman.

Finally, cut too is her gracious observation:

> Your lord does know my mind, I cannot love him,
> Yet I suppose him virtuous, know him noble,
> Of great estate, of fresh and stainless youth;
> In voices well divulg'd, free, learn'd, and valiant,
> And in dimension, and the shape of nature,
> A gracious person. But yet I cannot love him.
>
> (257–62)

The speech indicates Olivia's sensitivity as she lists his specific strengths. It is a remarkable statement to give to a young woman, since it suggests less an emotional reaction than a thoughtful evaluation of the man she rejects. She mentions none of his weaknesses but bases her decision only on her own taste: "I cannot love him," implying also that nothing in the future will change her mind. Adamant in her insistence that she will never love Orsino, the Countess repeats the words yet again near the scene's close. Viola understands and later attempts, unsuccessfully, to explain Olivia's point of view to Orsino.

Historically, most of the speech disappears from the stage. Kemble's version, setting the pattern for those to follow, combines the single opening line with the speech's closing, resulting in the cryptic, abbreviated message: "Your lord does know my mind, I cannot love him: / He might have took his answer long ago" (Kemble, 1810, p. 19). Conforming to the developing portrait of her in criticism, an arbitrary Olivia emerges here. Other acting texts follow Kemble's lead. Beerbohm Tree (1901) retains the first line of the speech. Augustin Daly (1893), Henry Irving (1884), and others retain its first three lines. These productions span almost an entire century and surely must have affected criticism.

In fact, in 1865, decrying this omission, Spedding writes:

> These lines are left out in the acting, which is surely a great mistake. As addressed by Olivia to Viola, they have a peculiar and pathetic meaning, and it is strange that the mixed emotions which they must have excited in her should not have been made one of the "points" in the play. (*Fraser's Magazine;* quoted in *Variorum Twelfth Night,* 90)

The lines not only affect Viola, who herself would like to "be his wife" (I.iv.42) but also illuminate the character of Olivia. She knows her own heart and mind; she can recognize virtue in others, even someone who is a bit foolish, like Orsino. Of course, she has only seen that side of him which is tangled in the conventions of wooing. Viola, on the other hand, hears a more relaxed man confiding his ideas not only about wooing and women but also about life generally. Employed as his page, she has also found him generous and trusting, having given her, an unknown youth, a position and quickly taken her into his confidence. Like Hermia and Helena, who encounter two different aspects of Demetrius in the early scenes of *A Midsummer Night's Dream,* Viola and Olivia encounter two different Orsinos.

Unmoved by the Orsino she knows, Olivia is captivated by his envoy, Viola. In this disguised woman of comparable background and wit, Olivia finds the perfect wooer—the one who verbalizes her own dream of what wooing should be: a challenging wit exchange between equals; honesty; and an absence of posing. Direct language can open a path to the heart. In scene 5, Viola adopts this method. Without realizing it, she once again departs from her "text" (232). This time she delivers an impassioned love lyric. Though meant to win Olivia for Orsino, it also reveals something of Viola's own feelings for the Duke: "If I did love you in my master's flame, / . . . I would. . . . / Make me a willow cabin at your gate, / . . . Hallo your name to the reverberate hills, / And make the babbling gossip of the air / Cry out 'Olivia'" (264–74).

The speech overwhelms the young Countess as it does the audience. Here are lines that differ from Orsino's flowery words; familiar images flood the language. One need not search for hidden meanings, merely visualize the youth standing before a simple cabin and hear him hallowing the name "Olivia." The air and the hills echo the name; the speaker captivates the listener, who admits in soliloquy after the young page leaves:

> How now?
> Even so quickly may one catch the plague?

> Methinks I feel this youth's perfections
> With an invisible and subtle stealth
> To creep in at mine eyes.[16] Well, let it be.
>
> (294–98)

But she doesn't "let it be." Instead, Olivia immediately sends Malvolio on a false errand, to return to the young Cesario a ring he never gave her. Each woman has been caught in an emotional response that will alter her self-perception and her desire for anonymity or privacy. No longer thinking of the brother she was mourning, Olivia seeks only to assure a return visit from Orsino's youthful page.

Perhaps squeamish about the possible impact of individual lines or simply choosing to cut at this point, actor-managers excised and revised. Charles Kean, the mid-nineteenth-century manager, for example, crossed out some of Olivia's speech above, specifically those lines expressing admiration for "this youth" (296–98). The intention was probably to remove any suggestion of Olivia's being homosexually attracted to Viola. In this comedy of mistaken identity, however, Shakespeare, not only suggests such an attachment, but then, through the sequential arrangement of scenes quickly offers an alternative possibility.

Olivia's startling emotional discovery precipitates an immediate scene change to the lost Sebastian, Viola's twin brother, who has survived the shipwreck. Derrida argues that the meanings of words are constantly being modified by the next signifier (Moi, 105–7). Building on Derrida's insight, I propose that meaning in drama derives not only from verbal signifiers, particularly the interaction of characters as they speak on stage, but also from the sequence of scenes as they unfold. This arrangement affects both our first, immediate response as well as the modification of that response. Moreover, because theater differs from the written text in at least one significant detail, it addresses a captive audience who must listen and react as the play progresses, this "deferral of meaning" occurs to a far larger extent with drama than with written literature since a reader may put down a book and stop reading.

The young Countess's comment about the disguised youth now takes on a different perspective with the introduction of Sebastian. His presence holds the promise of a possible new pairing, although audiences will have to wait to see when, and if, Sebastian meets Olivia and how that meeting will develop. The striking physical similarity between the twins will eventually resolve Olivia's dilemma. She will later woo Sebastian as Cesario although, as Heilbrun points out, Shakespeare, himself the father of opposite sex twins, surely knew such an indistinguishable resemblance to be impossible (37).

Similarities do, however, exist. Like Viola, Sebastian is first introduced with a sea captain, Antonio, who rescued him. Also like her, Viola's brother arouses intense feelings of affection, in his case from Antonio, who would serve the youth. And again like her, Sebastian stubbornly resists. "If you will not undo what you have done, that is, kill him whom you have recover'd, desire it not" (II.i.37–39), the young man insists before departing. Left alone on stage, Antonio, in soliloquy, first blesses the youth: "The gentleness of all the gods go with thee!" then reveals the intensity of his feelings.

> I have many enemies in Orsino's court,
> Else would I very shortly see thee there.
> But come what may, I do adore thee so
> That danger shall seem sport, and I will go.
>
> (II.i.44–48)

The speech suggests a strong, even if one-sided, affection. The captain will risk capture for the pleasure of following Sebastian.

Brother, like sister, rejects an implied homosexual relationship. Unlike Viola, however, Sebastian is not suffering from a misreading of his sexual identity since no disguise exists. And so the soliloquy is seldom heard on stage. The Bell version retains only a form of the first line, "The gentleness of the Gods go with thee!" (335), after which the two men "exeunt severally" (335). Kemble's text, followed by the French edition (*TN* 18) and others, transforms Antonio's first line into part of a brief dialogue, Sebastian answering with an invented line, "Fare ye well."

This first scene between Sebastian and Antonio often changes not only its shape, but also its place in the sequence. Despite its importance in the pattern of alternating scenes that illuminate the development of the two principal women characters, actor-managers and directors have often reshuffled the text—sometimes to simplify plot, sometimes to stress Malvolio's role (although it is shorter than those of Viola and Olivia), and sometimes to sustain a contrast between the women, favoring the disguised youth in breeches. Again Kemble's text set the example, transposing the

Folio sequence by placing Malvolio's scene with Viola immediately after Olivia's order to "return the ring," although the introduction of Sebastian interferes with such a smooth narrative sequence.[17] Other directors, such as Irving, who played Malvolio, have withheld Sebastian's surprise appearance until later in the play.[18] Focusing on his own role, Irving also abbreviated the women's lines.[19] Other actor-managers tended to fall into similar patterns, sometimes stripping the scene of most of its intense lines with their homoerotic implications, sometimes transposing the sequence, and often doing both.

Occasionally, as in the Sothern and Marlowe production at the beginning of the twentieth century, the scene was even merged with the second brief Sebastian-Antonio scene even though each of these functions differently. The first creates that happy shock of recognition of the physical resemblances between the twins; it also introduces the relationship between the two men. The second adds important plot elements: the captain decides to remain in Illyria, despite the hazards, then lends his purse to Sebastian, later seeking to retrieve it from Sebastian's double, Viola. The scene also testifies to the intensity of Antonio's affection for the youth. Sequentially, the second scene separates Maria's description of Malvolio in yellow garters from his actual appearance on stage.

In contrast, the Sothern-Marlowe merged scene (II.ii. in typescript—*TN* 31) retains only the factual information necessary for the plot's later development. It begins with the opening of Shakespeare's second of the two scenes (III.iii.1–15) where Antonio reveals his decision to accompany the young man, but it excises specific references to his love for Sebastian. Next follows the youth's disclosure of his identity, plucked from the earlier scene (II.i), thus confirming as well Viola's upper-class background. Finally, returning to the later scene, this new mongrel concludes with Antonio giving his purse to Sebastian. Sequentially, it follows Malvolio's outburst to the drunken Sir Toby and Sir Andrew (II.iii) and precedes Viola's debate with Orsino on love (II.iv). Although in many ways the Sothern-Marlowe version defeats the purposes of the two separate scenes, it does not subvert the play's ability to construct strong parallels between two wealthy, young, single women who have lost father and brother. That was Daly's contribution and he achieved it by opening the play with Sebastian's arrival in Illyria. This assured audiences that the relationship between Olivia and

Viola was just a game and that Viola's early quest for independence had no reality since her brother lived.

Shakespeare, however, not only raises this issue of independence but also further develops it in Viola's retort to Malvolio when he delivers the ring. For the dramatist here offers a significant example of women bonding. Knowing she never gave Olivia a ring, the disguised page nevertheless answers the steward: "She took the ring of me, I'll none of it" (12). Although the line has puzzled some editors, it seems consistent with Viola's constant makeshift attempts both to conceal her disguise and to reveal her insights as a woman into another woman's actions. This will occur again two scenes later when she attempts to explain to the Duke Olivia's feelings for him, but instead nearly trips over her own identity. Clearly in her scene with Malvolio, Viola understands what has occurred, as her soliloquy, following his brusque departure, indicates: "I left no ring with her. . . . / Fortune forbid my outside have not charm'd her" (II.ii.17–18). Indeed it has. But Sebastian's arrival may promise a "happy ending," even while the play continues to explore the women's struggles, whether in breeches or skirts, to assert their sense of self.

In the scenes that follow, Olivia's struggle once more comes to the fore, again through hearsay and inference as Shakespeare thrusts us ever more intimately into the dynamics of her household. Again the challenge to her independence grows out of her position as a marriageable, wealthy young woman. When the drunken Sir Toby and Sir Andrew wobble in, raucously singing, Maria first reprimands them, invoking the name of her mistress, but then later joins them. Less flexible, Malvolio, awakened from sleep by this boisterous crew, more vehemently chastises them, again invoking Olivia's name:

> My lady bade me tell you, that though she harbors you as her kinsman, she's nothing allied to your disorders. If you can separate yourself and your misdemeanors, you are welcome to the house; if not, and it would please you to take leave of her, she is very willing to bid you farewell.
> (II.iii.95–101)

Since he never carries out the threat but is himself bested, his lines indicate his misreading of Olivia, exhibiting his lust for power and his method of exercising it. Betraying his ambition as well as his vulnerability to the gulling he will later suffer, his speech illuminates the extent and intensiveness of another of Olivia's pursuers.

He will readily adopt cross-garters and attempt to smile in his effort to win her hand and, with it, permanent power as her husband. Little disappears from this comic scene in staged versions—only the songs. First omitted from the Bell edition, they are later excised by Kemble and Irving who substitute other, briefer drinking songs.

A far different fate on stage meets the scene which follows: the debate between Viola and Orsino on men's and women's capacity for love. The scene loses much of its substance through cutting. It is full of inconsistencies and contradications in Orsino's arguments while stressing at the same time the complexity of Viola's position as she strives to convey to the Duke something of a woman's point of view. Filled with humor and further mockery of the conventions of the Petrarchan lover, it continues the portrait of Orsino begun in the first scene—a silly lover drowning in self-pity. Again, his desire for music opens the scene:

> that piece of song,
> That old and antique song we heard last night;
> Methought it did relieve my passion much,
> More than light airs and recollected terms
> Of these most brisk and giddy-paced times.

> (II.iv.2–6)

Still seeking to "relieve" his passion, Orsino sounds very much like the melancholy character we met earlier. But this request for music does not appear in the Bell edition, the Kemble edition, or the French edition, basically covering a century of staging. Instead, in those editions, the scene opens with Orsino attempting to warn his page of what to expect from love. "Come hither boy," the Duke instructs, "If ever thou shalt love, / In the sweet pangs of it remember me" (15–16). Observing Cesario/Viola's downcast expression, her master quizzes her about her beloved's appearance: "Of your complexion" and "about your years" (26, 28), confesses the disguised woman.

Her lines trigger Orsino's first dissertation on love, which will eventually be contradicted by his second. "[H]owever we do praise ourselves, / Our fancies are more giddy . . . Than women's are" (32–35), he claims, advising Cesario to choose a woman younger than himself. Later, however, when describing his own love for Olivia, the Duke contradicts himself, insisting, "no woman's heart / So big, to hold so much; they lack retention" (95–96). He also compares a woman's love which "may be call'd appetite" (97) with his own, which is "all as hungry as the sea" (100). Kemble and Bell omit the first assertion and Kemble, Bell, Irving, Daly, and Sothern and Marlowe omit its contradiction. As a result of these excisions, the Duke sounds consistent, a quality that Shakespeare denies him. The elimination of both groups of quotes by Bell and Kemble alters the scene's emphasis, losing much of its irony.

In these editions, reflecting stage performances, not only do the contradictions disappear, but also Orsino turns into a fairly direct, attractive man. Reduced, the text's long lecture on love becomes merely a brief comment to Viola/Cesario on her beloved, "too old, by heaven" (29), followed immediately by the direction: "Get thee to yond same sovereign cruelty" (80), Olivia. Covering a mere two pages in the Kemble text, the scene fails to develop the portrait of a melancholy and self-pitying Orsino resembling Shakespeare's Duke. Instead, it becomes a brief interlude of disagreement between the disguised page and the man she loves in which she stumbles when trying to fictionalize her love for him.

Juxtaposing the young page's clearly reasoned defense of Olivia against the Duke's confused and contradictory comments on men's and women's capacity to love, Shakespeare in this scene once again illustrates women bonding and also gives Viola rational arguments favoring a woman's right to free choice. Furthermore, the scene reaffirms Viola's sense of her own identity; she is always emotionally and intellectually clearly a woman. Attempting to deliver Olivia's message and sensitive to its intention, Viola tries to convince Orsino of its finality, transposing Olivia's words. "But if she *cannot love* you, sir?" (II.iv.87, emphasis added here and throughout this paragraph). In response, the Duke retains only the original "cannot." "I *cannot* be so answer'd" (88), he insists. Viola then cites the parallel of an imaginary woman (herself) in love with him. Suppose "*You* cannot love *her*" (91). The pronouns have shifted from that first expression by Olivia but the body of the line has been restored. The debate surrounding a woman's right to express or reject love on a plane equal to a man's is given clear expression through Viola as Cesario, the young lad, while the refusal of the man, Orsino, to respect Olivia's wishes resonates through the text.

In this scene, Viola seems torn between revealing her identity and maintaining her disguise. Earlier she had decided, "Time, thou must untangle this, not I" (II.ii.40). But here that resolve weakens, when, in trying to convince the Duke, she says, "My father had a daughter lov'd a man / As it might be perhaps, were I a woman, / I should your lordship" (II.iv.107–9). "And what's her history?" (109) the Duke quickly asks. Surely her answer, "I am all the daughters of my father's house, / And all the brothers too" (120–21), should have led to a full revelation. But the Duke is so self-absorbed in his own feelings that his ear is not keyed to Viola's words. And so she continues in her role as his messenger.

Having chosen her disguise almost whimsically, she finds its advantages quickly fading. First, her success in winning a place with the Duke has led to her appointment as his surrogate wooer although she confesses, in soliloquy: "Whoe'er I woo, myself would be his wife" (I.iv.42). Then her enchantment of Olivia further intensifies Viola's problem. Next, when she tries to explain the other woman's position to the Duke, he refuses to listen. Later, despite her protests, Sir Andrew challenges her to a duel for Olivia's hand, leading Viola to muse to herself: "A little thing would make me tell them how much I lack of a man" (III.iv.302–3). And finally, she must confront the issue of a dual identity, having become embroiled in the circle of pursued and pursuer. The problems Viola faces caused by her disguise are, if less life threatening, more subtle and emotionally complex than those that confront Shakespeare's other women in breeches: Rosalind of *As You Like It*, Imogen of *Cymbeline*, and Jessica of *The Merchant of Venice*, who choose disguise to evade pursuit; Julia of *The Two Gentlemen of Verona*, who concealed herself to pursue her lover; or Portia and Nerissa, who dress as lawyer and law clerk to save their husbands' friend.

If, however, Shakespeare were less interested in realistic reasons for the disguise than in the larger concept—the relationship of sexuality to women's economic independence—the silliness of the breeches controversy would be exposed by the similarities between the women's plights. Although differently dressed, both must revise their self-perceptions, modifying them to accommodate erotic urges as these affect women's lives in such a society. Viola's choice of disguise, like Olivia's choice of mourning, tests the limits of self-sovereignty when supported by economic independence.

Thus their new erotic interests conflict with their development of independence. Nevertheless, both women persevere in their chosen direction. Viola remains in service to Orsino, wooing Olivia, while she, in turn, continues her forthright pursuit of Cesario. Two other brief exchanges mark the women's time alone together. In the earlier one (III.i.93–164), Olivia apologizes for sending the false message and the ring and quite directly declares her love. In the second (III.iv.201–17), an exchange of less than twenty lines within a much longer scene, she acknowledges having compromised herself:

> I have said too much unto a heart of stone,
> And laid mine honor too unchary on't.
> There's something in me that reproves my fault;
> But such a headstrong potent fault it is
> That it but mocks reproof.

(201–5)

Recognition but not retraction leads to her next speech, "Here, wear this jewel for me, 'tis my picture" (208), promising Viola, "it hath no tongue to vex you" (209). Olivia is ready to embark on what appears to be a cross-class marriage to a young page. Is she using her wealth to lure a husband, who, in fact has the virtues of a woman and is, perhaps, therefore attractive? In the text, ambiguity then prevails. Does Viola accept the jewel? No hint appears in the language. Her response, like so many of her answers to Olivia, evades the subject, asking instead, "your true love for my master" (213).

Further evasion appears in promptbooks, many of which excise this brief moment between the disguised woman and the lady who openly vows her love. For example, the encounter is crossed out by Charles Kean, who used a Kemble text (*TN* 14). And the Irving version retains only the last four lines of the women's conversation. Their brief moment is then over: no apologies for having declared her love, and no giving Viola "this jewel" that contains Olivia's picture (*TN* 15, p. 52). Was Viola's behavior not exemplary enough for the adaptors? Was the intensity of Olivia's passion, directed as it was to a woman, embarrassing? Probably both. In the text, the exchange amplifies their portraits, which have been acquiring dimension with each new scene.

Like a juggler, Shakespeare keeps aloft the atmosphere of romance as well as the realities of drunks and duels and always, whether directly or through hearsay, he illuminates the challenges facing the two women. Perhaps nowhere more clearly than in the middle section of the play are we witness to this balancing act. Act 3, scene 2 includes the conning of Sir Andrew (into penning a challenge to Cesario) and the report on Malvolio's appearance (wearing yellow cross-garters)—both men wishing to win Olivia through their actions.

Opening in her garden, scene 4 of act 3 shows the Countess ranging from one interest to another in quick succession.

> I have sent after him; he says he'll come.
> How shall I feast him? What bestow of him?
> For youth is bought more oft than begg'd or borrow'd.
> I speak too loud.
>
> (1–4).

The excitement generated within this speech, even including the suggestion that it is spoken in a whisper reveals an altered Olivia—one neither disinterested nor in mourning. The Bell edition contains a footnote on her appearance: "Olivia should possess beauty of countenance, elegance of figure, grace of deportment, and sensibility of speech" [bottom, p. 357, vol. 5, of Bell edition]. The edition also records a seemingly slight alteration in the opening line, but one which changes the idea. It reads: "I have sent after him; *say he will come,* / How shall I feast him? What bestow on him?" (emphasis added, p. 357). The conditional here contradicts the straight assertion in the Folio. Her lines reflect her excitement.

She then changes the subject, "Where's Malvolio?" (5).[20] Asking for him and commenting that his sad state suits her well, Olivia learns from Maria that he is as one "possessed." When he appears before her in yellow garters and smiling, she attempts to understand this sudden change, but the arrival of Cesario cuts short the interview, leading Olivia to assign Malvolio to Maria and Sir Toby—thus asking his gullers to be his handlers. After the steward's triumphant soliloquy celebrating what he believes to be his new status—the prospective husband to Olivia—the scene moves without a pause to Sir Andrew's timidly worded letter of challenge to Cesario. Here both Viola and Olivia are the subjects—the one's problems created by her disguise, the other's by her lack of disguise, but clearly her marriageability. Thus both illuminate challenges to the women's pursuit of their own independence. The brief interlude between the two women follows.

The focus then shifts to Viola. Suddenly her resemblance to her brother fades as she faces the "terror," Sir Andrew, an equally reluctant adversary. Their swords at the ready, both participants back off from one another, even as Antonio, mistaking Viola for Sebastian, interrupts their duel, finds himself under arrest by officers, requests his purse of "Sebastian," and denied, offers Viola her first inkling that her brother lives.

> He nam'd Sebastian. I my brother know
> Yet living in my glass; even such and so
> In favor was my brother, and he went
> Still in this fashion, color, ornament,
> For him I imitate.

(379–83)

We discover how completely Viola has mimicked her brother and are prepared for the confusion that will result.

The dramatist next adds depth and shading to the design, for the following scene has the cinematic quality of a "double take." "Will you make me believe that I am not sent for you?" (IV.i.1–2), challenges the Clown to Cesario's double, Sebastian. But we have already witnessed the interview between Viola and Olivia. Replaying an earlier moment, the Clown's confrontational attack seems to precede the previous scene. But the take is skewed. The line is addressed to Sebastian, not Viola/Cesario, and the outcome differs from the expected. We are caught in Shakespeare's double time as he confirms, through witnesses, the extraordinary resemblance between the twins. Sir Andrew and Sir Toby provide the next testimony. Again challenging the character they assume to be Orsino's page, they little realize they are encountering a different adversary. Finally, Olivia rushes out to save one she believes to be Cesario, but instead overwhelms Sebastian: "Let fancy still my sense in Lethe steep; / If it be thus to dream, still let me sleep!" (IV.i.62–63). Brother, like sister, uses a classical allusion. Just as a painter places small dabs of similar colors strategically throughout his painting to orchestrate its parts and help unify it, the writer paints resemblances through language and literary references.

Culminating in Olivia's "Would thou'dst be rul'd by me!" (64), this scene has carried the accidental disguise motif to its climax, when Sebastian replies, "Madam, I will," and Olivia joyously exclaims, "O, say so, and so be!" (65) and departs to plan a wedding. In contrast, a scene of intentional disguise follows, its darkness contrasting with the light of the previous scene as well as the subsequent one. Both literally and figuratively, darkness prevails as Sir Toby, Maria, and the Clown seek to frustrate Malvolio and convince him he is mad while keeping him imprisoned in darkness and calling it light. Again, Olivia, though absent is present: hearsay and hope, Malvolio's hope of marriage, keep her in the audience's consciousness.

Darkness then gives way to light. "This is the air, that is the glorious sun" (IV.iii.1), Sebastian marvels in soliloquy at Olivia's gifts, then later follows her to church to exchange vows. The soliloquy wanders over several topics, but always with Olivia at its core. Wondering what has happened to Antonio and wishing for his advice, the youth speculates,

> For though my soul disputes well with my sense,
> That this may be some error, but no madness,
> Yet doth this accident and flood of fortune
> So far exceed all instance, all discourse,
> That I am ready to distrust mine eyes,
> And wrangle with my reason that persuades me
> To any other trust but that I am mad,
> Or else the lady's mad.
>
> (9–16)

Debating with himself as to whether she is mad, he concludes this to be impossible—else she could not run her house, command her followers, and manage her affairs with such skill and "stable bearing" (19). Here in the testimony of a stranger who has observed the lady in action we are told of her ability.

But again the glorification of Olivia falls before the actor-manager's or director's pen. Since she is here challenging patterns of patriarchy, these producers of the play seem to assert that her more positive features need not be emphasized. Cuts in Sebastian's soliloquy appear in early promptbooks or acting versions and continue well into the twentieth century although they outline her skills. Clearly, the lines testify to her never having left this world, but merely having divorced herself from availability to suitors. And so, acting texts excise.[21] Kemble omits the lines as do the Oxberry and the French texts (*TN* 9). By the time we reach the Sothern-Marlowe version the soliloquy has been reduced to its first four lines, followed by its last two. With only its skeleton remaining, this abbreviated scene is then attached to the beginning of the closing scene (V.i) without a break.

Meanwhile, Viola is confronting the clear possibility that her brother lives. Although a joyous prospect, it will end her adventure into independence just as Olivia's decision to marry will end hers. In the single scene in act 5, Shakespeare, for the last time, presents the challenges the two single young women face and weaves together fact and fantasy, for this is Illyria.

Maria, too, has won her objective. Although she does not appear in the scene, we learn that through her successful plot to ensnare Malvolio "at Sir Toby's" wish, he hath "In recompense . . . married her" (363–64). A strong character, Maria differs from the other two women, having persistently sought marriage. Viola and Olivia, however, have had a momentary chance at self ownership.

The conflict between the qualities referred to by de Beauvoir— the sense of the self being primary, and the "erotic urges and social pressures" to conform—is dramatized. By refusing to sacrifice the sense of self being primary, Olivia wins a husband; but he is only a facsimile of the "man" she pursued. However, because Sebastian's easy compliance to Olivia's proposal of marriage sharply contrasts with the passion of his rejection of Antonio earlier, one must question its reality. It is almost as if the dramatist were sending a signal to the audience to observe the character of the twin so as to realize the challenge to realism in the ending.

Critics have noted the weakness of this ending—its basic disregard for logic.[22] Anne Barton, for example, observes that in *Twelfth Night* "Shakespeare began to unbuild his own comic form at its point of greatest vulnerability: the ending" (171). The brief scene between Antonio and Sebastian at the beginning of act 2 contributes to the absence of logic in the ending. In the earlier scene, the youth exhibits qualities clearly out of character with his impulsive actions near the comedy's close. One need only compare the attitude of Bertram to Helena with that of Sebastian to Olivia, a total stranger who asks him to marry her thinking he is Cesario, to see Shakespeare's lack of interest in a realistic ending. Nor do audiences react negatively to this strange and speedy marriage where the characters do not know one another. Because this is a comedy and because the young man himself does not object, we accept the convention of marriage as the outcome and delight that here in Illyria, Viola's twin brother shows up at just the right moment.

We also realize that the relationship between the two people to be married is inconsequential in this play, as is the need for a realistic reason for Viola's decision to disguise. Rather, the comedy seems to concentrate more closely on the changes in the women's self-perception from "primary" to "other" as they accept their identities as sexual beings in a male-dominated world. Attire, whether breeches or skirts, fades in importance as the dramatist explores the potential for independence by single women with wealth when unhampered by brothers or fathers.

Large group scene of the citizens welcoming home the victorious Theseus with his captive bride, Hippolyta—from the 1934 Reinhardt film *A Midsummer Night's Dream*. Courtesy of the Museum of Modern Art/Film Stills Archive.

CHAPTER SEVEN

Conclusion

THE GREAT GLOBE ITSELF

Created for plays at the Theatre and later at the Globe across the Thames, Shakespeare's women characters move beyond that restricted world into the great globe itself. They burst the limits of the Renaissance stage and illuminate issues which women still face. For even today women must confront rejection or domination in a patriarchal society; they must wrestle, too, with the burdens of poverty or wealth, the one making them susceptible to male political power, the other making them susceptible to the ambitions of the fortune hunter. Women still fall into the role of "other" in a society that considers man "primary"; and women, too often, learn self-hatred, adopting the views of the dominant group. In their varied roles as daughters, sisters, lovers, wives, mothers, and widows—but even when single, celibate, and unattached to men—women come to life in Shakespeare's plays, raising questions about sexual, political, familial, and economic patterns in the world around them.

Although acted by boys on the Elizabethan stage, these women characters capture with verisimilitude the emotional ambiguities of women in the larger globe. They show us the confusion of women such as Gertrude—mother, wife, widow, and queen; or Ophelia—daughter, sister, beloved, and king's subject; or of Lady Macbeth—devoted wife without scruples; or even of Lady Macduff—a wife questioning her husband's morality. In the comedies too, women must face decisions, questions of allegiance, and problems concerning behavior. Helena, of *All's Well That Ends Well*, like her adoptive mother, the Countess of Rossillion, must choose between herself and her husband just as the Countess must choose between her daughter-in-law and her son. And Hermia, of *A Midsummer Night's*

247

Dream, must decide whether to oppose her father and her ruler, fleeing Athens, or allow them to determine her future. Finally, Viola and Olivia, of *Twelfth Night,* raise troubling questions about wealth and independence even while they eventually opt for marriage.

Whereas the dramatist asks questions about women's choices and decisions, later productions often did not. Consider the effect of Lady Macbeth's absence from the discovery scene, because, we are told, Garrick's audience would have laughed, even at the great Mrs. Pritchard in the role when she asks "Help me hence, ho!" (*Macbeth,* II.iii.118). But the questions raised by her presence, and by these lines, offer insights not only into a wife's reaction when she is so completely tied to her husband and his fate but also to her sudden loss of importance in this man's world. Thus Shakespeare's great globe kept expanding to the greater globe where women lived lonely lives when cut off from other women, relying solely on their husbands for support and moral judgment.

The dramatist continued to ask questions, even while he created exciting theater. On his stage, Helena danced from one young man to another in the King's court of *All's Well That Ends Well,* but later productions limited her world. Must Helena be played as unattractive because brains and beauty stereotypically may not be found in one woman? And what of that capable, generous, and wealthy woman who also aggressively pursues a husband? Must Olivia, too, be relegated to a laughing stock because aggressive wealthy women are frowned upon by producers of the plays as well as by their audiences? Or even worse, must the women's roles be reshaped to enhance those of the male characters as often occurs in the staging of *Hamlet* and *Macbeth*?

Since every age brings certain prejudices and subjective responses to the reading of a text, one may ask, "Why object to this particular warping?" The answer lies in the persistence of patriarchy and of its values. These impinge on and skew a text's meaning. Although the dramatist lived in a patriarchal age, and questions arise as to how much his own value system incorporated the attitudes of that age, I believe that his plays transcend their time. They offer insights into experiences of both genders. Nevertheless, the constant alteration of women's roles tends to deprive us of the complete view of these characters. For women are neither angels nor fiends, chaste virgins nor whores, wise seers nor crones. Rather, like men, the women characters in Shakespeare's plays reflect the human range—wise and foolish; alert and slow; bright and dull; attractive and plain; questioning and accepting; challenging and complying; laughing and weeping; confident and diffident; proud and self-hating. Presented against the backdrop of a patriarchal society, the women in the plays incorporate this diversity.

Frequently, however, societal attitudes towards women have prevailed instead. As I have illustrated throughout this book, acting versions tend to simplify women's roles so that "accepted" norms of behavior dominate and deviation is condemned. If this means altering the text, actor-managers and producers in the theater have obliged, often through excision of lines, transposition of scenes, or even costuming and stage directions. As a result, stereotypes tend to replace the plays' more complex portraits, and ambiguities disappear.

In addition, a consistency in interpretation of the women characters persists from one generation to the next. As we discovered, for example, Olivia and Viola have been presented on stage as contrasts: a rich, arrogant young woman versus a poor, modest one. Or a fiendish Lady Macbeth confronts us in the theater, the witches fading in importance and Lady Macduff often disappearing, while literary criticism concentrates on Lady Macbeth's manipulativeness. But what drives women to undiscerning support of their husbands? And how can *Macbeth* offer insights into husband-wife relationships even as it goes beyond the realistic into the world of fantasy and witchcraft? Or, in a different context, what might Cressida, if a study were concentrated on her rather than her relationship only with Troilus, illuminate about women's jarring experiences in a society which uses them for barter? Speaking of Cressida, is Shakespeare in that play suggesting an alternative to Ophelia's choice, one that promises a woman survival rather than madness and death? Probing the range of women's lives, the plays explore the dimensions of patriarchal power and their counterpart for women—the extent of women's self-respect and self-love or self-hate.

On stage we are supposed to be entertained by a spellbound Titania entwining her arms around an ass whereas we seldom hear her intense and earnest evaluation of the emotional cost of conflict between the sexes whether fairy or human. And we watch a weak, pliable Ophelia with a comic, rather than overbearing, father since his insidious instructions to Reynaldo are usually excised. All of this takes some textual high jinks, directorial liberties, or critical blindness. When Tyrone Guthrie cheapens the women of Florence despite the lines of the text, audiences, unaware of the bias, depart from the theater with a misconception about the play.

Therefore, reacquainting ourselves with the texts means not only examining the plays themselves but also their acting versions— whether printed or in promptbooks. Noting excisions and scene transpositions helps highlight moments often missed in the reading and overlooked on stage. The subtlety of characterization of the women then emerges: whether of the more familiar Gertrude or the enigmatic Hippolyta. The derision usually found in portrayals of Olivia in *Twelfth Night* or Helena in *All's Well That Ends Well* reveals either an insensitivity to the complexity of these characters' personalities, a hostility to strong, independent women, or perhaps merely a concentration on other more easily acceptable roles— Viola's or Parolles's or even Malvolio's, a role frequently played by a star. However, both Olivia and Helena, although differing from one another, have in common an innate sense of themselves as primary and have seldom, until recently, been presented sympathetically on stage.

When criticism concentrates on the women characters, new equations must result. While new fields have opened as critics have explored the roles of women both in the plays and in the society of Shakespeare's time, there has also been a movement to dismiss his women characters as representative of women's experiences because boy actors played women's roles. But the sex of the performer seems to be transcended by the insights of the characterization. Generations of actresses have found validity in these stage portraits whether, like Ellen Terry, they have sought to bring a Lady Macbeth to life on stage or, like Lillian Gish, have tried to better understand Ophelia's descent into madness.

Economics, too, enters the picture as an Orson Welles receives backing for a filmed *Macbeth* and creates a highly sympathetic hero—his Lady's role shrunk and distorted; or a Max Reinhardt imposes ideas about women onto interpretations of Hippolyta; or a Liviu Ciulei, some fifty years later, seeks to rethink the play's direction. In asking for a closer look at the women characters, I am not asking for a rewriting of the text as occurred in Zefferelli's *Hamlet*. Rather I believe that the plays continue to speak to us although filtered through different lenses, bringing us insights into our own worlds even as some of the worlds for which they were written have disappeared. For men and women still function in power relationships—and women still confront a hostile environment. The plays offer the multiple reactions of women characters to those power plays. As they explore the life around them—the strange Illyria where they suddenly discover themselves and must make decisions—women may find in Shakespeare's plays hints about the self-sovereignty they must achieve.

Distorted portraits of the women characters sometimes emerge from contemporaneous reviews. Again *Twelfth Night* provides an example, this time of Viola in Daly's production. Writing of the play in the *Boston Advertiser* (1893), H. A. Clark details the staging while indicating the accepted perspective on the disguised young woman:

> I must remonstrate with Mr. Daly for his scheme of separating Olivia and Viola upon the stage in the second act, in order that the former may declaim her declaration of love from a portico at the head of a flight of stairs, or the latter may declaim a refusal back from the foot of the stairway. Olivia would not have put the coy Cesario at such a distance at such a moment.[1]

Why did he call her "the coy Cesario"? Did the reviewer choose the term because of the production or because of a preconceived notion about the character? The close interweaving of the two reveals the impact of attitudes in the larger culture on textual interpretation.

Because of his skill as a dramatist, Shakespeare could consider issues of equality and economic independence in a comedy even while couching them in the larger entertainment. Thus *All's Well That Ends Well* contains a strong role for the comedian who plays Parolles, offers a diversionary love interest in Diana, moves audiences from France to Italy and back, and, at the same time presents a bridegroom of such questionable worth that one may ask, "What does Helena see in him?" dismissing the larger issue of women's equality raised by the play. *Measure for Measure*, too, provides diversion in the comedy of both Lucio and Elbow even as it examines the problem of "sexual harassment" within its unseemly context.

What then was life like for women in Shakespeare's time that he could pose such questions? We are just beginning to find out. "The woman of the Renaissance is many women—mother, daughter, widow; warrior, manager, servant; nun, heretic, saint, witch; queen, martyr, seeker" (xiii), writes Margaret L. King in her comprehensive new study of women in the family, women and the church, and women and High Culture between 1350 and 1650. In some ways, King paints a bleak picture, echoing and enlarging upon Joan Kelly-Gadol's famous essay, "Did Women Have a Renaissance?" which concludes with a no. Nevertheless, King does sound one optimistic note, and it relates indirectly to Shakespeare's plays. She cites the conclusion of another scholar working in the area, David Herlihy, who believes, "Something changed in the Renaissance in women's sense of themselves, even if very little changed or changed for the better in their social condition" (238). Women gained a stronger sense of self—and Shakespeare's plays reflect that greater awareness.

Although in such plays as *Hamlet,* and *Macbeth,* we see women who are unaware of their potential as individuals unattached to men, the women do grow as each of the plays progresses. However, the plays also reflect the disastrous consequences of a woman's failure to rely on her own judgment. Thus the importance of self-knowledge and individual integrity surfaces in both works. The example of Lady Macduff, who appears so briefly and yet acts as a mirror for Lady Macbeth, illustrates the value of that integrity. In addition, as I point out in chapter 5, the artistry with which Shakespeare places her particular scene speaks to the fallibility of the male value system. While Margaret Fuller, so much later, wrote of women's need to know themselves—separating themselves, if necessary, from the world of men—Shakespeare's plays also illustrate, if less directly, the importance of that self-knowledge.

The dramatist also raises questions about the rules and patterns of his own society regarding marriage. King describes the confused messages women received at the time:

> The wife who had married, willing or unwilling, had to develop a relationship with her husband negotiated between contradictory injunctions. On the one hand, she was expected to be a companion to her husband, but on the other, she was his subordinate and the object of restrictive regulations imposed by him and other male authorities.
>
> The theme of companionship is sounded by the male theorists of marriage with unvarying enthusiasm: Catholics and Protestants alike shared the same vision of marriage and adopted the same priorities. (35)[2]

However, she also writes of the "tensions inherent in a Renaissance marriage" because, despite the constant references to "conjugal union," the husband had the authority. On stage too, tensions break out between husbands and wives. As I point out in chapters 4 and 5, on *Hamlet* and *Macbeth*, the conflict between a woman's role as partner and as subordinate also exists in the plays. That partnership role is frequently illusory, however. And the dramatist shows how women, at their peril, fail to realize the importance of retaining, recapturing, or even gaining for a first time a clear sense of their own identity. Although, as Catharine R. Stimpson writes, "No matter what her class, and class did matter intensely, a woman was the sinful daughter of Eve, a carrier of the viruses of lust and licentiousness. Church, state, father, and husband had to control her" (King, x), Shakespeare's plays question rather than accept that opinion.[3] For he creates bright, sensitive, skeptical, and assertive women as well as those who falter, or who, like Lady Macbeth, doom themselves. Moreover, his plays allow us to observe women who grow in self-knowledge and self-understanding.

Finally, the plays provide examples of women supporting women—women bonding. Often to achieve such results, the dramatist invents characters not present in any of his sources. Thus the Countess of Rossillion provides the early support for Helena; Celia bonds with Rosalind in *As You Like It;* and Beatrice bonds with Hero in *Much Ado About Nothing.* Although Helena and Hermia of *A Midsummer Night's Dream* quarrel in the enchanted forest, their close friendship reemerges when they leave the woods. Frequently, women bond with their mistresses, as does Nerissa with Portia in *The Merchant of Venice.* More impressive, however, is the bonding of women who are strangers to one another: those women of Florence to Helena; Viola to Olivia; and the potential for Hippolyta's bonding with Hermia at the beginning of *A Midsummer Night's Dream.*[4] The dramatist's reliance on this relationship between women suggests that such bonding existed in the Renaissance just as it does today, belying the too-frequent emphasis on women as competitors with one another.

Throughout this book, I have frequently referred to stage versions, particularly those of the more famous actor-managers or directors. Many of them—David Garrick, John Philip Kemble, Henry Irving, and Augustin Daly, to name a few—left not only promptbooks as records of their productions but also printed acting versions. Thus their productions were not single, peculiar examples of alterations of women's roles but reflected a general attitude and point of view since those printed versions were widely used by others as the basis for productions from the mid eighteenth into the twentieth century. Although occasionally a singular version such as Orson Welles's *Macbeth* occurred, the other pattern was more usual. I have also emphasized the moderating ability of music, song, dance, and spectacle to draw attention away from the verbal conflicts in the text.

As we move into the twenty-first century, it would be nice to think that we are returning once more to Shakespeare's full text, noting its nuances, recouping its excised passages, reevaluating its women characters. Diverse, these characters spark issues that have a relevance for us today. They question conventional patterns for women's actions. Individualized, they cause audiences to wonder about women's limited roles.

For them, Illyria proves a challenging new place where they seek to test their strengths and learn the boundaries of their world. Often that world is unexpectedly complicated and intense. For some, Illyria is not a distant isle or country at all, but rather an inner space where a sense of self-worth must grow even as a character discovers the power of patriarchy to shape and reshape her life.

Shakespeare captures women's voices as they interact with others. Centuries of productions acting synergistically with criticism may quiet but cannot eradicate those voices. They ask questions, illuminating complex characters. That the plays challenge contemporary ideas of a particular time, the criticism of some of those women and the absence of staging of some of the plays confirm. By returning to the underperformed and overlooked passages we will recapture their nuances and reacquaint ourselves with the richly drawn women and men characters that Shakespeare created. They may give us new insights into the plays as well as into our own Illyrias.

Notes

CHAPTER 1. *INTRODUCTION:* WORLDS WITHIN WORLDS

1. Recent feminist criticism has suggested that a totally new discourse is needed to define the nature of the human struggle. Harding and Hintikka warn that rather than building on accepted definitions, we need new ones so that we may not only better understand women's lives but also men's. Although I am not rewriting the definition of the "human struggle," I am offering a new tool for examining Shakespeare's plays, one that I hope will provide new insights into his artistry. Harding and Hintikka write:

> Within the theories, concepts, methods and goals of inquiry we inherited from the dominant discourses we have generated an impressive collection of "facts" about women and their lives, cross-culturally and historically—and we can produce many, many more. But these do not, and cannot, add up to more than a partial and distorted understanding of the patterns of women's lives. We cannot understand women and their lives by adding facts about them to bodies of knowledge which take men, their lives, and their beliefs as the human norm. Furthermore, it is now evident that if women's lives cannot be understood within the inherited inquiry frameworks, then neither can men's lives. . . . A more fundamental project now confronts us. We must root out sexist distortions and perversions in epistemology, metaphysics, methodology and the philosophy of science—in the "hard core" of abstract reasoning thought most immune to infiltration by social values. (ix)

2. While it is true that men too must adapt to superior power—of a lord, a king, a master—even such men have power over women, specifically their wives and daughters. As Karen Newman observes, although men in the early modern period, were "also subjects" . . . "contemporary feminists' focus on women had, and continues to have, enormous strategic importance" (*Fashioning Femininity,* xix).

3. In the Renaissance, the word *vocation* had a somewhat different meaning than it has today. The conduct books of the time, for example, used the term *vocation* to refer to marriage. Kelso writes: "In renaissance theory it is true to say, only one vocation, marriage, was proposed for the lady. Occasional reference to a choice before the girl, or rather before her father, between marriage and dedication to the church was made, only to be dismissed as extremely limited in possible practice because of the small chance of the girl's fitness for the nun's life, and also because of more important, material considerations, for in fact the lady is purely a secular figure" (78). Vives, early in the sixteenth century, in a work widely reproduced, Whately, in 1617, and Gouge, in 1622, among many others, illustrate in their works this use of the term as they dictate proper conduct for the married woman.

4. See Joseph Price, *The Unfortunate Comedy: A Study of "All's Well That Ends Well" and Its Critics.*

5. See Howard C. Cole's discussion of contemporary reactions to the idea of wardship in his analysis of Bertram as a ward of the king (35).

6. Norman Rabkin's famous article, "Rabbits, Ducks, and *Henry V,*" discusses the play's ambiguities and the alternative possible interpretations.

7. The Folger Library Prompt of *Macbeth* (*Mac* 20) is a transcription of "Macready's Drury Lane promptbook made by George Ellis in 1846 and sent by him to Charles Kean in America" (Shattuck, *Shakespeare Promptbooks,* 242).

8. Schanzer quotes Lascelles Abercrombie, "A Plea for Liberty of Interpreting," in *Aspects of Shakespeare,* 236.

9. The reference to R. W. Chambers comes from his book *Man's Unconquerable Mind: Studies of English Writers, from Bede to A. E. Housman and W. P. Ker,* 292. Cassandra is the Isabella character in George Whetstone's *Promos and Cassandra* (1578).

10. See Geoffrey Bullough, ed., *Narrative and Dramatic Sources of Shakespeare,* II: 400–404, and 442–513.

11. During the Restoration, Davenant created a version by combining *Measure for Measure* with *Much Ado About Nothing,* calling his play *The Law Against Lovers* (1673). Charles Gildon wrote another version in 1700 called *Beauty the Best Advocate.* When the play finally reappeared on the stage, excisions abounded, eliminating most of the "offensive underworld matter" (Odell, II, 23) and adding new lines at the close (Hogan, I, 301).

12. Unless otherwise noted, the text used throughout is *The Riverside Shakespeare.* For the sake of clarity, the square brackets appearing in the Riverside text have been eliminated. When used in this book, square brackets indicate interpolation by the author.

13. The concept of a precontract has been explored in much twentieth-century criticism, where the distinction has been made between promises, "de praesenti" betrothals, effective immediately, such as that of Claudio and Juliet, and "de futuro" betrothals, promises taking place in the future. According to Karl P. Wentersdorf, both are "spousals" (129). See also Margaret Loftus Ranald, *Shakespeare and His Social Context,* who writes that spousals whether "de praesenti" or "de futuro" did not confer all the physical rights of marriage.

14. A 1977 headline in *The New York Times* read "Brother and Sister Buried After Both Die Violently." The sister had died "on the Atlantic City Expressway when she leaped from a speeding car to avoid sexual advances from a man who had picked her up while she was hitchhiking." The brother was killed when returning from the memorial services for her, his motorcycle having collided with a car (*NY Times* 25 August 1977, p. 34). The contemporaneity and modernity of the motorcycle and expressway contrast with the timelessness of the young woman's actions in an attempt to escape rape.

A more recent example of the reference to sexual harassment occurred in the testimony of Anita Hill at the confirmation hearings on Clarence Thomas to become a justice on the United States Supreme Court (October-November, 1991). I believe it is significant that following these hearings students, for the first time, understood Isabella's plight, and, without exception, could hear the modern resonances in her exchange with Angelo.

15. See Lawrence Stone; Louis B. Wright, especially, chap. 13; Jonathan Gold-

berg; Louis Montrose; Debora Kuller Shuger; Margaret Loftus Ranald; and *Women in the Renaissance,* ed. Kirby Farrell, Elizabeth H. Hageman, and Arthur F. Kinney.

16. See, for example, the work included in the volumes edited by Margaret Patterson Hannay, Margaret L. King, Katharina M. Wilson, Moira Ferguson, and Betty Travitsky for an indication of the research being done in this area.

17. See Sandra K. Fischer "Elizabeth Cary and Tyranny," in Hannay, ed., *Silent But for the Word,* 225–37.

18. See Whately on the duties of a wife. But see also Debora K. Shuger's recent work where she questions the application of the term *patriarchy* to male despotism (218). Rather, Shuger suggests that "'Patriarchy' does not primarily refer to the actual behaviors of fathers toward their wives and children but rather to a cultural ideal. The English Renaissance was a patriarchal society because fatherhood came to symbolize an ideal of domestic, political, and religious order. The ideal was not unrelated to actual behavior, but it is the normative and symbolic value of fatherhood during this period, its significance as a conceptual category, that designates the culture as patriarchal. It follows that patriarchy principally refers to the relation between father and child, not husband and wife" (219).

19. Jensen emphasizes the importance of the total theatrical experience as vital to our appreciation and enjoyment of the work. He points out the folly of limiting the meaning of a comedy to its ending.

20. See Philip McGuire's chapter "The Final Silences of *Measure for Measure*" (63–96) in *Speechless Dialect* for a detailed discussion of the different ways in which five noted directors—between 1969 and 1978—have presented the last scene on stage, affecting audiences' responses to the play.

21. See Alan Hughes's *Henry Irving, Shakespearean,* 88–116.

22. See Schweikhardt article on the importance of the gender of the critic.

CHAPTER 2. *WHEN WOMEN CHOOSE:* ALL'S WELL THAT ENDS WELL

1. Kelso discusses her use of the term *lady* as follows:

> . . . there was no such thing as the lady so far as theory went . . . distinguished either from the gentleman or from any other woman. . . . [M]any books of a theoretical sort were written for and on the lady . . . but beyond the dedications to ladies, duchesses, or queens, the contents . . . apply to the whole sex rather than to any favored section of it. The lady, shall we venture to say, turns out to be merely a wife. (1)

See chapter 1, note 3 for further discussion of Kelso's book. See also Renaissance conduct manuals such as Juan Luis Vives's *A Very Fruitful and Pleasant Booke, called the Instruction of a Christian Woman,* which went into many printings during the sixteenth century, and William Whately's *A Bride-Bush, or A Wedding Sermon* (1617). See chapter 3, note 1 for excerpts from Whately's work. For a selection of the writings as well as a discussion of them, see Joan Larsen Klein's *Daughters, Wives, and Widows: Writings by Men about Women and Marriage in England, 1500–1640.*

2. According to George Winchester Stone, Jr., we do not know whether Garrick "supervised any revisions of the texts. . . . However that he was closely concerned with their production cannot be doubted" ("Garrick's Handling of Shakespeare's

Plays. . . ." I:320). According to Pedicord and Bergmann, Garrick "produced but did not act in *All's Well That Ends Well*" (3:xiv). No specific Garrick version exists. I will therefore refer to changes in *All's Well That Ends Well* at that time as the Bell text, the Drury Lane production, or the 1773 text, since the Bell text records the play "as performed at the Theatre-Royal, Drury Lane (London: John Bell, 1773)." Folger prompt *AW3* uses this edition although it is marked with later changes by an unknown hand (n.d.).

3. In *Love's Labour's Lost*, a similar kind of error in coupling of characters occurs. There, we tend to parallel characters because they are love-matched couples, for example, Berowne and Rosaline. In reality, however, the primary intellectually and verbally matched couple is Berowne and the Princess of France. For a full discussion of this, see chapter 2 of Irene Dash's *Wooing, Wedding, and Power.*

4. In some ways Helena's lines, with their hesitation and emotional intensity, resemble Leontes's in I.ii of *The Winter's Tale* when he is tormented by thoughts of his wife's unfaithfulness (108–46, 185–206 continuing intermittently to 333). As Susan Snyder observes, the exact meaning of this passage has been debated. Some scholars even believe that lines have been omitted and "recent textual work has uncovered signs of authorial second thoughts" (68). Snyder offers a detailed analysis of various interpretations of this section.

5. According to the *Concordance,* Helena and Parolles have an almost equal number of speeches, lines, and words, thus dominating the action. Whereas Helena has more lines and words (15.8 percent of each) than Parolles (12.8 percent and 13.25 percent), he has the greater number of speeches (15.0 percent to her 11.6 percent). Spevack, *Concordance* 1:1015–1121.

6. See David Haley's discussion of the role of alchemical medicine in this play, especially 58–101, 224–37.

7. These lines appear in the Kemble 1793 acting text (5). However, after having reduced the soliloquy to these two lines (121 and 129 in Shakespeare's text), Kemble then found them sequentially weak and transposed them in his 1811 version (10).

8. See, for example Farnham and Lundberg's *Modern Woman: The Lost Sex* (1947), a popular work of the time.

9. See Joseph Price's excellent book for a review and analysis of the criticism.

10. See chapter 5, "A Woman Tamed," on *Othello* in *Wooing, Wedding, and Power* for a discussion of the problems in criticism of the play and the frequent failure of critics to recognize Desdemona as a complex woman character entering an unorthodox marriage.

11. When the Princess of France warns the King of Navarre, "your Grace is perjur'd much, . . . / Your oath I will not trust" (*LLL* V.ii.790, 794), she is saying in a comedy what Juliet says in a tragedy when she warns Romeo "Do not swear at all" (*Rom* II.ii.112). The dramatist in each case is illustrating the ease with which men swear and the skepticism of women. For further discussion, see chapters 2, 4, and 8 in *Wooing, Wedding, and Power.*

CHAPTER 3. *MALE MAGIC:* A MIDSUMMER NIGHT'S DREAM

1. Such popular works as Vives's *Instructions of a Christian Woman* and Whately's *A Bride-bush,* although slightly later in time (1617), address the obligations

of the bride. *Love* appears on this list. In speaking of marriage and its obligations, he speaks of mutuality, at least obliquely:

> 6. The mutuall therefore (that wee may speake of them in order) are requyred both of man and wife, though not in an equall measure of both. For in all these common duties, the husband should bee most abundant, knowing that more of every grace is looked for from him, then from the weaker vessell. Wee call them not therefore common or mutuall, because both should have a like quantity of them; but because both must have some of all, and the husband most of all. And for these common duties, you must know in generall, that whatsoever is requyred of all men and women, generally towards other, by the Law of Christianity and Charity, as they bee men and neighbors; the same is in an higher degree and larger measure requyred from the husband toward the wife, and from her to him. (6)

Unfortunately he then writes of persuasion of a wife to yield to the husband's authority, although earlier he wrote of love being a very important ingredient in the relationship.

> Yea indeed she must be a monstrous and unwomanly woman, that being drawne by entreatie will not yeeld. Authority is like the arts of Logick and Rhetoricke, that must in speaking be used, and yet concealed: and then they most prevaile when being used, they are least seene. . . . Men that ride horses have a wand and a spurre, both; they wil rather set forward their horses with the whisk & sound, or perhaps little touch of the smal stick, then with the sharpnesse of their iron spurre. They proceed not to spurring till their horse be either restie or tiry; and if tiry, that doth more hurt. So the husband should governe his wife, & provoke her to accomplish his will with quiet, pleasing and insinuating termes, rather than open and expresse, much lesse violent commandings, unlesse shee bee more then ordinarily unruly. Christ beseecheth his Church most an end, which hee might with most right command. (29)

Having finally finished writing of the duties of the husband, Whately then turns to the duties of the wife:

> The whole duty of the wife is referred to two heads. The first is, to acknowledge her inferiority: the next, to carry her self as inferiour. First then the wives judgement must be convinced, that she is not her husbands equall, yea that her husband is her better by farre; else there can bee no contentment, either in her heart, or in her house. If shee stand upon termes of equality, much more of being better than he is, the very root of good carriage is withered, and the fountaine thereof dryed up. (36)

2. *The Fairies* (1755) was billed as an opera. It "is made up from the first four acts only, of Shakespeare's play" and does not include references to Bottom and his troop. It also includes twenty-eight songs added to the text. Some are from the play, some from other plays or other sources, such as Milton's "L'Allegro." It was a success (Stone, *MND*, 469–72). In 1763 a version of *A Midsummer Night's Dream*, attributed variously to Garrick and Colman but which Stone faults Colman for, appeared for one night and failed. It was subsequently followed by *A Fairy Tale*, which consists of two short acts, "centering about the Oberon-Titania dispute and includes Bottom and his fellows" (Stone, *MND*, 480–81). For a complete discussion of the adaptations variously attributed to David Garrick and George Colman, see Stone, "*A Midsummer Night's Dream*"; and Pedicord and Bergmann, eds. *The Plays of David Garrick*, vol. 4, 420–31. Depending upon which version I am discussing, I refer either to Garrick or Garrick-Colman as the adaptors.

3. The first *Pyramus and Thisbe,* adapted by Richard Leveridge, 1716, contained their early scenes of planning as well as the actual play-within-a-play; the second, adapted by John Frederick Lampe, 1745, retained only the fifth-act production but omitted the court personnel (Hogan, I.339). Departing further from Shakespeare's *A Midsummer Night's Dream,* but adopting its adventures of the workmen, Charles Johnson, in 1723, inserted a "Pyramus and Thisbe" comic segment into his version of *As You Like It* calling his work *Love in a Forest* (Hogan, I.339). We are not here dealing with Shakespeare's *A Midsummer Night's Dream,* merely with bits and pieces.

4. Generally, but inconclusively, attributed to Elkanah Settle, its music definitely written by Henry Purcell, *The Fairy Queen* was a lavish production costing £3000 (*LS*,1:lv). Its closing was capped by a dance with "twenty-four Chineses" (Odell, 1:194).

5. The nineteenth-century dedication to massive staging may have contributed to this shift. According to Gary Jay Williams the transposition of text and the scenic effects may also reflect the general celebration of empire at the time, with Theseus as the triumphant victor.

6. Reinhardt here drew on his 1927 stage production at the Century theater, in New York, in which Hippolyta appears with a group of large dogs.

7. These are some of the numbered "shots" in the script.

8. That script, although designated as "Final" was not incorporated into the finished film. Nor has any copy of this visual sequence of film—a first reel—been found. Robert H. Ball, in seeking to document this same information, found, in 1971 that "no indication of reels until 15 reel version" existed. This comment appears on a chart he made of the different versions, identifying them as "R= Reinhardt; K=Kenyon + McCall; 15=15 reel dial; 12=12 reel dial." In addition, his K list has "(marked 'Final')" and corresponds exactly with the material I found in the Warner Brothers archives at Princeton. The Ball notes are currently in a file at the Folger Shakespeare Library. It also contains an earlier correspondence between Ball and Joel Swensen at Warner Brothers in 1947. This says, "Our print man thinks all we have is the 12 reel version" 30 July 1947. An earlier letter from Henry Blanke, at Warner Brothers in California, to Joel Swensen, states, "As far as I can recall, the 15 reel version of *A Midsummer Night's Dream* ran all over the country, except that very much later on a certain re-issue it was cut down to 12 reels. However, neither the 15 nor the 12 reel version will completely correspond with the script as many sequences contained in the script were eliminated—as is usually the case in motion pictures—before their release. So the closest thing to go by or to get a comparison to the script would be the dialogue sheets that were put out with the original 15 reel version." The letter is dated 14 July 1947.

9. The full text of Fuller's comment is:

> In every-day life, the feelings of the many are stained with vanity. Each wishes to be lord in a little world, to be superior at least over one; and he does not feel strong enough to retain a life-long ascendency over a strong nature. Only a Theseus could conquer before he wed the Amazonian queen. Hercules wished rather to rest with Dejanira, and received the poisoned robe as a fit guerdon. The tale should be interpreted to all those who seek repose with the weak. (43)

10. Aside from having been eliminated from the Garrick-Colman and Reynolds versions, the references also disappeared in whole or part from the printed acting

texts of the nineteenth and twentieth centuries such as French's (*MND* 20), Charles Kean's edition (*MND* 9), Augustin Daly's (*MND* 5), and from the typescript of Henry Jewett's for a 1915 production (*MND* 12). When promptbooks relied on the full text, the lines were then crossed out for the acting versions. Among the latter were the recording of the Burton performance of 1854 (*MND* 21), the Beerbohm Tree production of 1900 (*MND* 7), and the Samuel Phelps production of 1861 (*MND* 13). The Reinhardt film retains only a small section of the speech.

11. Excisions persisted over a long period of time beginning with the earliest record, the Smock Alley prompt, sometime before 1700, where the lines are crossed out. Garrick eliminated them from his preparation copy of 1763. They do not appear in Reynolds's 1816 version, are crossed out in Charles Kean's (*MND* 9) and eliminated by Daly in 1888 as well as by Herbert Beerbohm Tree for the 1900 production (*MND* 7), to name just a few characteristic productions.

12. Literally, the lines (136–49) were not printed in the French acting texts (*MND* 15, *MND* 20) and Charles Kean's text of 1869 (*MND* 9). In the Burton text of 1854 (*MND* 21), the lines appear but are then crossed through.

13. They are excised from the French text (Prompt *MND* 15, 20), the Charles Kean text (*MND* 9), the Daly text (*MND* 5), and are crossed out or blocked for omission in the Burton prompt (page 9, *MND* 21), the Tree prompt (page 5, *MND* 7). In the Phelps prompt (page 311, *MND* 13), it is more difficult to be certain of whether or not the section was excised since there are two different sets of markings here—some in brown ink, others in pencil. This section has a penciled bracket on the left. Since another passage immediately above it on the page has been crossed through, the question remains of whether this passage was in fact excised.

14. The *Variorum* also notes that Halliwell "afterwards modified" this "by the reflection (p.36, folio ed.) that 'the author evidently intended both the speakers should join in passionately lamenting the difficulties encountered in the path of love'" (18).

15. Having removed this section from the printed text, the Kean book (prompt *MND* 9) indicates even further excision, penciling out still more of the beginning of this exchange between the two women. It is also excised from the Phelps promptbook (*MND* 13). Earlier, Garrick, who had cut the lines of the speech, nevertheless retained the character of Helena here whereas Reynolds, despite his promise to restore more of the play in 1816, eliminated her completely from the scene.

16. The excisions occur in the following prompts: *MND* 9, *MND* 20, *MND* 21, *MND* 15, and others.

17. The handwriting has been identified as Garrick's. See also Stone article on *A Midsummer Night's Dream,* discussed in note 2.

18. In a Charles Calvert promptbook of an 1865 production (*MND* 1), for example, after her line, "For I upon this bank will rest my head" (40), her speech continues with "and good night, sweet friend / Thy love ne'er alter, till thy sweet life end!" (60–61). Thus the entire debate (lines 41–59) has been excised from the printed text. Kean too (*MND* 9) follows this format. Tree (*MND* 7) crosses out text, retaining only one line of Lysander's—"One turf shall serve as pillow for us both,"(41)—and then, once again, Hermia's "Nay good Lysander; for my sake" (43) precedes the jump to the conclusion "so far be distant, and good night, sweet friend: / Thy love ne'er alter till thy sweet life end!" (60–61). Lysander's innocuous

"Amen" and the few brief lines of good night precede their finally falling off to sleep, which closes this section of the scene. Phelps's book, too (*MND* 13), cuts the debate. Gone is Lysander's sophisticated argument in favor of one bed, along with her "Lysander riddles very prettily . . . " (42, 43b-56a). Daly, too (*MND* 5), includes Lysander's "One turf . . ." (41–42) and Hermia's brief response "Nay good Lysander . . ." (43–44) then jumps to line 60, "So far be distant; and good night sweet friend. / Thy love ne'er alter, till thy sweet life end!" (60–61).

19. As a sampling, they are crossed out in Burton's text (22–23) (*MND* 21) and Phelps's of 1861 (328–29) (*MND* 13); and are omitted from George Colman and David Garrick's 1763 version (*MND* 19), Charles Kean's (*MND* 9), Augustin Daly's, 1888 (*MND* 5), Herbert Beerbohm Tree's (*MND* 7), French's (*MND* 15), and the edition recording performances at the Broadway Theatre (*MND* 20), as well as Henry Jewett's 1915 typescript (*MND* 12). Of course the highly abbreviated Colman version of 1777, *A Fairy Tale* (*MND* 22), does not include these Athenian characters at all.

20. Seldom the subject for criticism, Helena has the largest percentage of lines (10.4) and words (11.2) of any woman character in the play although Hermia has more speeches (9.5 percent to Helena's 7.14). Hermia's fewer lines (7.5 percent) and words (7.9 percent) suggest the difference in the pattern of the women's speeches. Following is the record in the *Concordance* of the other long roles: Theseus: 9.5 percent speeches, 10.9 percent lines, 10.7 percent words; Bottom 9.9 percent speeches, 9.7 percent lines, 10.3 percent words; Oberon 5.7 percent speeches, 10.2 percent lines, 9.9 percent words. Spevack, *Concordance* 1:666–713.

21. Many fine references appear in this article, including one to Gayle Rubin's "The Traffic in Women." Marshall asks questions: "How are we to take Demetrius' recovery from the 'sickness' of abandoning Helena and loving Hermia since it is just as much the product of enchantment as Lysander's abandonment of Hermia and love for Helena? Are we to be pleased by the success of Helena's subjection of herself to Demetrius or Titania's sudden and manipulated surrender to Oberon? What about Hippolyta's marriage to the soldier who vanquished her? . . . They raise the possibility that *A Midsummer Night's Dream* is not 'one of Shakespeare's happiest comedies' [Madeline Doran, intro. in Penguin *Complete Works*] but rather a 'most lamentable comedy' (I.ii.11–12) and 'very tragical mirth' (V.i.57)" (548).

Marshall also takes exception to C. L. Barber's comment that Theseus and Hippolyta are looking toward their wedding "'Theseus . . . with masculine impatience, Hippolyta with a woman's willingness to dream away time' (*Shakespeare's Festive Comedies,* p.128)" (548). Marshall asks how Barber knows this since the language doesn't say it. "I don't know how Barber manages to assign genders to these feelings" (548).

Of David P. Young's comment (*Something of Great Constancy: the Art of "A Midsummer Night's Dream",* New Haven: Yale University Press, 1966, 109), "It is appropriate that Theseus, as representative of daylight and right reason, should have subdued his bride-to-be to the rule of his masculine will. That is the natural order of things (p. 99)," Marshall comments," This *may* have been the ruling ideology in the sixteenth century or in 1966—I don't see that it has ever been the *natural* order of things—but it is not necessarily the ideology of *A Midsummer Night's Dream*" (550).

22. The typescript of Henry Jewett's 1915 production (*MND* 12), for example, directs Titania to take the boy to her side (14). In the elegant Daly version, when

Titania enters, her "attendant fairies . . . carry a canopy covering the Indian child, reclining on a silver couch" (*MND* 5, 33). In this cut version, there is even the printed stage direction, "Oberon orders his attendants to advance, and he dashes toward the couch to seize the child. He tears aside the curtains, and finds that it has disappeared" (34). Crossed out in pencil by a later manager, the action dramatizes the hostility between king and queen although simplifying the portraits.

23. The comment is by Thomas Hailes Lacy for the 1840 text. Actually Mendelssohn first wrote the overture for an 1827 revival in Berlin (Campbell, 546). However it was the Vestris production, claiming to present the play "almost as Shakespeare wrote it, for the first time since 1642," that was such a huge success (Campbell, 546). According to Odell, no version this close to Shakespeare's had appeared since Davenant's in the seventeenth century (II.204). Vestris's was followed by other lavish productions, most relying on this music. Only Phelps eschewed the music.

24. The popularity of *A Midsummer Night's Dream* at mid nineteenth century extended from London to New York, two rival productions appearing in February, 1854: at Burton's and the Broadway theaters. Both claimed Mendelssohn's music.

25. See Stevie Davis's sensitive analysis of Titania and of her relationship with the mother of the boy before his birth (125–29).

26. See the following promptbooks: *MND* 5, *MND* 9, *MND* 20, *MND* 21, *MND* 13, *MND* 15. Although, according to Allen, "all but 300 lines of the original" were excised by Phelps, in prompt *MND* 13, believed to be a record of his production, huge chunks of Titania's speeches were cut. In fact only the first seven lines (81–89) remain of the speech beginning "These are the forgeries of jealousies." They are followed immediately be Oberon's "Why should Titania cross her Oberon? / I do but beg a little changeling boy, / To be my henchman" (119–21). A single line is cut from his speech. Again Titania's description of the boy's mother is also crossed through. Thus, the "restoration" hardly affects the lines of Titania. In II.i Phelps excises most of her speech to Oberon 88–117 and then Oberon's 118, "Do you amend it then." Again the actor-manager excises "When we have laugh'd to see the sails conceive . . . did die," 128–35.

27. Crossed out in Burton's text (*MND* 21), and in Samuel Phelps's (*MND* 13), her lines disappear from the Kean printed text (*MND* 9), the Daly text (*MND* 5), and others.

28. Marilyn Williamson refers to the need to be aware of the historical contexts in which the plays were written. Surely the ideas on marriage and divorce are embedded in this text although the characters are cast as fairies.

29. Circled for excision from *MND* 6 (by Garrick), therefore gone from 1763 text (*MND* 19), and from Reynolds's 1816 text (*MND* 18); Burton (*MND* 21) 1854; (*MND* 9); Daly (*MND* 5); the lines are circled for excision in Phelps *MND* 13. Also excised from typescript of Jewett's, 1915 (*MND* 12).

30. Here again Phelps's prompt (*MND* 13) has excised lines as have the texts of 1763, 1854, and Tree, etc. The whole section referring to "reason" in Lysander's speech has also been eliminated from the 1856 printed text (*MND* 9); most of the lines have been excised from Jewett's 1915 typescript (*MND* 12) and from Daly's 1888 text (*MND* 5); finally, the section has been crossed out in the 1853 (*MND* 13) and 1854 versions (*MND* 21), Tree's in 1900 (*MND* 7) (and probably other contemporaneous ones that I did not examine).

31. Kean (*MND* 9). He emphasizes her unique role as "a spirit of no common rate" and retains only the first line (152) of the quote, following it immediately with "For I do love thee," a variant on the text's "And I do love thee" (156). In that version, neither Bottom nor the audience is told of her power to keep him from leaving.

32. See chapter 3, "Challenging Patterns," in Irene Dash's *Wooing, Wedding, and Power: Women in Shakespeare's Plays,* 33–66.

33. In Prompt *MND* 8, this section has been crossed through in pencil.

34. According to Shattuck (323), this is a Kemble edition (1816) although nowhere on the title page or elsewhere does the usual attribution appear. Some of the alterations, however, do appear in later acting versions.

35. Among the other versions that excised, once the longer play appeared are the 1935 film, the Beerbohm Tree version, and the 1854 version.

36. According to Hogan (II.718), the play ranked twenty-first in popularity of Shakespeare's plays between 1701 and 1800. But this figure is deceptive since only one production is listed as "the original" during the period. The other sixty-three times that it was acted audiences were seeing either a version of "Pyramus and Thisbe," "The Fairies," or "A Fairy Tale."

CHAPTER 4. *CONFLICTING LOYALTIES:* HAMLET

1. For an interesting analysis of this speech and its contradictory elements, see Booth, "On the Value of *Hamlet,*" 148–49.

2. Smock Alley *Hamlet.* This prompt is based on F3 (1663) and is believed to have been used for performance in the 1670s (Part 1, 1–2). Other texts suggesting the prevalence of the tradition are discussed below. *Hamlet, Prince of Denmark,* London: J. and P. Knapton, T. Longman, C. Hitch, et al., 1747). This was the text used by Garrick for 1772 revisions (Folger prompt *Ham* 16). *Hamlet, Prince of Denmark,* London: Hawes, Dodd, et al., 1763. Pedicord and Bergmann in *Garrick's Adaptations of Shakespeare 1759–1773,* vol. 4 of *The Plays of David Garrick,* identify this as a text "we are certain was Garrick's," 432. The excisions are not crossed out as they would be in a promptbook, but are omitted from this printed text. Here we see the influence of prompts on the texts which then were used as the basis for later productions. For the similarities among the various versions of the period, see Hogan, *Shakespeare in the Theatre: 1700–1800* 2, 187–90. Shakespeare's *Hamlet,* a tragedy, revised by J. P. Kemble (1804) is another printed edition that had a long life in the theater, having been used during most of the nineteenth century; *Hamlet,* no. xviii Modern Standard Drama, edited by Epes Sargent (New York: Berford and Co., 1847) (Macready prompt *NCP 1847); Irving's version presented at the Lyceum theater on Monday, 30 December 1878. These are a few of the many acting texts that follow the same pattern. How an actor would handle the lines remains problematic, since they seldom reach the stage.

3. This occurs either in promptbooks, where the lines are crossed out—such as the Smock Alley, Garrick's 1772 book, and the George Frederick Cooke prompt for a production of *Hamlet* at Chester in 1785—or in printed acting texts where the omissions are less apparent since no marks occur but speeches are simply abbreviated. In this category are such texts as Henry Irving's of 1874 (Souvenir Promptbook. Harvard Theatre Collection TS–2272.75) and 1878 as well as typescripts such as the twentieth-century McClintic version, *Hamlet* 1936 (notebook).

This is a pasteup of the printed text, cut and pasted into the book (New York Public Library, *NCP 1936). Later books (*NCP 1937 Books 1 and 2 Guthrie McClintic) have stage directions and are typescripts. Texts are the same but vol. 1, the stage manager's copy, has the most up-to-date text. It has been retyped, cutting out omitted material. The Leslie Howard-John Houseman (1936) and the Richard Burton (1964) *Hamlets* omit selected sections of the speech. As Charles H. Shattuck observes of Cooke's book, it contains "Cuts, calls, copious stage business and notes on *customary stage practices,* cues for effects" (italics mine), 92. See William P. Halstead's *Shakespeare as Spoken* for an extensive list of the many texts that excise this for the stage.

4. 1767; 1839; both of Irving's; Sothern-Marlowe promptbook (unidentified as to exact date. This could be the record of one or more performances between 4 October 1904 and 1920 when Julia Marlowe stopped playing Ophelia); McClintic, 1936; Olivier, *Hamlet,* 1948; Burton, 1964.

5. This appears following the title page in the 1897 text above and is signed "Johnston Forbes Robertson." He also writes, "I have ventured to transfer the scenes taking place in the house of Polonius to the Castle of Elsinore, in order to avoid as much as possible a change of scene." Illustrations in his edition reinforce the stage directions which have the mad scene taking place in the orchard of the palace (71 and photograph on facing page).

6. *Riverside,* 1,194; Michael Allen, 606.

7. Carlisle, 136–69 and passim. This work offers a fine summary of different interpretations by performers.

8. See chapter 2, "Oath-Taking" in *Wooing, Wedding, and Power* for a full development of this idea.

9. The word is being used in the sense of "being resentful toward another on account of known or suspected rivalry; . . . apprehensive of being displaced in the love or goodwill of someone" (*OED*).

10. See the discussion of this play in Dreher, 76–84 and passim.

11. At the beginning of the play (I.ii), Capulet, preferring to have his daughter wait before marrying, answers Paris's "Younger than she are happy mothers made" (12) with "And too soon marr'd are those so early made" (13). Later, in III.v., even when Capulet has decided on an immediate wedding, he pleads concern for her:

> God's bread, it makes me mad! Day, night, work, play,
> Alone, in company, still my care hath been
> To have her matched.

> (176–78)

See chapter 4 in *Wooing, Wedding, and Power* for further discussion of the shifting father-daughter relationship.

12. *Othello,* III.iv.100–106. See chapter 5 in *Wooing.*

13. The cabinet photograph of Ellen Terry (Folger Shakespeare Library) and the photograph of Julie Harris as Ophelia and Robert Burr as Hamlet in the New York Shakespeare Festival *Hamlet* (1964), produced and directed by Joseph Papp (Billy Rose Theatre Collection, New York Public Library).

14. Photograph of Aubrey Mather and Pamela Stanley (Billy Rose Theatre Collection, New York Public Library).

15. Photograph of Maurice Evans and Frances Reed (Billy Rose Theatre Collection, New York Public Library).

16. Shakespeare's Tragedy of *Hamlet* Prince of Denmark (Folger prompt *Ham* 30). In this book, we learn that the ghost does not enter but that a blue light is used to signify the ghost. Excisions occur in Laertes's instructions to Ophelia; at III.ii. the whole Rosencranz and Guildenstern section is cut including the recorders. III.iii, "R & G to England" is cut. As so often occurs in the closet scene, here too there is major cutting of Hamlet's attack on his mother. In the section where he tells her to "confess herself to heaven" (III.iv.170), to her question, "What shall I do?" the stage direction is "Looking out to audience," then Hamlet's entire speech is cut until his line "I must to England." The following four scenes are also cut. Act 3 begins at IV.v, the "mad scene." Also cut is the Queen's description, "There is a willow grows aslant a brook." Critics praised this *Hamlet* for its completeness.

17. See John Webster's *The Duchess of Malfi* and Thomas Middleton and William Rowley's *The Changeling*. Although both works belong to the Jacobean period and appeared after *Hamlet*, they offer outstanding illustrations of the use of mad scenes and lunatics on the stage during the beginning of the seventeenth century.

18. Photograph by Francis Bruguiere (Billy Rose Theatre Collection, New York Public Library).

Chapter 5. *Dependent Identities:* Macbeth

1. The *OED*, 1989 ed., offers a range of definitions of *moral*. While they are related to one another, the first definition offers the widest range and comes closest to my meaning. "Of or pertaining to character or disposition, considered as good or bad, virtuous or vicious; of or pertaining to the distinction between right and wrong, or good and evil, in relation to the actions, volitions, or character of responsible beings; ethical."

2. All Terry manuscript notes are from her copies of the play at Smallhythe. Hencefore, all references to material on interleaves will be identified by "opp." indicating "opposite" a specific page.

3. See chapter 2 of *Wooing, Wedding, and Power*, which explores this topic in depth.

4. Although her thesis differs from mine, Marilyn French, too, notes the tendency of critics to apply different standards to Lady Macbeth and Macbeth. French observes that "the word most frequently used for the lady is 'unnatural.' Macbeth is a good man gone wrong; he is judged ethically. Lady Macbeth violates 'nature,' and is judged mythically" (fn. 47, 360).

5. See especially De Quincey's essay, "On the Knocking at the Gate in *Macbeth*."

6. At the bottom of page 21 in an Ellen Terry copy of the play, this quote from a letter from "F=Philadelphia" appears. The writer may have been Furness.

7. Lady Macbeth is absent from this scene in the 1773 Bell edition (prompt *Mac* 13), the Kemble edition (1803), the Oxberry edition of 1823, which includes printed cast lists with Kean as Macbeth at Drury Lane and Macready in the role at Covent Garden (prompt *Mac* 39), and the Cumberland edition, which also records cast lists for the 1820s at both Drury Lane—Kean in 1824 and Macready in 1827—and at Covent Garden with Warde as Macbeth in 1827 (*Mac* 3). The Modern Standard Edition (n.d.) with cast lists for 1823 showing Young as Macbeth

at Drury Lane and Macready at Covent Garden also records a production with Forrest as Macbeth at the Park, in 1847 (Prompts *Mac* 1, 10). This shows the pervasiveness of the pattern in performances well into mid century.

8. The earlier influence of Alexander Pope's edition, which had had an impact on the Bell edition and probably on Garrick's text, had been incorporated and transformed by acting tradition. In Pope's text, the porter section of II.iii (Pope's II.iv), is moved to the bottom of the page (5:541) and continued at the bottom of the next page (5:542), indicating Pope's conviction that the lines were probably not Shakespeare's or that they did not belong here, or that they were offensive (see my dissertation, "Changing Attitudes," chapter 3). Pope includes lines 1–37 in the small type at the bottom of the page. Thus Pope's scene begins with "Is thy master stirring?" Bell's acting text, however (Garrick's probably), excises only the Porter's soliloquy, thus opening with the line "Was it so late, friend, ere you went to bed, / That you do lie so long?" Then follows a section in italics, before the query "Is thy master stirring" (Pope's opening). A note at the bottom of the page, probably in deference to Pope and Hanmer, but also recognizing the needs of the theater, explains:

> The part of the porter is properly omitted; and the Italic lines, by transposition, judiciously introduced to give *Macbeth* time for change of appearance, of which, even now, he is allowed too little. (Bell ed. 1773, p. 25 [*Mac* 13])

Such a logical concern, however, no longer had an influence on Kemble's edition and the many through the nineteenth century that followed his pattern. Time for change of clothes seems not to have been a concern. Kemble's scene opens with two speeches omitted by Pope, Macduff's "Was it so late, friend, ere you went to bed, / That you do lie so late?" and the response, "'Faith, sir, we were carousing till the second cock" (*Mac* 19, p. 26), then jumps to the query "Is thy master stirring?"

9. A Thomas Hailes Lacy edition with the 1853 cast list for a Charles Kean production includes manuscript notes on an interleaf (Folger *Mac* 9) describing Mme. Ristori's performance (probably 1857, in Italian. [Carlson, 25–32, Morley, 158–62.]) According to Odell, Ristori played Lady Macbeth at the Lyceum in July 1857 and spoke in Italian. This is probably the performance being described here (Odell, *Shakespeare*, ii, 262).

10. See previous chapter, "Conflicting Loyalties," for a fuller discussion of Gertrude in *Hamlet*, III.

11. Although I was not aware of his work when I wrote this, James L. Calderwood in *If It Were Done* also argues for a relationship between *Hamlet* and *Macbeth*. However, his point of view differs from mine. He perceives *Macbeth's* debt to *Hamlet* as deriving not from similarities but "because they are almost systematically opposed" in "modes and structures of presentation" (ix).

12. Garrick's (Bell, p. 33) and Kemble's (1803, *Mac* 19, p. 32) texts. Absorbing her lines into his speech, Macbeth's half-line grows to three effusive lines of insincerity. The excision also appeared in the many texts deriving from Kemble's. Following his lead, those texts also continued Macbeth's speech so as to include his next two lines.

13. In contrast, the twentieth century production of E. H. Sothern and Julia Marlowe (FO 8) opens the scene as a social gathering of men and women. "Discov-

ered: Lennox with 2 ladies is up R. Ross with Lady and gentleman down L. 2 ladies and gentleman below arch R. 6 soldiers across stage at back. As curtain rises, Ross with his Lady and Gentleman cross up L. Enter Banquo, with Fleance—L.I.E. At entrance all men raise their R arms in greeting to Banquo. Fleance runs to Ross and his group and all engage in seeming conversation with each other and do not observe Banquo during his soliloquy. . . . Banquo crosses to below table R. C. and leans against it." He then begins the soliloquy. At its close, there are more women present as king and queen enter accompanied by lords and ladies. It is a mass court scene without any of the sense of the solitariness of Lady Macbeth as a woman in a world of men.

14. Garrick, Kemble, Kean, Irving, Inchbald, Lacy, and Campbell set the pattern during each period.

15. The speeches are absent from the Bell and Kemble texts and those deriving from them, as well as the Irving text in the nineteenth century and, among others, the Orson Welles *Voodoo Macbeth* (1936) in the twentieth.

16. The direction to her to entertain Banquo at the banquet was excised by Garrick, Irving, Lacy, Kean, and *Mac* 28 (1873) among others.

17. Although the Garrick text appears to retain the third murderer, in a prompt-book said to "reflect Garrick's practice" (*Mac* 13), only two lines remain: the first murderer's "Tis he. Follow me" and Banquo's warning to Fleance to fly (*Mac* 13). In another 1773 text, what little remains of the scene is then crossed through (*Mac* 43).

18. This appears in a marked-up acting copy of a Charles Kean text (*Mac* 9), owned by Cowper.

19. In prompt *Mac* 48, with notes by Percy Fitzgerald assembled for Henry Irving (1888 book according to Shattuck no. 90) appears the suggestion that the ghost should not appear. "How much more effective the empty chair, than the sight of a man rising or walking in. The ghost in Hamlet is seen by everyone and talks: so he ought to have a visible presence. Here he is seen by none save Macbeth and does not speak. When Macbeth says 'The table's full'—I fancy he has not yet noted Banquo's presence, but only that he cannot see his place. He is confused and bewildered.—If the actual ghost is to appear, he should not sit stolidly as is customary.–but–in a mournful picturesque attitude at the front corner of the table, leaning on his elbow, as if abstracted from all." According to Bartholomeusz, "Banquo's ghost, as a physical presence, was banished from Drury Lane and then from Covent Garden, when Kemble moved there in the autumn of 1803, until, London audiences clamouring for the restoration of a visible ghost, Kemble was forced to resurrect him, as he told Joseph Farrington, against his better judgement" (113). The footnote for this is Joseph Farrington, *Diary*, 8 November 1811.

20. Stephen Booth argues for the proposition that people reexperience certain responses to literature despite knowing the outcome: "How it is that we are capable of such reexperience does not much matter. The reason we can do it, I think, is that, as a familiar literary construct passes across our understandings, the promissory signals that deceived us the first time still signal what they signaled the first time and evoke again the expectations they evoked before, evoke them in us even when those expectations coexist with knowledge that they will be frustrated" (125). The sudden appearance of Banquo's ghost has this effect on the audience. If the play is effectively produced, the ghost surprises and shocks whenever he appears.

21. Using the same terminology as de Beauvoir, Bamber perceives as "Other" only those women who represent what she calls the "feminine" (93) and not all women. She therefore considers Lady Macduff, but not Lady Macbeth, as "Other"(93). To me, they both represent woman as Other, Shakespeare presenting the types of problems different women face and showing how both are excluded from the male world.

22. This reference to Banquo was excised in the books of Garrick, Inchbald, Kemble, Lacy (Prompt *Mac* 28), Kean, and Irving among others, suggesting the prevalence of the excision during the eighteenth and nineteenth centuries.

23. Scholars have questioned the authenticity of the Hecate scene as Shakespeare's (see, for example, Kenneth Muir's introduction to the Arden edition, xxxv). It is, therefore, often omitted from productions. However, the need for the contrast between the mortal and unearthly has led producers to substitute the next witch scene (IV.i) for the Hecate scene (III.v). Because IV.i includes the parade of apparitions, further sequential revision then results. The new theory of Taylor and Jowett that collaboration was the norm and that at least four plays, including *Macbeth*, contained passages not by Shakespeare may alter perceptions of producers as they look at the whole play as an organized entity (225, 311).

24. Among the productions that eliminated both the Hecate scene and the Lennox scene that follows (III.v. and vi) were those of Irving (1888), Sothern-Marlowe (1911), Benson (1923), Webster (1941), and Glen Byam Shaw (1955), and the 1920 production with Mrs. Pat Campbell.

25. See chap. 5, "A Woman Tamed," in *Wooing, Wedding, and Power* for further discussion of this.

26. I realize that there is also a religous bias to her words since her reference to "earthly world" implies a "heavenly" world where good deeds are rewarded. Nevertheless, she goes beyond this to relate such reward patterns to women's conduct and to reject such simplistic thinking. For the audience, there is also the ironic underpinning here where she equates good deeds with "womanly defense."

27. For an extensive discussion of this play, see chap. 6, "Courageous Wives" in *Wooing, Wedding, and Power*, also Dash's "A Penchant for Perdita on the Eighteenth-Century Stage."

28. Squared to indicate excision (pages 51–52) for a later production in one 1773 prompt (*Mac* 13) and crossed out in another (*Mac* 43), the entire scene disappears from the Kemble printed text (1803), the Lacy text (*Mac* 9), the Inchbald text (1808), the Cumberland text, Modern Standard Drama (*Mac* 10), the crystal palace production text (1874), the Oxberry text (1823), the Prompt-Book, edited by William Winter, with Edwin Booth's version (1878) (*Mac* 25), the Irving text (1888), the Forbes-Robertson text (1898), and the Sothern-Marlowe production (1911), among others. In *Mac* 28 (using the text of Chalmers's edition of *Works*, vol. 4, 83–188), the entire scene is squared for excision, pin marks indicating nonperformance of those pages and Lady Macduff's absence from the cast list confirming this.

29. The scene was retained by Webster (1941), Shaw (1955), and Nunn (1976), to name some of the more famous producers.

30. Among the many productions that excised this question were those of Garrick, Irving, Sothern-Marlowe (FO8), and the one with Mrs. Patrick Campbell in 1920 (*Mac* 11).

31. Bullough concludes that Shakespeare deviates from his source, Holinshed's

Chronicles, where "Macduff apparently knows of his wife's death before he approaches Malcolm," and keeps Macduff "in ignorance until after he has persuaded Malcolm to attack Macbeth" so as to make Macduff's "motive more purely patriotic and less personal" (7:450). However, as I suggest, this revision, particularly since it also includes a scene of the murder of Lady Macduff, leaves us with a Macduff whose standards of behavior are open to question.

32. David Norbrook writes of the political undercurrents of the time as expressed in histories of Scotland. Here we see how the absence of the Lady Macduff scene can strip the play of some of its breadth and move the concentration to the question of the legitimacy of murdering the tyrant.

33. See Erasmus's *The Education of a Christian Prince,* "[T]he prince should take special care not to sin, because he makes so many followers in his wrongdoings, but rather to devote himself to being virtuous" (157). He stresses the idea that a prince is a Christian. Nor should the prince protest, "'I am not a priest. I am not a monk.' Think rather in this fashion: 'I am a Christian and a prince'" (153). Although this is much earlier than Shakespeare's play, it was a popular work and surely provided some ideas as to the virtues of the "ideal prince."

34. Trader Faulkner, who played Malcolm, is quoted as saying: "I started to play the role as a young, virile, resolute man of impeccable principles. I felt that he must be absolutely honest. . . . He [Glen Byam Shaw] said he saw him as a rather effete young man without very much strength—rather decadent." According to Michael Mullin, an argument ensued finally calmed by Olivier (Glen Byam Shaw, 252).

35. Just as Antony, absent from the last act of *Antony and Cleopatra* nevertheless haunts it, driving much of the action, so I feel, the shriek of the women in attendance, Macbeth's reaction, and that momentary reference to Macduff's family, as well as the witches' prediction, all contribute to our awareness, as audience, of the women's presence.

36. The *OED* (second edition, 1989) has over five pages of notes on the word *cast.* Although the phrase has been generally believed to refer to "casting urine"— analyzing urine for disease—the *OED* specifically contains the expression "Casting the water by hand out of a boat" in the first definition of the word as a verb. At no. 40 (949c) and indicated as obsolete, is "to cast water: to diagnose disease by inspection of (urine). Also fig. Obs. or dial." The problem is that the definition in one place has been picked up by editors and retained as standard, without questioning.

37. Even Kittredge, who analyzes the line "Cure her of that!" as "That is the very thing of which I wish to cure, I called you to the castle for that very purpose" (956) accepts the concept that Macbeth here is thinking of himself:

> Macbeth first expresses his disappointment at the Doctor's failure and his contempt for the whole art of medicine; then he repeats the order to "send out" which he gave in l.35; then he turns back to the Doctor with a familiar and confidential remark; then he reiterates his command to the squire who is arming him; and finally he addresses the Doctor once more and compares Scotland to a patient in need of medical treatment, interrupting himself with another impatient order to the squire. . . . "cast . . . land": make a diagnosis of the disease from which Scotland is suffering. A medical figure from examination of a patient's urine. (957)

38. For a portrait of an independent woman who, believing she, rather than an uncle, should have been the inheritor of her father's land, see the excerpt from

the diary of Ann Clifford (Graham, 35–53). Particularly interesting is her rejection of the intervention of King James:

> The King asked us all if we would submit to his judgment in this case. My uncle Cumberland, my cousin Clifford, and my lord answered they would, but I would never agree to it without Westmoreland [the estate]. At which the king grew in a great chaff, my Lord of Pembroke and the king's solicitor speaking much against me. At last when they saw there was no remedy, my lord, fearing the king would do me some public disgrace, desired Sir John Digby would open the door, who went out with me and persuaded me much to yield to the king" (46).

Nevertheless, she steadfastly refused. Eventually she succeeded to the land after her uncles died (35).

Although this was written in 1617, several years after the performance of *Macbeth,* it is close enough in time to suggest that such women, possible models for a Lady Macduff, existed.

CHAPTER 6. *CHALLENGING CONVENTIONS:* TWELFTH NIGHT

1. Louis B. Wright, 491–507 and passim. Juliet Dusinberre ascribes the debates on women's rights in the late sixteenth century to the rise of Puritanism, which encouraged mutual respect between husband and wife. See especially the introduction and 231–40. Linda T. Fitz, although less optimistic about women's achieving new rights, believes that the magnitude of the literature dictating what women should do indicates that they were not following prescribed paths: "the irrepressible spirit of those Renaissance English women . . . made sober treatises necessary" (18). Preceding the earliest production of *Twelfth Night,* works such as Jane Anger's (1589) appeared and, as late as 1620, the John Chamberlain letter records the king's "express commandment . . . to inveigh vehemently against the insolencie of . . . women." See Edward Phillips Statham, 182–83. See also Lisa Jardine, 9–36, where she also discusses the censuring of boys playing women's roles. She also quotes a letter of John Rainoldes in 1592 citing Scripture that says: "a woman shall not weare that which pertaineth to a man, nether shall a man put on womans raiment: for all that do so are abhomination to the lord thy god" (14).

As Linda Woodbridge writes:

> In 1620, a controversy about women which had been simmering for nearly fifty years came to a boil in two essays, "Hic Mulier," an attack on women who wear masculine clothing, and "Haec-Vir," an answering defense which attacks male foppishness. In the unpromising context of fashion, the two essays really joined combat on the nature of the sexes. . . . The transvestite controversy began, as nearly as we can tell, in about the 1570s, when some women began adopting masculine attire. (139)

Woodbridge then cites George Gascoigne's satire *The Steele Glas,* 1576; Phillip Stubbes's *Anatomy of Abuses,* 1583; and William Averell's *A mervailous combat of contrarieties,* 1588 (Woodbridge, 140). She concludes that because the movement received no attention in the 1590s and early 1600s it "was apparently quiescent," comments not arising again until 1606 when Henry Parrot's *The Mous Trap* and Richard Niccols's *The Cuckow* appeared. According to Woodbridge, the movement then gained momentum, "climaxing between 1615 and 1620" (141). This supposes that because we have no literature during the intervening years, either none existed or women suddenly gave up this attire only to don it again around 1615 when Swetnam's *Arraignment of Lewd, Idle, Froward and Unconstant Women* appeared, followed by the anonymous *Hic Mulier; or, The Man-Woman: Being a Medicine to cure the Coltish Disease of the Staggers in the Masculine-Feminines of our Times,* 1620, and the anonymous response a week later, *Haec-Vir; or, The Womanish Man: Being an Answere to the late Booke intituled Hic-Mulier. Exprest in a briefe Dialogue between Haec-Vir the Womanish Man, and Hic-Mulier the Man-Woman* (Woodbridge, 142–46).

2. Although some critics use the terms *self* and *other* to describe Shakespeare's relationship to, or perception of, his male and female characters, my reference is to de Beauvoir's use of these terms as they describe the self-perceptions of men and women.

3. See the chapter "Growing Up," on *Romeo and Juliet,* in *Wooing, Wedding, and Power.*

4. Aside from the scene transposition, which I discuss later, the following lines are excised in these works: the Bell edition; the Kemble edition and those deriving from it; the Irving edition where the scene is compressed with the later scene 4; the French edition; *TN* 21 (listed as "Ada Rehan's" but using the French text, not that of Augustin Daly, her manager); and the Sothern-Marlowe typescript—among others:

> O spirit of love, how quick and fresh art thou,
> That notwithstanding thy capacity
> Receiveth as the sea, nought enters there,
> Of what validity and pitch soe'er,
> But falls into abatement and low price
> Even in a minute. So full of shapes is fancy
> That it alone is high fantastical.

(I.i.9–15)

Also frequently cut are the scene's closing lines also spoken by the Duke:

> Away before me to sweet beds of flow'rs,
> Love-thoughts lie rich when canopied with bow'rs.

(39–40)

5. See Stephen Booth's article (*"Twelfth Night:* 1.1") on the verbal incongruities in this scene and the ways in which these incongruities prepare us for the rest of the play.

6. Robert Kimbrough, in an excellent article on androgyny, theorizes that Viola adopts male disguise to prevent being sent home immediately by the Duke (her father's friend) if she appear at his palace in her own attire ("Androgyny," 29).

7. Several versions that barely resembled Shakespeare's were presented during the seventeenth and early eighteenth centuries. However, no acting edition of the play appeared before 1750 although Hogan records productions, referring to several of these as "the original" (I:545–57). I suspect, however, that the Bell edition recorded what had been performed during the 1740s, prior to its publication. Odell notes only that: "both the Clown's songs, 'O Mistress mine,' and 'Come away, come away, Death,' with their surrounding context are omitted,

more's the pity, but nothing of importance, otherwise, is cast aside" (II.29). Obviously, to Odell, Viola's reference to gold was unimportant; to paraphrase Odell, "more's the pity."

8. As well as productions that used Kemble editions of 1810, 1811, and 1815 into the late 1850s, the Modern Standard Drama edition published by William Taylor and Company with Samuel French as general agent includes many of the same inserts and textual changes as do the Kemble editions. Because the French publications hardly ever bear a date, one must usually date them by the cast list for a particular production, which is printed in the edition. Among the books I have seen are those of William Burton, 1852, and Miss Neilson, dated 2/78. Thomas Hailes Lacy (1867) also followed Kemble's format. Charles Kean altered Kemble's 1811 edition of *Twelfth Night,* for the performance of 28 September 1850. See also Folger prompts *TN* 16, *TN* 17, *TN* 4, *TN* 5, *TN* 3, *TN* 18; also Shattuck, 469–89.

9. While Henry Irving's adaptation differs somewhat from Kemble's, it contains many of the same excisions and follows Kemble by beginning at scene 2. Irving, however, does not introduce scene 1 until after I.iv.7. Thus Viola is present during his mooning for Olivia although the scene itself is much abbreviated, containing only lines 1 to 8 and 16 to 38. See Folger promptbooks *TN* 13, *TN* 15.

10. See Schochet, 65–66, for a discussion of the heirarchical structure in the patriarchal family in Renaissance England. Obviously the dramatist was drawing on generally accepted patterns in his society. In this play, however, both Viola and Olivia have temporarily been freed from this pattern.

11. Salingar's article has many fine insights, particularly where he compares Shakespeare's play with his sources. As a matter of fact, Salingar may have made this statement because he was transferring the identity of a source character for Olivia to Shakespeare's Olivia.

12. The illustration is taken from Cassell, Petter & Galpin (G. Greatbach, Sculpt. [i.e. engraver]; C. Green, Pinxt [this word means he drew the original illustration]). Greatbach flourished in mid nineteenth century.

13. Daly's illustrations of the performance have a warmer and younger looking Olivia than appears in the designs for the role.

14. Folger prompts: 16, 17 (Kemble); 15 (Irving); 10, 21, 29 (Daly). University of Bristol: HBT 138 (Tree).

15. Excised by Irving (*TN* 15).

16. Although some critics have read this phrase as an indication that she has formerly been weeping and now her eyes are tearing for joy, I believe that she is referring to the image of Cesario that is creeping into her heart through her eyes. The language is ambiguous.

17. Daly, Irving, Tree, and others followed Kemble's lead although often slightly altering the exact sequential revision. Henry Irving, after first adopting Kemble's opening with Viola's I.ii, then moved immediately to "Court-yard of Olivia's house" (11), with Sir Toby's line "What a plague means my niece, to take the death of her brother thus?" Since Irving played Malvolio, the play was reshaped to emphasize the comedic scenes, while yet retaining Viola's role, played by Ellen Terry. Orsino's Palace, the setting of the third scene, opens as does I.iv., where Viola as Cesario has already won her way into the Duke's favor. Only after having established this time sequence, does Irving insert Shakespeare's opening lines, "If music be the food of love, play on" (15), continuing with abbreviated

material from that first scene, and then moving on to Orsino's conversation with Cesario and his assignment to her to woo Olivia.

18. It follows the second interlude between Viola and the Duke (II.iv), where she almost discloses her identity (III.ii in Irving's version—*TN* 15).

19. According to the *Concordance,* Viola has 13.0 percent of the speeches, 13.0 percent of the lines and 13.2 percent of the words; Olivia has 12.7 percent of the speeches, 12.0 percent of the lines and 11.8 percent of the words. Actually the longest role belongs to Sir Toby who has 16.5 percent of the speeches, 14.0 percent of the lines, and 13.8 percent of the words, whereas Malvolio trails with 9.4 percent of the speeches, 11.0 percent of the lines, and 11.4 percent of the words. However Malvolio's role has frequently been taken by a lead actor since it allows for great antics and hamming. Spevack, *Concordance* 1:1162–1213.

20. Irving begins his scene here, eliminating the earlier reference to Cesario. Sothern-Marlowe too delete the reference although it clearly anticipates the later intense interview between the two young women. Rather, in the Sothern-Marlowe typescript Maria's description of Malvolio (in the text's III.ii) immediately precedes his actual appearance (in the text's III.iv) without a break.

21. Acknowledging the foolishness of excising the last six lines (16–21), the editor of the Bell edition even comments, "Why omit these lines? to us they seem necessary" (338), then prints them in small type at the bottom of the page. Daly also omits them. The entire soliloquy is crossed out in the Irving prompt, while Charles Kean (*TN* 14) cuts the entire scene.

22. Several critics have recently written on the importance of the impact of the full text rather than of the ending, noting an overemphasis on closure. See, for example, Belsey, 187–88, and Jensen, 99–117.

Chapter 7. *Conclusion:* The Great Globe Itself

1. Writing of the *Twelfth Night* productions of his predecessors, Winthrop Ames quotes this review by H. A. Clark of Daly's 1893 production. Reviews of other earlier productions are also included in Ames's notes.

2. This is footnoted with a reference to Natalie Zemon Davis's article, "Women in the Crafts in Sixteenth-Century Lyon." In *Women in Work in Pre-Industrial Europe,* ed. Barbara A. Hanawalt, 167–97. Bloomington: Indiana University Press, 1986; orig. *Feminist Studies* 1982, 8:47–80.

3. Stimpson's comment appears in the forward to King's book.

4. As I pointed out in chap. 3, Hippolyta's silence during most of the first scene allows for a range of possibilities in staging. Occasionally, as in Ciulei's production, this bonding appears in her actions.

Bibliography

Abercrombie, Lascelles. "A Plea for Liberty of Interpreting." In *Aspects of Shakespeare Being British Academy Lectures by Lascelles Abercrombie*. Oxford: Clarendon Press, 1933.

Adams, John F. "*All's Well That Ends Well:* The Paradox of Procreation." *Shakespeare Quarterly* 12 (1961): 261–71.

Adelman, Janet. "'Born of Woman': Fantasies of Maternal Power in *Macbeth*." *Cannibals, Witches, and Divorce: Estranging the Renaissance*. Selected Papers from the English Institute. Edited by Marjorie Garber, 90–122. Baltimore and London: Johns Hopkins University Press, 1987.

Allen, Michael J. B., and Kenneth Muir, eds. *Shakespeare's Plays in Quarto*. Berkeley, Los Angeles, London: University of California Press, 1981.

Allen, Shirley S. *Samuel Phelps and Sadler's Wells Theatre*. Middletown, Conn: Wesleyan University Press, 1971.

Ames, Winthrop. Typescript of production of William Shakespeare's *Twelfth Night*. With notes on interpretations by critics. Billy Rose Theatre Collection, New York Public Library. *NCP+1906.

Amussen, Susan Dwyer. *An Ordered Society: Gender and Class in Early Modern England*. Oxford & New York: Basil Blackwell, 1988.

Anger, Jane. *Protection for Women*. 1589.

Anglo, Sydney, ed. *The Damned Art: Essays in the Literature of Witchcraft*. London: Routledge and Kegan Paul, 1977.

Auerbach, Nina. *Ellen Terry: Player in Her Time*. New York: W. W. Norton, 1987.

Baker, Herschel, ed. *Twelfth Night* by William Shakespeare. New York: Signet, 1965.

Bamber, Linda. *Comic Women, Tragic Men: A Study of Gender and Genre in Shakespeare*. Stanford, Calif.: Stanford University Press, 1982.

Barber, C. L. *Shakespeare's Festive Comedy*. Princeton: Princeton University Press, 1959. (*FC*)

Barber, C. L. and Richard P. Wheeler. *The Whole Journey: Shakespeare's Power of Development*. Berkeley: University of California Press, 1986. (*WJ*)

Barber, Frances. "Ophelia in *Hamlet*." In *Players of Shakespeare 2: Further Essays in Shakespearean Performance by Players with the Royal Shakespeare Company*, edited by Russell Jackson and Robert Smallwood, 137–49. Cambridge and New York: Cambridge University Press, 1988.

Bartholomeusz, Dennis. *Macbeth and the Players*. Cambridge: Cambridge University Press, 1969.

Barton, Anne. "*As You Like It* and *Twelfth Night:* Shakespeare's Sense of an Ending." In Bradbury, 160–80.

———. Introduction to *All's Well That Ends Well*. In *The Riverside Shakespeare*, edited by G. Blakemore Evans, 499–503. Boston: Houghton, 1974.

[Barrymore, John.] *Hamlet* produced by Mr. Arthur Hopkins with Mr. John Barrymore and Company, Sam H. Harris Theatre, N.Y.C., 16 November 1922. *NCP+76–2597. Photos by Francis Bruguiere, Billy Rose Theatre Collection, New York Public Library.

Baylis, Lilian. *All's Well That Ends Well*, 1922. Acting Copy. Shakespeare Centre. 72.901 at 71.21.

Beauvoir, Simone de. *The Second Sex*. Translated and edited by H. M. Parshley. New York: Alfred A. Knopf, 1953. Reprint. Bantam Books, 1961.

Belsey, Catherine. "Disrupting Sexual Difference: Meaning and Gender in the Comedies." *Alternative Shakespeares*. Edited by John Drakakis, 166–90. London and New York: Methuen, 1985.

Benthall, Michael, dir. *All's Well That Ends Well*. Old Vic, London. September 15, 1953. Workbook. Enthoven Collection, Victoria and Albert Museum S679–1982 AW 1953–54.

Berry, Edward. *Shakespeare's Comic Rites*. Cambridge: Cambridge University Press, 1984.

Berry, Philippa. *Of Chastity and Power: Elizabethan Literature and the Unmarried Queen*. London and New York: Routledge, 1989.

Bevington, David. "'But We Are Spirits of Another Sort': The Dark Side of Love and Magic in *A Midsummer Night's Dream*." *Medieval and Renaissance Studies 7* (1975). Edited by Sigfried Wenzel, 80–92. Chapel Hill: University of North Carolina Press, 1978.

Boose, Lynda E. "The Father and the Bride in Shakespeare." *PMLA* 97 (1982): 325–47.

Booth, Stephen. "On the Value of *Hamlet*." In *Reinterpretations of Elizabethan Drama*, edited by Norman Rabkin, 137–76. New York: Columbia University Press, 1967.

———. *"King Lear," "Macbeth," Indefinition, and Tragedy*. New Haven and London: Yale University Press, 1983.

———. *"Twelfth Night:* 1.1: The Audience as Malvolio." In *Shakespeare's Rough Magic*, edited by Peter Erickson and Coppelia Kahn, 149–67. Newark: University of Delaware Press; London and Toronto: Associated University Press, 1985.

Bradbury, Malcolm, and David Palmer, eds. *Shakespearian Comedy: StratfordUpon-Avon Studies* 14. London: Edward Arnold Ltd., 1972.

Bradley, A. C. *Shakespearean Tragedy*. 1904. Reprint. New York: Fawcett, 1965.

Brook, Peter. *Peter Brook's Production of William Shakespeare's "A Midsummer Night's Dream" for the Royal Shakespeare Company*. Editing and Interviews by Glenn Loney. Chicago: The Dramatic Publishing Company, 1974.

Broun, Heywood. *New York World*, 16 November 1922.

Broverman, Inge K., et al., "Sex-Role Stereotypes and Clinical Judgments of Mental Health." *Journal of Consulting and Clinical Psychology* 34 (February 1970): 1–7.

Brown, John Russell. "The Presentation of Comedy: The First Ten Plays." In Bradbury, 9–30.

Brownmiller, Susan. *Against Our Will: Men, Women and Rape*. New York: Simon and Schuster, 1975.

Bryant, J. A., Jr. *Shakespeare and the Uses of Comedy.* University Press of Kentucky, 1986.

Bullough, Geoffrey, ed. *Narrative and Dramatic Sources of Shakespeare.* 8 vols. New York: Columbia University Press, 1957–75.

Burnim, Kalman A. *David Garrick: Director.* 1961. Reprint. Carbondale and Edwardsville: Southern Illinois University Press, 1973.

Burton, Richard. *Hamlet* (1964). Typescript New York Public Library, Lincoln Center no. 5821.

Calderwood, James L. *If It Were Done: "Macbeth" and Tragic Action.* Amherst: University of Massachusetts Press, 1986.

Campbell, Oscar James, and Edward G. Quinn. *The Reader's Encyclopedia of Shakespeare.* New York: Thomas Y. Crowell Co., 1966.

Carlisle, Carol Jones. *Shakespeare from the Greenroom: Actors' Criticisms of Four Major Tragedies.* Chapel Hill: University of North Carolina Press, 1969.

———. "Helen Faucit's Lady Macbeth." *Shakespeare Studies* 16 (1983): 205–33.

Carlson, Marvin. *The Italian Shakespearians.* Cranbury, N.J., and London: Associated University Presses, 1985.

Carroll, William C. *The Metamorphoses of Shakespearean Comedy.* Princeton: Princeton University Press, 1985.

Chambers, R. W. *Man's Unconquerable Mind.* London: Jonathan Cape, 1939.

Champion, Larry S. *The Evolution of Shakespeare's Comedy: A Study of Dramatic Perspective.* Cambridge: Harvard University Press, 1970.

Cole, Howard C. *The All's Well Story from Boccaccio to Shakespeare.* Urbana: University of Illinois Press, 1981.

Coleridge, Samuel Taylor. *Coleridge's Shakespearean Criticism.* Edited by Thomas Middleton Raysor. 2 vols. London: Constable, 1930.

[Colman, George]. *A Fairy Tale.* In Two Acts. Taken from Shakespeare. As it is Performed at the Theatre-Royal In Drury-Lane. London: Printed for J. and R. Tonson. 1763. (This only has the fairies and the mechanicals.) [According to Folger catalogue, "records Colman's 1777 production at the Haymarket.] Prompt MND 22.

Colman, George, and David Garrick. Mss. notes for Garrick's production. Folger mss. w.b. 469.

Cook, Ann Jennalie. *Making a Match: Courtship in Shakespeare and His Society.* Princeton: Princeton University Press, 1991.

[Cooke, George Frederick.] *Hamlet, Prince of Denmark:* A tragedy, written by William Shakspeare. Marked with Variations in the Manager's Book, at the Theatre-Royal in Drury Lane. London: C. Bathurst &c., 1782. Promptbook for 1785 production.

Cottrell, John. *Laurence Olivier.* Englewood Cliffs, N.J.: Prentice, 1975.

Cowl, Jane. *Twelfth Night* promptbook. New York Public Library. *NCP+1930.

Crawford, Patricia. "The Construction and Experience of Maternity in Seventeenth-Century England." In *Women as Mothers in Pre-Industrial England.* Edited by Valerie Fildes, 3–38. London and New York: Routledge, 1990.

[Daly, Augustin] Shakespeare's *All's Well That Ends Well.* Workbook, ca. 1882.

———. *Twelfe Night, or what you will,* by William Shakspere. Arranged to be played in four acts by Augustin Daly. Printed from the Prompt Book, and as produced at Daly's Theatre, 21 February 1893. With an Introductory Word by William Winter, Esq. Privately Printed for Augustin Daly, 1893. Folger Prompts *TN* 29, *TN* 10, *TN* 11.

Dash, Irene G. "Changing Attitudes Toward Shakespeare as Reflected in Editions and Staged Adaptations of *The Winter's Tale* from 1703 to 1762." Ph. D. Diss., Columbia University, 1971.

——. *Wooing, Wedding, and Power: Women in Shakespeare's Plays*. New York: Columbia University Press, 1981.

——. "A Penchant for Perdita on the Eighteenth-Century Stage." In Lenz, 271–84.

——. "*Macbeth* at the Public." *Shakespeare Bulletin* 8, no. 1 (1992): 10–11.

Davenant, Sir William. *The Law Against Lovers*. London: 1673.

——. *Macbeth, A Tragaedy*. With all the Alterations, Amendments, Additions, and New Songs. As it's now Acted at the Dukes Theatre. London: P. Chetwin, 1674. In *Five Restoration Adaptations of Shakespeare,* edited by Christopher Spencer. Urbana: University of Illinois Press, 1965.

Davies, Stevie. *The Feminine Reclaimed: The Idea of Woman in Spenser, Shakespeare, and Milton.* Lexington: University Press of Kentucky, 1986.

Davies, Thomas. *Dramatic Miscellanies:* consisting of Critical Observations on Several Plays of Shakespeare: With a review of his principal characters, and those of various eminent writers, as represented by Mr. Garrick, and other celebrated comedians. With anecdotes of dramatic poets, actors, &c. in three vols., vol. 2. Dublin: Printed for S. Price et al., 1784.

De Quincey, Thomas. "On the Knocking at the Gate in *Macbeth.*" *London Magazine* (Oct. 1823). Reprinted in *Shakespeare Criticism: A Selection 1623–1840,* edited by D. Nichol Smith. London: Oxford University Press, 1916. Reprint. 1961.

Desmet, Christy. "'Neither Maid, Widow, nor Wife': Rhetoric of the Woman Controversy in *Measure for Measure* and *The Duchess of Malfi.*" In *Another Country: Feminist Perspectives on Renaissance Drama,* edited by Dorothea Kehler and Susan Baker. 71–92. Metuchen, N.J. and London: Scarecrow Press, 1991.

Dessen, Alan C. *Elizabethan Stage Conventions and Modern Interpreters.* Cambridge: Cambridge University Press, 1984.

Donohue, Joseph. "Kemble and Mrs. Siddons in *Macbeth:* The Romantic Approach to Tragic Character." *Theatre Notebook* 22 (1967–68): 65–86.

Dreher, Diane. *Domination and Defiance: Fathers and Daughters in Shakespeare.* Lexington: University Press of Kentucky, 1986.

Dusinberre, Juliet. *Shakespeare and the Nature of Women.* London: Macmillan, 1975.

Eagleton, Terry. *William Shakespeare.* Oxford: Blackwell, 1986.

Erasmus, Desiderius. *The Education of a Christian Prince.* Translated by Lester K. Born. New York: Columbia University Press, 1936.

Evans, G. Blakemore, ed. *The Riverside Shakespeare.* Boston: Houghton, 1974.

Evans, Malcolm. *Signifying Nothing: Truth's True Contents in Shakespeare's Text.* Athens: University of Georgia Press, 1986.

Evans, Maurice. *Maurice Evans' G. I. Production of Hamlet by William Shakespeare,* Acting edition with a Preface by Mr. Evans. Written with George Schaefer.

Designer's sketches by Frederick Stover. New York: Doubleday, 1947. Photographs, Maurice Evans as Hamlet and Frances Reid as Ophelia, Thomas Gomez as Claudius, and Lili Darvas as Gertrude. Billy Rose Theatre Collection, New York Public Library.

Farnham, Marynia, and Ferdinand Lundberg. *Modern Woman: The Lost Sex.* New York: Harper, 1947.

Farrell, Kirby, Elizabeth H. Hageman, and Arthur F. Kinney, eds. *Women in the Renaissance.* Amherst: University of Massachusetts Press, 1988.

Felheim, Marvin. *The Theater of Augustin Daly.* Cambridge: Harvard University Press, 1956.

Ferguson, Moira, ed. *First Feminists: British Women Writers, 1578–1799.* Bloomington: Indiana University Press, 1985.

Fischer, Sandra K. "Elizabeth Cary and Tyranny." In Hannay, 225–37.

Fitz, L. T. "Egyptian Queens and Male Reviewers: Sexist Attitudes in *Antony and Cleopatra* Criticism." *Shakespeare Quarterly* 28 (1977): 297–316.

———. "'What Says the Married Woman?': Marriage Theory and Feminism in the English Renaissance," *Mosaic* 13, no. 2 (1980): 1–22.

Fitzgerald, F. Scott. *The Letters of F. Scott Fitzgerald.* Edited by Andrew Turnbull. 1963. Reprint. New York: Bantam, 1971.

Foakes, R. A., ed. *A Midsummer Night's Dream.* Cambridge: Cambridge University Press, 1984.

———. "Images of Death: Ambition in *Macbeth*." In *Focus on "Macbeth"*, edited by John Russell Brown, 7–29. London: Routledge and Kegan Paul, 1982.

Freedman, Barbara. *Staging the Gaze: Postmodernism, Psychoanalysis, and Shakespearean Comedy.* Ithaca and London: Cornell University Press, 1991.

French, Marilyn. *Shakespeare's Division of Experience.* New York: Summit, 1981.

Friedan, Betty. *The Feminine Mystique.* 1963. Reprint. New York: Dell, 1975.

Frye, Northrop. *Anatomy of Criticism.* Princeton: Princeton University Press, 1957.

Fuller, Margaret. *Woman in the Nineteenth Century.* 1845. Reprint. New York: Norton, 1971.

Furness, Horace Howard, ed. *A New Variorum Edition of Shakespeare, Hamlet.* 2 vols. 1877. Reprint. New York: Dover, 1963.

———, ed. *A New Variorum Edition of Shakespeare.* Vol. 13. *Twelfe Night, or What you will.* Philadelphia: J. B. Lippincott Co., 1901.

———, ed. *A New Variorum Edition of . . . Macbeth.* 1903. Reprint. New York: Dover, 1963.

———, ed. *A New Variorum Edition of Shakespeare.* Vol. 25. *A Midsommer Nights Dreame.* With a Supplementary Bibliography by Louis Marder. Reprint. New York: American Scholar Publications, 1966.

Garber, Marjorie. *Dream in Shakespeare.* New Haven: Yale University Press, 1974.

———. *Vested Interests: Cross-Dressing and Cultural Anxiety.* New York and London: Routledge, 1992.

Gardner, Helen. "*Othello:* A Retrospect, 1900–67." *Shakespeare Survey* 21 (1968):1–11.

Garrick, David. *The Fairies.* an Opera. Taken from *A Midsummer Night's Dream,* written by Shakespear. As it is Perform'd at the Theatre-Royal in Drury-Lane.

The Songs from Shakespear, Milton, Waller, Dryden, Lansdown, Hammond, & c. The Music composed by Mr. Smith. London: Printed for J. and R. Tonson and S. Draper in the Strand. 1755.

[————]. William Shakespear, *Hamlet, Prince of Denmark,* A tragedy, As it is now acted at the Theatres Royal, in Drury Lane, and Covent Garden. London: Hawes, Dodd, et al, 1763. According to Pedicord and Bergmann, this was the Garrick text.

[————]. William Shakespear, *Hamlet, Prince of Denmark,* As it is now Acted by His Majesty's Servants. London: J. and P. Knapton, T. Longman, C. Hitch, et al, 1747. This was the text used by Garrick for 1772 revisions. Folger Prompt Ham 16.

Gibbons, Brian, ed. *Measure for Measure.* Cambridge and New York: Cambridge University Press, 1991.

Gilder, Rosamond. *John Gielgud's Hamlet 1937: A Record of Performances.* New York and Toronto: Oxford University Press, 1937.

Gildon, Charles. *Beauty the Best Advocate.* London, 1700.

Giles, David, dir. *Hamlet.* With Ian McKellen as Hamlet, John Woodvine as Claudius, Faith Brook as Gertrude, Susan Fleetwood as Ophelia, and Pigott Smith as Laertes. Knightsbridge Television Enterprises, 1971.

Gilman, Charlotte Perkins. *Women and Economics.* Boston: Small, Maynard and Co., 1898. Selections reprint. in *The Feminist Papers,* edited by Alice S. Rossi, 572–98. New York: Columbia University Press, 1973. Reprint. Bantam, 1974.

Gish, Lillian. Correspondence. New York Public Library at Lincoln Center.

Gish, Lillian, with Ann Pinchot. *Lillian Gish: The Movies, Mr. Griffith, and Me.* New York: Prentice-Hall, 1969.

Gohlke, Madelon. "'I wooed thee with my sword': Shakespeare's Tragic Paradigms." In Lenz, 150–70.

Goldberg, Jonathan. *James I and the Politics of Literature.* Baltimore: Johns Hopkins University Press, 1983.

Gouge, William. *Of Domesticall Duties Eight Treatises.* London: Printed by John Haviland for William Bladen, 1622.

Graham, Elspeth, et al., eds. *Her Own Life: Autobiographical Writings by Seventeenth-century Englishwomen.* London and New York: Routledge, 1989.

Granville-Barker, Harley. *More Prefaces to Shakespeare.* Edited by Edward M. Moore. Princeton: Princeton University Press, 1974.

Greg, W. W. *The Shakespeare First Folio.* 1955. Reprint. London: Oxford University Press, 1969.

Guthrie, Tyrone, dir. *All's Well That Ends Well.* Stratford-upon-Avon, April 21, 1959. Workbook. Shakespeare Centre O.S. 71 21/1959A.

Haley, David. *Shakespeare's Courtly Mirror: Reflexivity and Prudence in "All's Well That Ends Well."* Newark: University of Delaware Press, 1993.

Halio, Jay L. "Nightingales That Roar: The Language of *A Midsummer Night's Dream.*" In *Traditions and Innovations: Essays on British Literature of the Middle Ages and the Renaissance,* edited by David G. Allen and Robert A. White. Newark, London, Toronto: University of Delaware Press, 1990.

Hall, Peter. "Directing *Macbeth.*" Interview with John Russell Brown. In *Focus on*

"Macbeth", edited by John Russell Brown, 231–48. London: Routledge and Kegan Paul, 1982.

Halstead, William P. _Shakespeare as Spoken._ Published for American Theatre Association by University Microfilms, 1977.

Hannay, Margaret Patterson, ed. _Silent But for the Word: Tudor Women as Patrons, Translators, and Writers of Religious Works._ Kent: Kent State University Press, 1985.

Harding, D. W. "Women's Fantasy of Manhood: A Shakespearian Theme." _Shakespeare Quarterly_ 20 (1969): 245–53.

Harding, Sandra, and Merrill B. Hintikka, eds. _Discovering Reality._ Dordrecht, Holland, Boston, London: D. Reidel Publishing Co., 1983.

Hazlitt, William. _Characters of Shakespeare's Plays._ London: Printed by C. H. Reynell, 21, Piccadily . . . , 1817.

Heilbrun, Carolyn. "The Character of Hamlet's Mother." _Shakespeare Quarterly_ 8 (1957): 201–6.

Heisch, Allison. "Queen Elizabeth I and the Persistence of Patriarchy." _Feminist Review_ (London) 4 (1980): 45–56.

Heller, Joseph. _Catch-22._ New York: Simon & Schuster, 1961.

Hibbard, G. R. "The Year's Contributions to Shakespearian Study." _Shakespeare Survey_ 22 (1969): 145–66.

Hogan, Charles Beecher. _Shakespeare in the Theatre, 1701–1800._ 2 vols. London: Oxford University Press, 1952–57.

Holinshed, Raphaell. _The First and second volumes of Chronicles,_ comprising 1. the description and historie of England, 2. the description and historie of Ireland, 3. The description and historie of Scotland: First collected and published by Raphaell Holinshed, William Harrison, and others: Now newlie augmented and continued (with manifold matters of singular note and worthie memorie) to the year 1586 by John Hooker alias Vowell Gent. and others. STC 13569 copy 1 v. 1.

Holland, Norman N. "Hermia's Dream." In _Representing Shakespeare,_ edited by Murray M. Schwartz and Coppelia Kahn, 1–20. Baltimore and London: Johns Hopkins University Press, 1980.

Horner, Matina. "Fail: Bright Women." _Psychology Today_ 3 (1969): 36–39.

Howard, Leslie, and John Houseman, dirs. _William Shakespeare's Hamlet_ Prince of Denmark. Adapted in Three Acts and Nine Scenes by Schuyler Watts for the Leslie Howard production, 1936. Settings and costumes by Stewart Chaney. Music by Virgil Thomson. Mime of Players' Scene by Agnes de Mille. Typescript University of California at Los Angeles Houseman Box 13. Photograph of Aubrey Mather as Polonius and Pamela Stanley as Ophelia, Billy Rose Theatre Collection, New York Public Library.

Hubler, Edward, ed. _Hamlet,_ by William Shakespeare. New York: NAL, 1963, Signet edition.

Hughes, Alan. _Henry Irving, Shakespearean._ Cambridge and New York: Cambridge University Press, 1981.

Hunter, G. K. Introduction to _All's Well That Ends Well._ The Arden Shakespeare. London: Methuen, 1967.

Inchbald, E. S., ed. *The British Theatre.* Vol. 5. London: Longman, Hurst, Rees, and Orme, 1808.

[Irving, Henry]. *Hamlet* Souvenir Promptbook of 1874. Harvard Theatre Collection TS–2272.75.

[———.] William Shakespeare, *Hamlet,* As arranged for the Stage by Henry Irving and presented at the Lyceum theatre on Monday, 30 December 1878. London: Printed at the Chiswick Press, 1878.

[———.] *Twelfth Night* by William Shakespeare. London: George Bell and Sons, 1882. Folger Prompt TN 13.

[———]. *Twelfth Night* by William Shakespeare, As Arranged for the Stage by Henry Irving and presented at the Lyceum theatre on 8 July 1884. London: Chiswick Press, 1884. Folger Prompt TN 15.

James VI of Scotland, I of England. *Daemonologie, in forme of a Dialogue, Divided into three Bookes.* Edinburgh: Printed by Robert Walde-grave Printer to the Kings Majestie. An.1597.

Jardine, Lisa. *Still Harping on Daughters.* Totowa, N.J.: Barnes & Noble Books, 1983.

Jensen, Ejner J., *Shakespeare and the Ends of Comedy.* Drama and Performance Studies Series. Bloomington and Indianapolis: Indiana University Press, 1991.

Johnson, Samuel. ed. *The Plays of William Shakespeare.* In eight volumes, with corrections and illustrations of Various Commentators; To which are added Notes by Sam. Johnson. London: Printed for J. and R. Tonson. . . . 1765.

———. *Johnson on Shakespeare.* Edited by Arthur Sherbo. Vols. 7 and 8 of *Works of Samuel Johnson.* New Haven: Yale University Press, 1968.

Kahn, Coppelia. *Man's Estate: Masculine Identity in Shakespeare.* Berkeley: University of California Press, 1981.

Keene, Laura. *Shakespeare's play of a 'Midsummer Night's Dream'.* Arranged for representation at Laura Keene's theatre. . . . New York: O. A. Roorback, Jun'r. 346 & 348 Broadway. 1859. Wm. Seymour Collection. Princeton University.

Keller, Evelyn Fox. *Reflections on Gender and Science.* New Haven: Yale University Press, 1985.

Kelly-Gadol, Joan. "Did Women Have a Renaissance?" In *Becoming Visible,* edited by Renate Bridenthal and Claudia Koonz, 137–64. Boston: Houghton Mifflin, 1977.

Kelso, Ruth. *Doctrine for the Lady of the Renaissance.* Urbana: University of Illinois Press, 1956.

[Kemble, J. P.] Shakespeare's *All's Well That Ends Well,* with Alterations by J. P. Kemble, As . . . Performed . . . [at] the Theatre-Royal, Drury-Lane. London: J. Debrett, 1793.

[———.] Shakespeare's *All's Well That Ends Well,* Adapted . . . by J. P. Kemble . . . as acted at the Theatre Royal in Covent Garden. London, 1811. Folger prompt *AW* 2.

[———.] Shakespeare's *Hamlet,* a tragedy, revised by J. P. Kemble, and now first published as it is acted at the Theatre Royal in Covent Garden. London: Printed for the Theatre, 1804.

[———.] *Twelfth Night; or What you will.* A Comedy. Revised by J. P. Kemble; & now first published as it is acted at the Theatre Royal in Covent Garden.

London: Printed for the theatre, 1810 Folger prompts _TN_ 16 (ms. cast list for 1818; bookplate and autograph of Walter Lacy; bookplate of Sir Henry Irving), _TN_ 38.

[————.] No t.p. 1810 or 1811. "Mr. Charles Kean. Prompt Copy" (embossed on cover). Charles Kean altered this edition of _Twelfth Night,_ for the performance of 28 September 1850. Souvenir promptbook made in 1859 by T. W. Edmonds, the prompter. Folger prompt _TN_ 14.

[————.] _Twelfth Night; or, What you will._ A comedy. Revised by J. P. Kemble; & now first published as it is acted at the Theatre Royal in Covent Garden. London: Printed for the Theatre. 1811 "Operatic version" by Frederick Reynolds, 1820 at Covent Garden. Folger prompt _TN_ 17.

[————.] _Twelfth Night; or What you will:_ a comedy. Revised by J. P. Kemble; and now published as it is performed at the Theatres Royal. London: Printed for John Miller, and sold in the theatres, 1815. Folger prompts _TN_ 4 (in ink at top of p. 5: "Mr. J. B. Buckstone . . . 1859." ms. cast list for "July 2d 1856 Haymarket"), _TN_ 6.

Kimbrough, Robert. "Androgyny Seen Through Shakespeare's Disguise." _Shakespeare Quarterly_ 33 (1982): 17–33.

————. "Macbeth: The Prisoner of Gender." _Shakespeare Studies_ 16 (1983): 175–90.

King, Margaret L. _Women of the Renaissance._ Chicago and London: University of Chicago Press, 1991.

Kirsch, Arthur. "The Integrity of _Measure for Measure._" _Shakespeare Survey_ 28 (1975): 89–105.

————. _Shakespeare and the Experience of Love._ Cambridge: Cambridge University Press, 1981.

Klein, Joan Larsen, ed. _Daughters, Wives, and Widows: Writings by Men About Women and Marriage in England, 1500–1640._ Urbana and Chicago: University of Illinois Press, 1992.

————. "Lady Macbeth: 'Infirm of purpose.'" In Lenz, 240–55.

Kliman, Bernice W. "Isabella in _Measure for Measure._" _Shakespeare Studies_ 15 (1982): 137–48.

————. _Hamlet: Film, Television, and Audio Performance._ Rutherford, N. J.: Fairleigh Dickinson University Press, 1988.

Kott, Jan. _Shakespeare Our Contemporary._ Translated by Boleslaw Taborski. Preface by Peter Brook. London: Methuen and Co. 1965. Reprint. New York: Norton, 1974.

Lawrence, W. W. _Shakespeare's Problem Comedies._ New York: Macmillan, 1931.

Leech, Clifford. _Twelfth Night and Shakespearian Comedy._ Toronto: Dalhousie University Press and University of Toronto, 1935.

Leggatt, Alexander. _Citizen Comedy in the Age of Shakespeare._ Toronto: University of Toronto Press, 1973.

Lenz, Carolyn Ruth Swift, Gayle Greene, and Carol Thomas Neely, eds. _The Woman's Part._ Urbana: University of Illinois Press, 1980.

Levin, Richard A. "_All's Well That Ends Well,_ and 'All seems well.'" _Shakespeare Studies_ 13 (1980): 131–44.

Lothian, J. M., and T. W. Craik, eds. *Twelfth Night*. The Arden Shakespeare. London: Methuen, 1975.

McClintic, Guthrie, dir. *Hamlet,* at The Empire Theatre, New York, 8 October 1936. notebook. This is a pasteup of the printed text, cut and pasted into the book. New York Public Library, *NCP 1936. Later books have stage directions and are typescripts. *NCP 1937 Books 1 & 2 Guthrie McClintic. Texts are the same, but vol. 1, the stage manager's copy, has the most up-to-date text. It has been retyped, cutting out omitted material. Photographs of John Gielgud as Hamlet, Judith Anderson as Gertrude, and Lillian Gish as Ophelia: Billy Rose Theatre Collection, New York Public Library.

McElroy, Bernard. *Shakespeare's Mature Tragedies*. Princeton: Princeton University Press, 1973.

McGuire, Philip C. *Speechless Dialect: Shakespeare's Open Silences*. Berkeley, Los Angeles, London: University of California Press, 1985.

————. "Egeus and the Implications of Silence." In *Shakespeare and the Sense of Performance*, edited by Marvin and Ruth Thompson, 103–15. Delaware: University of Delaware Press; London and Toronto: Associated University Press, 1989.

MacLean, Ian. *The Renaissance Notion of Woman*. Cambridge: Cambridge University Press, 1980.

Mahood, M. M., ed. *Twelfth Night* by William Shakespeare. Middlesex, England: Penguin Books, 1981.

Malcolmson, Cristina. "'What You Will': Social Mobility and Gender in *Twelfth Night*." In *The Matter of Difference: Materialist Feminist Criticism of Shakespeare*, edited by Valerie Wayne, 29–57. Ithaca: Cornell University Press, 1991.

Marsh, Ngaio. "A Note on a Production of *Twelfth Night*." *Shakespeare Survey* 8 (1955): 69–80.

Marshall, David. "Exchanging Visions: Reading *A Midsummer Night's Dream*." *Journal of English Literary History* 49 (1982): 543–75.

Merchant, W. Moelwyn. "His Fiend-like Queen." *Shakespeare Survey* 19 (1966): 75–81.

Middleton, Thomas. *The Witch*. Malone Society Reprints. Oxford: Oxford University Press, 1950.

Middleton, Thomas, and William Rowley. *The Changeling*. Edited by George W. Williams. Lincoln: University of Nebraska Press, 1966.

Midsummer Night's Dream, A. The Old Vic Company. Souvenir Book. New York: Artcraft Litho. and Printing Co., 1954.

Millais, Sir John Everett. "Ophelia" (1852), Tate Gallery, London.

Millett, Kate. *Sexual Politics*. New York: Doubleday, 1970.

Moi, Toril. *Sexual/Textual Politics: Feminist Literary Theory*. London and New York: Methuen, 1985.

Montrose, Louis. "'Shaping Fantasies': Figuration of Gender and Power in Elizabethan Culture." *Representations* 1, no. 2 (1983): 61–94.

Morley, Henry. *The Journal of a London Playgoer*. London, 1866. Reprint. Leicester: Leicester University Press, 1974.

Muir, Kenneth. Introduction to *Macbeth*. The Arden Shakespeare. Cambridge: Harvard University Press, 1957.

Mullaney, Steven. *The Place of the Stage: License, Play, and Power in Renaissance England.* Chicago and London: University of Chicago Press, 1988.

Neale, John E. *Elizabeth and Her Parliaments, 1584–1601.* London: Jonathan Cape, 1957.

Nevo, Ruth. *Comic Transformations in Shakespeare.* London and New York: Methuen, 1980.

Newman, Karen. *Shakespeare's Rhetoric of Comic Character: Dramatic Convention in Classical and Renaissance Comedy.* New York and London: Methuen, 1985.

———. *Fashioning Femininity in English Renaissance Drama.* Chicago and London: University of Chicago Press, 1991.

Nicoll, Allardyce. *Restoration Drama, 1660–1700.* Vol. 1 of *A History of English Drama, 1660–1900.* 4th ed. London: 1923; Cambridge University Press, 1952. Reprint. 1965.

Novy, Marianne. "Shakespeare's Female Characters as Actors and Audience." In Lenz, 256–70.

Odell, George C. D. *Shakespeare from Betterton to Irving.* 2 vols. 1920. Reprint. New York: Dover, 1966.

———. *Annals of the New York Stage.* 15 vols. New York: Columbia University Press, 1927–49.

Olivier, Laurence, dir. and prod. *Hamlet.* A Two Cities Production. Post-Production Script. 11 May 1948. Printed in England.

Otten, Charlotte F. *English Women's Voices, 1540–1700.* Miami: Florida International University Press, 1992.

Papp, Joseph, dir. and prod. New York Shakespeare Festival *Hamlet* (1964), with Julie Harris as Ophelia and Robert Burr as Hamlet. Billy Rose Theatre Collection, New York Public Library.

Parker, R. B. "War and Sex in *All's Well That Ends Well.*" *Shakespeare Survey* 37 (1984): 99–113.

Payne, B. Iden, dir. *All's Well That Ends Well.* Stratford-upon-Avon, 23 April 1935. Workbook. Shakespeare Centre 71.21/1935A.

Pearlman, Elihu Hessel. "Malcolm and Macduff." *Studies in the Humanities* 9 (1981): 5–10.

Pearson, D'Orsay W. "Male Sovereignty, Harmony and Irony in *A Midsummer Night's Dream.*" *Upstart Crow* 7 (1987): 24–35.

Pedicord, Harry William, and Fredrick Louis Bergmann, eds. *Garrick's Adaptations of Shakespeare.* Vols. 3 and 4 of *The Plays of David Garrick.* Carbondale and Edwardsville, Illinois: Southern Illinois University Press, 1981.

Pinciss, Gerald M., and Roger Lockyer, eds. *Shakespeare's World.* New York: Continuum, 1989.

Polanski, Roman, dir. *Macbeth.* Great Britain: Playboy Productions/Columbia Pictures Industries, 1971. Screenplay: Roman Polanski and Kenneth Tynan.

Pope, Alexander, ed. *The Works of Mr. William Shakespear.* 6 vols. London: J. Tonson, 1723–25.

Pope, Alexander, and William Warburton, eds. *The Works of Shakespear.* 8 vols. London: J. & P. Knapton et al., 1747.

Power, Tyrone. Ms notes, 17 October 1907, in *The Elizabethan Shakspere: Macbeth*. New York: Doubleday, Page & Co., 1903. Prompt *Mac* 34.

Price, Joseph. *The Unfortunate Comedy: A Study of "All's Well That Ends Well" and Its Critics*. Toronto: University of Toronto Press, 1968.

Proser, Matthew N. *The Heroic Image in Five Shakespearean Tragedies*. Princeton: Princeton University Press, 1965.

Rabkin, Norman. *Shakespeare and the Common Understanding*. New York: Free Press, 1967.

———. "Rabbits, Ducks, and *Henry V*," *Shakespeare Quarterly* 28 (1977) 279–96.

———. *Shakespeare and the Problem of Meaning*. Chicago: University of Chicago Press, 1981.

Ramsey, Jarold W. "The Perversion of Manliness in *Macbeth*." *SEL* 13 (1973): 285–300.

Ranald, Margaret Loftus. *Shakespeare and His Social Context: Essays in Osmotic Knowledge and Literary Interpretation*. New York: AMS, 1987.

[Reinhardt, Max.] *A Midsummer Night's Dream*. Final 12/6/34. Warner Brothers. Script. Correspondence. William Seymour collection, Princeton University.

[———.] Shakespeare, William. *A Midsummer Night's Dream*. Warner Brothers Presents (film). Directed by Max Reinhardt. 1934.

[———.] *A Midsummer Night's Dream*. Warner Brothers Presents (film). 1935. Kenyon and McCall. MFLM +.

[Reynolds, Frederick.] *A Midsummer Night's Dream*. Written by Shakspeare: with Alterations, Additions, and New Songs; As it is performed at the Theatre-Royal, Covent-Garden. London: Printed for John Miller, 25, bow-street, covent-garden; By b. McMillan, Bow-Street, Covent-Garden. 1816. Prompts *MND* 18, 8.

Richards, David. "A 'Carousel' for the 90's, Full of Grit and Passion." Review of *Carousel*, music by Richard Rodgers, book and lyrics by Oscar Hammerstein 2d. Vivian Beaumont Theater, Lincoln Center, New York. *New York Times* 25 March 1994, C1.

Roberts, Jeanne. *The Shakespearean Wild: Geography, Genus, and Gender*. Lincoln and London: University of Nebraska Press, 1991.

Rose, Mary Beth. *The Expense of Spirit*. Ithaca and London: Cornell University Press, 1988.

———, ed. *Women in the Middle Ages and the Renaissance: Literary and Historical Perspectives*. Syracuse, New York: Syracuse University Press, 1986.

Rosenberg, Marvin. *The Masks of Macbeth*. Berkeley, Los Angeles, London: University of California Press, 1978.

Rothman, Sheila M. *Woman's Proper Place: A History of Changing Ideals and Practices, 1870 to the Present*. New York: Basic Books, 1978.

Rutter, Carol. *Clamorous Voices: Shakespeare's Women Today*. New York: Routledge/Theatre Arts Books, 1989.

Salingar, L. G. "The Design of *Twelfth Night*." *Shakespeare Quarterly* 9 (1958). Reprint in *Dramatic Form in Shakespeare and the Jacobeans*. Essays by Leo Salingar. London and New York: Cambridge University Press, 1986.

Schanzer, Ernest. "Isabella Reproved." In *The Problem Plays of Shakespeare*. New York: Schocken Books, 1963. Reprinted in *20th Century Views of "Measure for*

Measure," edited by George L. Geckle. Englewood Cliffs, N.J.: Prentice-Hall, 1970.

Schochet, Gordon J. *Patriarchalism in Political Thought.* New York: Basic Books, 1975.

Schweickart, Patrocinio P. "Reading Ourselves: Toward a Feminist Theory of Reading." In *Gender and Reading: Essays on Readers, Texts, and Contexts,* edited by Elizabeth A. Flynn and Patrocinio P. Schweickart, 31–62. Baltimore and London: Johns Hopkins University Press, 1986.

Selbourne, David. *The Making of "A Midsummer Night's Dream."* 1982. Reprint. London and New York: Methuen, 1983.

Shakespear, William. *A Midsummer-Night's Dream.* London: Printed for J. Tonson, and the rest of the Proprietors; and sold by the Booksellers of London and Westminster. 1734. Prompt *MND* 6.

Shakespeare, William. *All's Well That Ends Well,* as performed at the Theatre-Royal, Drury Lane. London: John Bell, 1773. Folger prompt *AW* 3 uses this edition marked with later changes by an unknown hand (n.d.). In chapter 2, I refer to this text using the name of the publisher, "Bell," the date, "1773," or the place of production, "Drury Lane."

———. *All's Well That Ends Well,* Cumberland's British Theatre, vol. 18. London, 1828.

———. *All's Well That Ends Well,* Thomas Hailes Lacy [n.d.]. The title page reads "Printed from the Acting Copy, with Remarks, Biographical and Critical, by D. G. . . . . As Performed at the Theatres Royal, London." Cast given is for Covent Garden, 1811. This looks like the Kemble edition of 1811. The reference to "late Lacy's" on the cover suggests that the Kemble text was being used late in the century in a French's acting edition. The Folger card catalogue dates it "1843–73" since that was the period of Lacy's edition. Therefore, if the cover of this French edition tells us anything, it is that although the text is Kemble's 1811 (apparent when comparing this edition with Kemble's), the printing was much later, probably around 1873, because of the words "Late Lacy's" on the cover.

———. *All's Well That Ends Well,* Memorial Theatre Edition, 1888. Edited by C. E. Flower. London: Samuel French. Shakespeare Centre.

———. *All's Well That Ends Well.* London: British Broadcasting Corp., 1981. Elijah Moshinsky, dir. BBC—TV.

———. *All's Well That Ends Well.* Directed by Trevor Nunn. RSC. Martin Beck Theatre, 13 April 1983.

———. Tragedy of *Hamlet* Prince of Denmark. East Aurora, N.Y.: Roycroft Shop, 1902. Folger prompt *Ham* 30.

———. *Hamlet,* no. xviii Modern Standard Drama, edited by Epes Sargent. New York: Berford and Co., 1847. Macready prompt. *NCP 1847.

———. *Hamlet* as arranged for the stage by Forbes Robertson and presented at the Lyceum Theatre on Saturday, 11 September 1897, with illustrations by Hawes Craven. London: Nassau Press, St. Martin's Lane, W. C.; and Southwark, S. E. 1897. Collection, Huntington Library, CA.

———. *Macbeth* (n.p., n.d.) Catalogue entry reads: "Notes and suggestions for Macbeth" assembled for Henry Irving by Percy Fitzgerald. A few pencil notes by Irving. Copious notes refer to Garrick, Mrs. Pritchard, Edmund Kean, Macready, and Others. Bookplate of Henry Irving. [Shattuck dates this with production of 29 December 1888 (no. 90, 255).] Folger prompt *Mac* 48.

————. *Macbeth*. London: Simpkin, Marshall & Co., 1839. Catalogue entry reads: p. 3–59 (Hinds' English Stage) Interleaved. A transcript of Macready's Drury Lane promptbook. Note at top of page 9: Mr. Charles Kean's private prompt copy. Marked, & c.—by George Ellis prompter. Theatre Royal, Drury Lane, July 1846. Folger prompt *Mac* 20.

————. *Macbeth, A Tragedy*. As Performed at the Theatre-Royal, Drury-Lane. . . . An Introduction, and Notes Critical and Illustrative, are added by the Authors of the Dramatic Censor. London: John Bell, 1773. Folger prompts *Mac* 13, 43.

————. *Macbeth: A Tragedy*. To which are added all the Original Songs. As performed at the Theatres Royal In Drury-Lane, and Covent-Garden. London: Printed for W. Bowen, Bookseller, at Dock-head, Southwark, 1776. Folger PR 2823 l776a Copy 1 Sh. Col.

————. *Macbeth, A Tragedy*. Revised by J. P. Kemble: And now first published as it is acted at The Theatre Royal in Covent Garden. London: Printed for J. Ridgway, 1803. Folger prompts *Mac* 19, 53.

————. *Macbeth; A Tragedy*, in five Acts. As performed at the theatres Royal, Covent Garden and Drury Lane. . . . With remarks by Mrs. Inchbald. London: Printed for Longman, Hurst, . . . (1808). Notes by George Joseph Bell. Folger w.a. 70.

————. *Macbeth. A Tragedy*. London: Thomas Hailes Lacy [n.d.] (Notes on Ristori performance). Prompt *Mac* 9.

————. *Macbeth*. Boston: Oxberry's edition, 1823.

————. *Macbeth*. London: John Cumberland [n.d.] (According to Shattuck, interleaves marked 1841). This records production of Henry Beatty, 3 January 1845, at Covent Garden. Prompt *Mac* 3.

————. *Macbeth*. New York: Modern Standard Drama, No.L [n.d.]. (Shattuck dates this as 1850 because it includes a cast list for September 1850 with Charlotte Cushman.) Prompt *Mac* 10.

————. *Macbeth*. New York: Modern Standard Drama, No. L [n.d.]. Probably 1880, Leslie Allen production. Prompt *Mac* 1.

————. *Macbeth*. New Stage Arrangements under the direction of Mr. William Creswick. Sydenham: Crystal Palace Company, 1874.

————. *Macbeth*. The Prompt-Book. Edited by William Winter. Shakespeare's Tragedy . . . As Presented by Edwin Booth. New York: Printed for William Winter by Francis Hart & Company, 1878 Folger *Mac* 25.

————. *Macbeth*. (Proof copy of Irving edition, 1888. Smallhythe, with notes by Ellen Terry.)

————. *Macbeth, A Tragedy* for the Stage by Henry Irving. London: 1888. Ellen Terry's studybook.

————. *Macbeth*. No title page. (A Henry Irving prompt—for the 1888 production). Folger prompt *Mac* 48.

————. *Macbeth*. As arranged for the stage by Henry Irving, and presented at the Lyceum Theatre, 29 December 1888, with music by Arthur Sullivan. London: "Nassau Steam Press," 1889. Folger prompt *Mac* 14.

———. *Macbeth* as arranged for the stage by Forbes Robertson and presented at the Lyceum Theatre on Saturday, 17 September 1898. London: Nassau Press, 1898.

———. *Macbeth*. Preparation copy by Frederick Kaufman, general manager. E. H. Sothern and Julia Marlowe. Loose leaf notebook. 1910. Folger *Mac* Fo 8.

———. *Macbeth*. Acting Prompt, E. H. Sothern and Julia Marlowe, 1911. Folger *Mac* Fo 2.

———. *Macbeth*. Shakespeare's Tragedy. Edited by William J. Rolfe. New York, Cincinnati, Chicago: American Book Company, 1905. Preparation copy for Mrs. Patrick Campbell production, 1920. Prompt *Mac* 11.

———. *Macbeth*. n.p., n.d. Dir. Margaret Webster, starring Maurice Evans and Judith Anderson. (Photostat of original; records production of 1941.) Folger prompt *Mac* Fo 10.

———. *Macbeth*. Dir. Trevor Nunn. Promptbook, Warehouse. Originally used for the Other Place production, 1976 and for its revival at the R. S. T. 1977. Shakespeare Centre.

———. *Macbeth*. Dir. Philip Casson of Trevor Nunn production of Royal Shakespeare Company's *Macbeth* with Ian McKellen, Judi Dench, John Bown. Great Britain: Thames Television, 1976.

———. *A Midsummer Night's Dream*. With Alterations and Additions, and Several New Songs. As it is Performed at the Theatre-Royal in Drury-Lane. London: J. & R. Tonson, 1763. (Version by George Colman, the elder, and David Garrick.) Folger prompt *MND* 19.

———. *A Midsummer-Night's Dream*. A Comedy, in Five Acts. Thomas Hailes Lacy, Wellington Street, Strand London. (verso of t.p. "As performed at the Theatre Royal Covent Garden, Monday, 16 November 1840. Preceded by Mendelsohn's [sic] celebrated Overture.") Includes Vestris as Oberon. *NCP 18___.

———. *A Midsummer Night's Dream*. [No title page. According to Folger catalogue: London. Printed for F. C. and J. Rivington; J. Johnson; R. Baldwin; H. L. Gardner, etc. 1805, p. 303–87 (from vol. 2 of *The plays* edited by A. Chalmers). Records of Samuel Phelps, probably made for his 1861 revival.] Prompt *MND* 13.

———. *A Mid Summer-Night's Dream*. A Comedy in Three Acts. With Cast of Characters, Stage Business, Costumes, Relative Positions, etc. etc. Mendelssohn's Music of this Play may be had of T. Goodwin, No 7 Vandam St. New York. Samuel French. n.d. French's American Drama No. 1. Prompt *MND* 15.

———. *A Midsummer-Night's Dream*. In three Acts. To which are added A Description of the Costume—Cast of the Characters—Entrances and Exits—Relative Positions of the Performers on the Stage, and the whole of the Stage Business, as performed with great success for upwards of sixty consecutive nights at The Broadway Theatre. Mendelssohn's Vocal and Instrumental Music of this play may be had of W. T. Goodwin, no. 7 Vandam-street, N.Y. New York: Samuel French, 121 Nassau-street. French's American Drama. The Acting Edition. No. CVI. Prompt *MND* 20.

———. *A Midsummer Night's Dream*. Arranged for Representation at The Princess's Theatre, with Historical and Explanatory Notes, by Charles Kean. London: Printed by John K. Chapman and Co., 5, Shoe Lane, and Peterborough Court, Fleet Street. Prompt *MND* 9.

————. *A Midsummer-Night's Dream*. As arranged for the stage by Henry Jewett. Typescript. (According to Shattuck, 1 March 1915.) Prompt *MND* 12.

————. *A Midsummer Night's Dream*. Edited by William Aldis Wright, M. A. Oxford: At the Clarendon Press, 1888. (Herbert Beerbohm Tree prompt). Prompt *MND* 7.

————. *A Midsummer Night's Dream*. Directed by Liviu Ciulei, at the Guthrie Theatre, Minneapolis, 1985; Performing Arts Center, SUNY Purchase, 1986.

————. *A Midsummer Night's Dream*. Directed by A. J. Antoon. Music composed and directed by Michael Ward. The Public Theatre, New York, January 1988.

————. *Twelfth Night*. As Performed at the Theatres-Royal. London: John Bell, 1773.

————. *Twelfth Night or What You Will;* a comedy in five acts. As performed at the Theatres Royal, Drury Lane and Covent Garden. Printed under the authority of the managers, from the promptbook. With remarks by Mrs. Inchbald. London: Longman, Hurst, Rees, and Orme, 1808.

————. *Twelfth Night; or What You Will:* A comedy. With prefatory Remarks. The only edition existing which is faithfully marked with the stage business and stage directions; as it is performed at the Theatres Royal. by W. Oxberry, Comedian. London. Published for the proprietors, by W. Simpkin, and R. Marshall, stationers' Court, Ludgate-street; and C. Chapple, 59, Pall-mall. 1821. Folger prompt *TN* 20 (marked by Samuel Phelps and W. C. Williams, also reference to 1857 production on p. 69) (Shattuck dates this 1848).

————. *Twelfth Night; or What You Will:* A Comedy, In five Acts. London: Samuel French, publisher 89 Strand. New York: Samuel French & Son, publishers, 122 Nassau street. [n.d.]. (Autograph on front cover "Arranged by Miss Neilson 2/78"). Folger prompt *TN* 18.

————. *Twelfth Night; or What You Will:* A Comedy in five acts. With the stage business. New York: Wm. Taylor & Co. Modern Standard Drama no. 58. S. French, general agent. 151 Nassau Street. [n.d.]. [Folger prompt *TN* 5 (In ink on front paper cover, "Prompt Book Twelfth Night Burton's Theatre." In the hand of John Moore. According to Shattuck, the production was March 1852). Prompt *TN* 9 (cut and paste in a notebook: on cover in autograph "Twelfth Night Prompt Book Augustin Daly")].

————. *Twelfth Night; or What you will:* a comedy, in five acts. London, Thomas Hailes Lacy. [n.d.]. Folger prompt *TN* 3 (on first page: J. B. Buckstone . . . Theatre Royal, Haymarket, 1867).

————. *Twelfth Night; or What you will*. London, Edinburgh, & New York: Thomas Nelson and Sons. [n.d.]. P.359–428 from vol. 2 of *Dramatic Works*. Folger prompt *TN* 1, Viola Allen preparation copy for 1904 production.

————. *Twelfth Night*. Typescript of Winthrop Ames's production. *NCP+1906.

————. *Twelfth Night*. Herbert Beerbohm Tree workbook, 1901. University of Bristol Collection.

————. *Twelfth Night*. Published playscript. With producer's preface of Harley Granville-Barker. Produced at the Savoy Theatre, London. Opened 15 November 1912. London: William Heinemann, 1912.

————. *Twelfth Night*. As presented by Sothern-Marlowe [n.p., n.d]. Typescript (some notes refer to 1923 production). Folger prompt *TN* 31.

————. *Twelfth Night*. Joseph Papp, presents. New York Shakespeare Festival. Wilford Leach, director. Delacorte Theatre, Central Park, Summer 1986.

————. *Twelfth Night*. Stratford, Canada. 2–8 August 1988.

Shakspere, William. *All's Well That Ends Well*. London: J. Dicks. [n.d.]. Poel prompt. Enthoven Collection, Victoria and Albert Museum S 660–A 1982.

————. *A Midsummer Night's Dream* A Comedy in Five Acts. . . . Arranged for Production at Daly's Theatre, by Augustin Daly. Produced for the First Time. Privately Printed, 1888 (Copyright, 1887). Prompt *MND* 3.

————. The Comedy of *A Midsummer Night's Dream*. Arranged for Representation at Daly's Theatre, by Augustin Daly. Produced there for the First Time, 31 January 1888. Privately Printed for Mr. Daly, 1888. (An elegant illustrated souvenir book used as a prompt by later producers.) * NCP 1888; Prompt *MND* 5.

Shakspere's Beautiful Comedy of *Midsummer Night's Dream*. Some account of the Grand Performance at Burton's Theatre, Chambers Street. Universally conceded to be the Best Shaksperian Revival and the Most successful Exhibition ever recorded in the history of the Stage. With the Published Opinions of the Best Critics connected with the New York Press. [first produced on Friday, 3 February 1854.] . . . graced for the first time on any stage with Mendelssohn's Music! Performed by the Fine Orchestra of this Establishment, (all Solo Players,) with some additions for this occasion. The whole arranged by Mr. John Cooke, Director of Music. . . . The Comedy produced under the immediate direction of Mr. Burton, Materially aided by Mr. J. Moore, Stage Director. [Then follows a cast list with Burton as Bottom. The succeeding pages have quotes from sixteen reviews, some in dailies, some Sunday, some in periodicals.] Prompt *MND* 21.

Shakspere's Play of *A Midsummer Night's Dream*. Arranged for representation at the Prince's theatre, Manchester. by Charles Calvert. As First Performed on Saturday, 2 September 1865. Prompt *MND* 1.

Shattuck, Charles H. *The Shakespeare Promptbooks*. Urbana and London: University of Illinois Press, 1965.

Shaw, George Bernard. *Our Theatres in the Nineties*. 1932. Reprint. London: Constable and Co. 1948.

————. *Shaw on Shakespeare*. Edited and introduced by Edwin Wilson. New York: Dutton, 1961.

Shaw, Glen Byam. *Macbeth Onstage: An Annotated Facsimile of Glen Byam Shaw's 1955 Promptbook*. Edited by Michael Mullin. Columbia and London: University of Missouri Press, 1976.

Shepherd, Simon. *Amazons and Warrior Women: Varieties of Feminism in Seventeenth-Century Drama*. Brighton, Sussex: Harvester Press, 1981.

Shuger, Debora Kuller. *Habits of Thought in the Renaissance: Religion, Politics, and the Dominant Culture*. Berkeley: University of California Press, 1990.

Simon, John. Review of *A Midsummer Night's Dream*. *New York Magazine*, 25 January 1988, 71.

[Smock Alley]. *Hamlet* reproduced in *Shakespearean Prompt-Books of the Seventeenth Century*. Edited by G. Blakemore Evans. Vol. 4, parts 1 and 2. Charlottesville:

Bibliographical Society of University of Virginia, University Press of Virginia, 1966.

[———]. *Macbeth* reproduced in *Shakespearean Prompt-Books of the Seventeenth Century.* Edited by G. Blakemore Evans. Vol. 5, parts 1 and 2. Charlottesville: Bibliographical Society of University of Virginia, University Press of Virginia, 1970. (Based on 3rd Folio, 1664)

[———]. *Midsummer Night's Dream* Collation in *Shakespearean Prompt-Books of the Seventeenth Century.* Edited by G. Blakemore Evans. Vol 3, pt. 1. 27–35. Charlottesville, Bibliographical Society of the University of Virginia: University Press of Virginia, 1964.

Snyder, Susan. "*All's Well That Ends Well* and Shakespeare's Helens: Text and Subtext, Subject and Object." *ELR* 18 (1988): 66–77.

Sothern, E. H., and Julia Marlowe. *Hamlet* promptbook. Unidentified as to exact date. This could be the record of one or more performances between 4 October 1904 and 1920, when Julia Marlowe stopped playing Ophelia. *NCP 19— (Shattuck no. 139).

Spevack, Marvin. *A Complete Concordance to the Works of Shakespeare.* 6 vols. Hildesheim, Germany: George Olms, 1968–70.

Stallybrass, Peter. "*Macbeth* and Witchcraft." In *Focus on "Macbeth"*, edited by John Russell Brown. London: Routledge and Kegan Paul, 1982.

Statham, Edward Phillips. *A Jacobean Letter-Writer: The Life and Times of John Chamberlain.* London: 1920.

Stone, George Winchester, Jr. "Garrick's Long Lost Alteration of *Hamlet*," *PMLA* 49 (1934): 890–921.

———. "*A Midsummer Night's Dream* in the Hands of Garrick and Colman." *PMLA* 54 (1939): 467–82.

———. "Garrick's Handling of Shakespeare's Plays and His Influence upon the Changed Attitude of Shakespearian Criticism During the Eighteenth Century." Ph.D. diss., Harvard University, 1940.

Stone, Lawrence. *The Family, Sex, and Marriage in England, 1500–1800.* New York and London: Harper, 1977.

———. *Road to Divorce: England 1530–1987.* Oxford and New York: Oxford University Press, 1990.

Styan, J. L. *Shakespeare in Performance: All's Well That Ends Well.* Manchester: Manchester University Press, 1984.

Taylor, Gary, and John Jowett. *Shakespeare Reshaped, 1606–1623.* Oxford: Clarendon Press, 1993.

Teague, Frances. *Shakespeare's Speaking Properties.* Lewisburg: Bucknell University Press. London & Toronto: Associated University Presses, 1991.

Terry, Ellen. Letter to William Winter, 28 October 1895. Folger ms. collection, Folger Shakespeare Library.

———. Cabinet photograph. The Walter Hampden-Edwin Booth Theatre Collection and Library, the Players Club.

———. *Ellen Terry's Memoirs.* Edited by Edith Craig and Christopher St. John. London, 1932. Reprint. New York: Benjamin Blom, 1969.

———. Correspondence. Folger ms. collection.

Thirsk, Joan. Foreword to *Women in English Society, 1500–1800*. Edited by Mary Prior. London and New York: Methuen, 1985.

Thomas, Vivian. *The Moral Universe of Shakespeare's Problem Plays*. London and Sydney: Croom Helm, 1987.

Travitsky, Betty. *The Paradise of Women*. 1981. Reprint. New York: Columbia University Press, 1989.

Tree, Herbert Beerbohm. *Twelfth Night* promptbook, 1901. Tree collection, University of Bristol, HBT 138.

Van Lennep, William, et al., eds. *The London Stage, 1660–1800*. 5 parts in 11 vols. Carbondale: Southern Illinois University Press, 1960–68.

Vincinus, Martha. "Sexuality and Power: A Review of Current Work in the History of Sexuality." *Feminist Studies* 8 (Spring 1982): 133–56.

Vives, Juan Luis. *A Very Fruitful and Pleasant Booke, called the Instruction of a Christian Woman*. Translated by Richard Hyrde. London: Printed by Robert Walde-grave, 1585.

Waith, Eugene M. "Manhood and Valor in Two Shakespearean Tragedies." *ELH* 17 (1950): 262–73.

Warnicke, Retha M. *Women of the English Renaissance and Reformation*. Westport, Conn.: Greenwood Press, 1983.

Webster, John. *The Duchess of Malfi*. Edited by Fred B. Millett. Arlington Heights, Ill.: Harlan Davidson, 1953.

Webster, Margaret. *Shakespeare Without Tears*. Cleveland and New York: World, 1942.

Welles, Orson. *Macbeth*. Conceived * Arranged * Staged by Orson Welles. Managing Producer, John Houseman. Typescript. Federal Theatre. 1936. *NCP 1936 (Often referred to as the "Voodoo" *Macbeth*.)

———, dir. *Macbeth* Typescript. 26 March 1947.

———, dir. *Macbeth*. USA. A Mercury Prod., released by Republic Pictures, 1948.

———. Manuscripts Department, Lilly Library, Indiana University, Bloomington, Indiana.

Wentersdorf, Karl P. "The Marriage Contracts in *Measure for Measure*: A Reconsideration." *Shakespeare Survey* 32 (1979): 129–44.

Whately, William. *A Bride-bush, or A Wedding Sermon:* Compendiously describing the duties of Married Persons: By performing whereof, Marriage shall be to them a great Helpe, which now finde it a little Hell. Printed at London by William Jaggard, for Nicholas Bourne, and are to be sold at his shop at the entrance into the Royall Exchange, 1617.

Wheeler, Richard P. *Shakespeare's Development and the Problem Comedies: Turn and Counter Turn*. Berkeley: University of California Press, 1981.

Wiesen, Pearl. "A Study of Original Promptbooks and Acting Editions of Shakespeare's *Twelfth Night*." Master's thesis, Hunter College, New York: 1958.

Williams, Gary Jay. "The Scenic Language of Empire: *A Midsummer Night's Dream* in 1816." *Theatre Survey* 34 (1993): 47–59.

Williamson, Marilyn. *The Patriarchy of Shakespeare's Comedies*. Detroit: Wayne State University Press, 1986.

Williamson, Sandra L., and James E. Person, Jr., eds. *Shakespearean Criticism*. Vol. 12. Detroit, New York, London: Gale Research, 1991.

Wilson, Katharina M., ed. *Women Writers of the Renaissance and Reformation*. Athens: University of Georgia Press, 1987.

Woodbridge, Linda. *Women and the English Renaissance: Literature and the Nature of Womankind, 1540–1620*. Urbana and Chicago: University of Illinois Press, 1984.

Woodbridge, Linda and Edward Berry, eds. *True Rites and Maimed Rites: Ritual and Anti-Ritual in Shakespeare and His Age*. Urbana & Chicago: University of Illinois Press, 1992.

Woolf, Virginia. *A Room of One's Own*. New York: Harcourt, 1929.

Wright, Louis B. *Middle Class Culture in Elizabethan England*. Chapel Hill: University of North Carolina Press, 1935.

Wylie, Philip. *Generation of Vipers*. New York: Farrar and Rinehart, 1942.

Young, David. *Something of Great Constancy: The Art of "A Midsummer Night's Dream."* New Haven and London: Yale University Press, 1966.

Index

Page numbers in boldface indicate illustration pages.